URI

Journal of the Mystery of Uri Geller

URI

Journal of the Mystery of Uri Geller

ANDRIJA PUHARICH

www.whitecrowbooks.com

URI

Copyright © 1973, 2023 by Lab Nine Ltd. All rights reserved.

Published by White Crow Books; an imprint of White Crow Productions Ltd.

The moral right of the author has been asserted in accordance with the Copyright, Design and Patents act 1988.

No part of this book may be reproduced, copied or used in any form or manner whatsoever without written permission, except in the case of brief quotations in reviews and critical articles.

For information, contact White Crow Books by
e-mail: info@whitecrowbooks.com.

Cover Design by Astrid@Astridpaints.com
Interior design by Velin@Perseus-Design.com

Paperback: ISBN: 978-1-78677-250-3
eBook: ISBN: 978-1-78677-251-0

Non-Fiction / Parapsychology / UFOs & Extraterrestrials / Unexplained Phenomena

www.whitecrowbooks.com

Contents

Acknowledgments		7
Preface		9
Introduction		13
CHAPTER ONE:	"Uri" Means Light	37
CHAPTER TWO:	The Gordian Knot	60
CHAPTER THREE:	Dakashem	78
CHAPTER FOUR:	Spectra	111
CHAPTER FIVE:	When Time Stood Still	123
CHAPTER SIX:	Eye of the Hawk	145
CHAPTER SEVEN:	Seven Pillars of Fire	168
CHAPTER EIGHT:	The Battle for the Truth	201
CHAPTER NINE:	Why	231
EPILOGUE:	"It Is Only the Beginning"	244
Appendix One:	The Nine	251

Appendix Two:	Text of Stanford Research Institute Film	263
Appendix Three:	Clock, Time, and Prayer	272
Appendix Four:	Spacecraft Sightings	278
Author's Biography		283

Acknowledgments

I want to thank all of my friends mentioned in this book who know, beyond anything I could express, how much they gave in love, loyalty, and dedication. I also include friends and enemies not specifically mentioned who helped to make me wiser and stronger.

The tragedy of the death of Arigó, the great Brazilian healer, in 1971, awakened my consciousness to become a seeker. The seeking brought me to Israel, where I met Uri Geller, about whom this book is written. After I was convinced that Uri's abilities were genuine, I arranged to have him studied in the United States. Captain Edgar D. Mitchell, former astronaut, undertook the management of the first institutional research on Uri, and with Russell Targ, Harold Puthoff, and Wilbur Franklin carried out the initial experiments at Stanford Research Institute in late 1972.

I especially acknowledge the loyalty and talent of my close circle of working associates. We have been together for many years preparing for the advent of Uri Geller. To Luis Cortes for his brilliant medical research leadership in the work on Arigó in Brazil. To Melanie Toyofuku for her collaboration on research projects over the years and who was the first to welcome Uri in Europe when he left Israel. To Yasha Katz for his personal support of Uri in West Germany and elsewhere. To Solveig

Clark for her organizing work on our many research expeditions and her deep devotion. To Werner Schmid for organizing Uri's public appearances, and his vitality that carries us all along. To Byron and Maria Janis for their deep understanding and help in making it possible for Uri to demonstrate his paranormal powers in public. To Judy Skutch for her leadership in keeping alive the institutional research on Uri.

Ira Einhorn's imagination helped to formulate this book and to get it to the attention of publishers. Sharron McCann helped me through the agony of writing, typing, and editing the manuscript and served as a sounding board for many of the ideas and feelings herein. Bill Whitehead's cool judgment and courage got the book published. My greatest debt is to Uri for giving me the privilege of being his scribe.

Andrija Puharich

Preface

In late 1970 I read a report written by an Israeli army officer about a young man in Israel named Uri Geller. The letter described Geller's telepathic powers and his ability to make clock hands move without touching the clock. These alleged powers were so extraordinary that I could not believe the report. However, when this officer subsequently sent samples of metal broken by Geller's mental powers, and when the laboratory reports stated that this kind of metal fracture had not been seen before, my interest grew. I went to Tel Aviv, Israel, on August 17, 1971, to meet Uri Geller. My research with him convinced me that he was one of the most unusual men in the world. Why I think he is so unusual is the subject of this book.

I had suspected for a long time from my researches that man has been in communication with beings not of this earth for thousands of years. This personal opinion comes from a close reading of the record of ancient religions and from my own observations and data. What is not clear is why such communication has been kept secret for so long.

With the publication of this book, however, many of the cosmic secrets are now declassified. But the release of this knowledge in fact raises more questions than it answers.

One of the first of these new questions is an important one:

Why was Uri Geller selected to be the ambassador for an advanced civilization? And why did I become the principal witness to this ambassadorship and the chief scribe of its gradually unfolding revelations? These interrelated questions will be developed throughout this book.

My story involves three principal agents. The primary agent is not a single being, but a collegium of voices reaching man on earth. We have, in the beginning, the words of the Nine, who are directly related to man's concept of God. I shall develop the concept of the Nine in the Introduction. The controllers of the universe operate under the direction of the Nine. Between the controllers and the untold numbers of planetary civilizations in the universe are the messengers. It is the messengers who help to fulfill the destiny of creation by gentle accentuation where and when they are needed. Some of these messengers take the form of spacecraft, which in modern parlance are called unidentified flying objects, or UFOs. Uri and I have been reached mostly by the latter type of messenger, whose names and functions are varied. The intermediary between these messengers and earth people is Uri Geller. The function of chief witness to these interactions has fallen upon me.

If I am to get an attentive hearing, the reader should know that I have had many years of professional preparation and research experience in medicine, parapsychology, and laboratory and field investigations. I have only one interest in writing this book. That is to bring to people all over the world the facts about the existence of superior beings and what they want to say to man today. What follows is true, but it is not the whole truth. There are many things that my "editor in the sky" will not yet permit me to reveal. My editor on earth has advised me to delete material that could be considered too controversial or libelous. Events have been omitted for political reasons where governments have been involved. There are delicate questions concerning the relations between religions which have been avoided. In order to get the basic message in print, and out to the people, many diplomatic gestures have had to be made.

Perhaps someday, depending on the response of the public, my editors will allow the whole truth to be revealed.

Many people are mentioned in this book for the roles they played in the reported events. I have been in touch with these principals in order to compare my text with their recollections. The text that follows represents the agreement reached between each principal (whom I could reach) and myself. However, I want to make it clear that this does not mean that these individuals have necessarily endorsed the content or conclusions of this book. I stand alone with respect to the reporting of all events, interpretations, and conclusions.

INTRODUCTION

Once I realized I was involved in an event of immense importance, I began to retrace those incidents in my life which brought Uri and me together.

The first of these concerns Dr. D. G. Vinod, a Hindu scholar and sage from Poona, India, whom I briefly met by chance in New York City in December 1951. Two months later, on February 16, 1952, I had my first serious meeting with him. At that time he surprised me by asking permission to hold my right ring finger at the middle joint with his right thumb and index finger. He said that he used this form of contact with a person to read his past and his future. I agreed. He did this for about a minute, whistling between his teeth as though he were trying to find a pitch. Then he leaned back in his chair, and for an hour told me my life story with utter precision, as though he were reading out of a book. His accuracy about the past was extraordinary. He then predicted such a rosy future for me as an Arjuna figure that I was embarrassed. Nevertheless, I realized that here was intelligence on a scale I had not imagined to exist. I promised Dr. Vinod that I would call him to the laboratory in Maine as soon as my next experiment was ready.

As it turned out, this promised meeting was not to be held for nearly another year. On December 31, 1952, Dr. Vinod and I took a plane from New York to Maine. We landed in Augusta at

7:30 P.M., and Hank Jackson, the administrator of the laboratory, the Round Table Foundation, was there to meet us. We drove over the country roads in the snow, chatting all the way. We entered the great hall of the laboratory, and without saying a word or even taking off his overcoat, Dr. Vinod found his way to the library and sat down on a sofa. Hank and I followed him. We realized that he had gone into a trance. We sat opposite him, waiting expectantly. Curiously enough, the house was always bustling with activity, but on this New Year's Eve there was not a sound in the house from child, man, woman, or animal. There was the hushed silence of expectancy as Hank and I watched our entranced sage.

Then, at exactly 9 P.M., a deep sonorous voice came out of Dr. Vinod's mouth, totally unlike his own high-pitched, soft voice, saying in perfect English without an accent:

M calling: We are Nine Principles and Forces, personalities if you will, working in complete mutual implication. We are forces, and the nature of our work is to accentuate the positive, the evolutional, and the teleological aspects of existence. By teleology I do not mean the teleology of human derivation in a multidimensional concept of existence. Teleology will be understood in terms of a different ontology. To be simple, we accentuate certain directions as will fulfill the destiny of creation.

We propose to work with you in some essential respects with the relation of contradiction and contrariety. We shall negate and revise part of your work, by which I mean the work as presented by you. The point is that we want to begin altogether at a different dimension, though it is true that your work has itself led up to this.

I deeply appreciate your dedicatedness (sic) *to the great cause of peace which is a fulfillment of finitesimal existences. Peace is not warlessness. Peace is the integral fruitage of personality. We have designed to utilize you and thus to fulfill you. Peace is a process and will be revealed only progressively. You have it in plenty, I mean the patience which is so deeply needed in this magnificent adventure. But today, at the moment of our* advent, the most eventful and spectacular phase of your work begins.

Andrija Puharich (AP): "It is helpful to have your guidance."

We don't guide, nor do we seek guidance, although we appreciate the sense in which you mean it. All of us, including yourselves, can claim no better than being the expressive instruments and avenues of this purpose.

Einstein has privately felt the need of correcting himself. Infinitization of any mass, M_i, according to him,[1] can be achieved by equating it with:

$$M_i = \frac{m_0 c^2}{\sqrt{1 - \frac{v^2}{c^2}}}$$

An implication of this theorem, as yet unrevealed, will solve the problem of the superconscious.

The whole group of concepts has to be revised. The problem of psychokinesis, clairvoyance, etc., at the present stage is all right, but profoundly misleading—permit us to say the truth. Soon we will come to basic universal categories of explicating the superconscious. Just as Jesus said, "It is not work, but grace." A fruitful, creative approach to the superconscious is indeed a progressive reception of grace.

We cannot really go on with experimentation in this direction, but if we get seven times the electrical equivalent of the human body—if we get it seven times—do you know what would result? It would result in sevenon of the mass of electricity. That's a very strange term, but it's true. If it gains sevenfold, corresponding approximation to light velocity will be ninety-nine per cent. That is the point where human personality has to be stretched in order to achieve infinitization. This is one of the most secret insights.

See Appendix One for the philosophy of the Nine.

---

[1] This is a form of the well-known Lorentz-Einstein Transformation equation where c^2 is velocity of light squared, and v is velocity. Here, $M_i = E$, energy.

When Dr. Vinod awoke from his trance after some ninety minutes of speech by the Nine, he had no recollection or knowledge of what had been said. Hank and I worked for a month with Dr. Vinod, listening to the profound wisdom of the Nine. It was a deeply moving experience, and we really believed every word that we heard based purely on the internal evidence. This work was interrupted in February 1953 when I had to serve as a captain in the U. S. Army during the Korean War.

What was lacking in our study of Dr. Vinod and the Nine was some kind of external evidence for the reality of what was being said. Such evidence was forthcoming and occurred when I returned to the laboratory in Maine on a military leave.

On June 27, 1953, nine people met with Dr. Vinod at the Round Table Foundation in Maine. They were Henry Jackson, Georgia Jackson, Alice Bouverie, Marcella Du Pont, Carl Betz, Vonnie Beck, Arthur Young, Ruth Young, and I.

Dr. Vinod sat on the floor in the lotus posture holding in his hands a string of sacred beads, called *rakshas*. On his lap was a simple copper plate nine inches in diameter. On the floor to his side was a small statue of the Hindu god, Hanoum. Thus, Dr. Vinod was in the center of a circle made up of the nine people listed above. He entered a trance state at 12:15 A.M. He spoke for about fifteen minutes and then one of the Nine, R, spoke through him, saying:

Tonight we want to create Brahmins in this world. Brahmin means a person dedicated to Brahman.

At this instant all nine observers in the fully lighted room saw the appearance, in an instant, of what appeared to be a pile of cotton threads about three feet from Dr. Vinod. It seemed to this observer that the pile of thread had just popped right out of the wood floor. Dr. Vinod, still in a trance state, leaned over to pick up the threads. When he untangled them, he brought forth loops of finely woven cotton cord. He handed one to each person and there was exactly one loop for each. He asked each person to slip the loop over the right shoulder and under the left arm.

What we had witnessed was the appearance of a material sub-

Introduction

stance from nowhere! All present were quite sure that the large ball of cotton material had come from the floor and no place other than the floor.

R spoke:

Has everyone received one? This is called the Yadnyobavita. These are the sacred threads which Brahmins wear on their necks, as soon as they are through with the ceremony. We have to be born twice; unless we are threaded, we don't become Brahmins. This is the sacred thread which makes the human being the Brahmin. Each one of you becomes a Brahmin on this full-moon day.

Alchemy had three different areas of function. It really wanted to solve the problem of deterioration, disease, and death. All metals are really gold in one way, but deteriorated gold. So transformation of the lesser, grosser metals into gold was one idea. The second was to find an elixir to eliminate all disease from the human body, and the third was to produce the nectar to eliminate death. These three threads on this sacrificial thread stand for each of these functions—altogether there are fifteen threads. I don't know how many you have, that's perhaps the symbol of the full moon. Of course, you all know that alchemy is actually operative whenever we are forcing a crisis on ourselves, or permitting a crisis to be forced on us, we are exposed to alchemy. Of course, "Al" means God, and "Kem" means Egypt; therefore Alchemy is God of Egypt, and God of Egypt was this.

It's very strange that the life of Buddha had these same three crises in it; the sight of disease, and the sight of death, and the sight of old age, which is deterioration. He had never been exposed to these crises. He lived like a plant in a green room. Suddenly he came across these three instances, as he was passing through a street in a chariot. He came home and he couldn't rest and asked himself, "Why must the human body deteriorate? Why disease? Why death?" And he went out of his palace at midnight. He left a wife and newly born son.

I don't know why I'm speaking this, but I think it has some reference to some of you already exposed to emotional, spiritual, and perhaps financial crisis. An alchemist process to which we are addressed—let us welcome it. . . .

I cannot go into all the details of the meaning of these trance utterances by Dr. Vinod. The material that was given would fill another volume, and only a small sample is presented in Appendix One to give a synoptic view of the philosophy of the Nine. We took every known precaution against fraud, and the staff and I became thoroughly convinced that we were dealing with some kind of an extraordinary extraterrestrial intelligence. But for this belief we had no solid proof in 1953.

Three years later, I was called to Mexico to help solve an archaeological problem. With me was Peter Hurkos, one of the great telepathic talents of modern times. Peter and I arrived in the colonial village of Acámbaro, Mexico, on July 26, 1956. Rooms had been reserved for us at the only hotel in town. When we got there, we found that the only two good rooms in the hotel had been given to an American family by mistake. But it was late at night, so we accepted two strange windowless rooms and planned to get more decent accommodations by discussing the problem the next day with the Americans who had been given our rooms.

In the morning we met the Americans, a Dr. and Mrs. Charles Laughead from Whipple, Arizona. We could not understand why they were so happy to see us and why they so gladly gave up their lovely, sunny quarters in exchange for our drab, dark ones. When Dr. Laughead, who was a medical doctor, found out that I was an M.D. and that Peter was a psychic, he was beside himself with joy. He then told us the following story:

"Through the assistance of a young man, who is a very fine voice channel or medium, we have been in frequent communication for over a year with the Brotherhood of one of the ancient Mystery Schools in South America. These sessions covered a wide range of subjects, from ancient history and life origins on this planet to science and religion. This Brotherhood also served as a communication center for contacts with intelligences on other planets and star systems and on spacecraft. Some of these intelligences obviously were not human and operated on energy and life support mechanisms entirely foreign to our thinking. Their knowledge and wisdom far exceeded our comprehension. For simplicity, we referred to them as Space Beings or Space Brothers.

"In one of these sessions our attention was directed to the story of the arrival on earth of men from outer space in very ancient times. This landing took place on a small island near Easter Island, called Mangareva. We were then told that the clay figurines at Acámbaro, Mexico, would corroborate by certain clues the story about these early space travelers. We were then directed to search out a possible location for continuing study and research in Mexico, and on this scouting trip we naturally came to visit the library of figurines at Acámbaro.

"Because of the unusual nature of this meeting with you gentlemen and the work under investigation, we feel you must be related in some way to the unfolding story of the ancient mystery of man in space, even though at the present time you may not have recall of previous life cycles on this and on other planets.

"The voices of our mentors speaking through our young channel sounded so authoritative that we felt impelled to follow through with their suggestions and come to Mexico. And here we are, having arrived only an hour before you. Are you not brothers from space?"

Dr. Laughead stared at us so intently as he said this that for a moment I thought, "Maybe I am." But then Peter and I looked at each other and burst out laughing. The whole idea was just too absurd. Peter hastily said in his broken English, "Meester, I'm born right in my modder's bed. I'm no space mensch!"

We talked for an hour to these charming but naïve people, to no avail. They were firmly convinced of the authenticity of their message. They coaxed us to admit our true space origins. We gently but firmly backed away. We then bade them good-bye and went off to take care of our business. During our stay there we carefully avoided seeing the Laugheads again. This spacebrothers talk was just too wild for our tastes.

On August 15, 1956, I received a letter at the Round Table Foundation from Dr. Laughead, mailed on August 12, from Whipple, Arizona. The envelope was addressed to Dr. Andae

Poharits (misspelled). The letter, labeled by me as "Test No. 1," read as follows:

Test No. 1

Dear Dr. Pharits [again misspelled].

It was indeed a pleasant surprise for us on our recent Mexican trip to discover and make the acquaintance of others interested in the same things we are interested in, particularly to find another M.D. interested in and working in the field of parapsychological research.

As you well know, a professional man that dares to venture into this area is certain to have a lot of "pot shots" taken at him, and I admire your courage in devoting your full time to this study.

On the evening of August 11th, we received the two enclosed communications, each through a different channel, and we were instructed to forward them to you at once. [Author's note: I have labeled these enclosures "Test No. 2."]

We were told that you would understand and would know what to do concerning them. We were also instructed to send a copy to Mr. and Mrs. Arthur Young.

After leaving Acámbaro we visited the Chicomostoc ruins near Zacatecas where I had a pick up that my wife Lillian and I had lived there about 1200 A.D. as Indians and that we had been brothers at that time. We had started from there north on a journey which eventually took us as far as Mesa Verde in Colorado, visiting Indian tribes along the way. At Mesa Verde a great spacecraft landed and contact was made at that time with the brothers of space.

We trust that our paths shall cross again and that which began so strangely in an ancient Mexican town is but the beginning of an interesting association.

Fraternally,
[signed] Charles Laughead

I just couldn't believe what I was reading, especially when I read the enclosures that I shall describe shortly. I decided to use Peter Hurkos's proven ability at psychometry to assess this note.

"Psychometry" is an old term used to describe a form of extrasensory perception. In psychometry Peter takes an object in his hands and simply recounts whatever mental impressions he gets from it. (This is the way in which Peter would work with the police; by touching objects belonging to missing persons, he could get enough information so that the person would often be found.) With us was Harry Stone, another telepathic talent, who often worked with Hurkos.

At 2 P.M. I handed Peter Dr. Laughead's letter, Test No. 1, sealed in a brown opaque envelope. Here are Peter's psychometric impressions in English:

"I must tell you, Andrija, this is not a fake. No, it is not a fantasy. These people have found out something. There is a professor here. There is a doctor in here, engineers. They don't get pay from another country."

At this point Harry Stone wanted to participate in the reading. So we handed him the Test No. 1 envelope.

"I see two lines, like a blowtorch, but it is two jets. It was red in the beginning, but the fire turned blue. I see two rows of fire all shooting out with jets. The fire gets so violent that it starts searing me."

AP: "Harry, look into that fire."

Harry: "Now I see the eye of a hurricane turning around. I see two men—I think they are two men, but they don't want to show their faces to anyone. They were covering themselves somehow."

AP: "You said that you *think* they were men. Why did you say that? Can you draw what they look like?"

At this point Peter said he would like to make a drawing of what he saw. His drawing showed a figure in black with a pointed cap, but no arms or legs. Harry said that this is the same thing he saw.

Hurkos: "These are people in black, but I also couldn't see their faces. They are in a costume which can withstand thousands of degrees Centigrade heat. This is nothing to laugh at. It is all quite serious."

AP: "Is that all you get?"

Peter and Harry both said they were tired and didn't want to work anymore. I handed Dr. Laughead's letter and the two enclosures to Mrs. Ida Gold, the secretary, and asked her to transcribe them and the tape of the experiment into typescript. She went ahead with this task immediately.

An hour later she came to me in great puzzlement and said, "Dr. Puharich, I have been a bonded court secretary for thirty years and have never seen what I have seen just now. Here is the material you asked me to type. It covers twelve and one-half pages. I did not change the carbon paper but kept using the same one over and over again. Now, look at each of the carbon copies. Notice that page one carbon is black and clear. Pages two to nine are good but getting lighter and less clear. Note how pages ten and eleven are getting very light and still less clear. This continues on the top of page twelve where the first ten lines are really light and faint. Then as soon as I began to copy the first enclosure, Test Number Two, the carbon copy from line eleven and on got black and clear—just as it was on page one when the carbon paper was fresh. This is impossible—how can carbon paper suddenly get rejuvenated?"

I examined the sheets and she was absolutely right: the carbon copy of the first enclosure, Test Number Two, from Dr. Laughead was in clear bold black typescript:

Test No. 2

M calling:

At the moment of our advent, December 31, 1952, your most spectacular phase of work began. We are Nine principles and forces. The nature of our work is to accentuate certain directions as will fulfill the destiny of creation.

We used the body or brain of Dr. "V." We can and are using other bodies also.

Remember the formula:

$$\frac{1}{\sqrt{1-\frac{v^2}{c^2}}} = 7$$

Introduction

It is vital that you have a personal conference with Dr. "L" as soon as possible, for it was not accident that you met him in Mexico. We will have more—much more for you.

A very similar message (as the reader will recall) was given through Dr. Vinod almost four years before. I tried for two years to find out if this material had come into Dr. Laughead's hands from someone connected with my laboratory, but the search was fruitless. I talked thereafter many times with Dr. Laughead, and he stoutly maintained that the material had come directly from the mouth of a medium whom he did not want to name.

But even if Dr. Laughead had tried to commit some kind of a deception, it could not account for the rejuvenation of a worn-out sheet of carbon paper. I could only conclude that some kind of an intelligence had created this black imprint by means entirely unknown. I was even willing to admit that there might be some reality to Dr. Laughead's "contacts" with spacecraft.

But the second enclosure that came with Dr. Laughead's letter was an even deeper mystery. I could not understand this piece of writing until many years later when I was in Israel in 1971. I now give a faithful copy of this piece of writing sent to me by Dr. Laughead:

Test No. 2

Received evening of August 11, 1956
Laughead apartment
Whipple, Arizona

M: We are in the place where the first of the prophets have had their origins and wherein they shall be gathered in. And they shall be put into a place wherein are the people from the planets of many galaxies; and they shall be the gods which shall create worlds without end. And ye shall see them and ye shall be within the holy mount which is within the Galaxy of the Milky Way and the forest wherein the earth shall be put when she is anchored and wherein is the new berth which is prepared for her, and so shall the earth be delivered up. And the people therein shall be freed from the earth and they shall be put into another place wherein they shall be awakened.

These events, and those related to Dr. Vinod, were totally beyond my imagination to comprehend completely. At this point I was not fully convinced that these "intelligent beings" existed independently of the imaginations of all the witnesses who had shared these experiences. When this question was discussed with all of my colleagues—which we did many times—no one expressed the conviction that what had been said was really true and could be accepted as such. It boiled down to the simple fact that there was not enough proof to accept the explanation of the Nine for what they were. Now, although proof and therefore total conviction were lacking, I still found myself continually asking, "What if it were true?"

It was nearly six years later that I was to have my own experience with what seemed to be "other-worldly" sources. In 1963 I was living in Ossining, New York, commuting each day to New York City where I was working on an electronic invention which would help people with a hearing problem. On March 15 I came home from an exhausting day in the city with a splitting headache and, without eating dinner, fell asleep in a second-floor bedroom at the rear of the house.

I slept for about two hours. When I awakened, I looked at the luminous dial of my wristwatch in the dark and saw that it was 9:40 P.M. I lay there, awake and fresh, thinking about getting up and having some dinner. From my position in bed I could see the wintry clear night sky, full of stars. Then suddenly among them appeared a bright light. My first thought was that an oncoming plane had just turned on its landing lights. I slowly got out of bed, keeping my eyes on the light, and walked to the window. I now saw that the light was stationary and was located just over the first hill to the west, which was about three hundred yards from where I stood. The light was like a flattened egg in shape, about the size of a full moon and of a steady blue-green color. The color, in fact, was the same color as one sees in a mercury vapor streetlamp. I stared at the light object.

I began to have a profound feeling of the gravity of this moment. I knew that the light was very, very real, and it gave me the feeling of a living thing. Normally in this kind of situation I would have taken my movie camera and gone outdoors to take pictures of the thing I saw. But now I had no desire to prove anything or to document what I saw. This was for me "pure experience." It was like nothing that had ever happened to me before, nor was there anything that I could associate with it.

I stood there for twenty minutes (by clock time) staring unblinkingly at this light object. I saw that it was only light; there seemed to be nothing solid associated with it. I could see nothing inside of the light as I stared at it. Suddenly the light was out. There was no movement; it just went out. I stood there staring at the bright night sky for another hour, but the light did not return.

After I had recovered from the emotional intensity of being in the presence of the light, I tried to analyze what this meant. I first thought of all the reports I had read about or had been told about concerning unidentified spacecraft. I concluded that what I had just seen and witnessed did not fit the general description that went with the most commonly reported types of UFOs. I recalled what Dr. Laughead had given me as a description of the spacecraft he had seen. I again recalled what Peter Hurkos had once described to me as "flying saucers" he had seen (or, the way he pronounced this phrase, "flying sausages"). None of these descriptions fit my experience. I finally concluded that what I had seen had to stand by itself, that I could not fortify it by getting assurance that others had also had the same experience.

The experience to me was very real, and the memory of it stayed with me. But I talked to no one about it. It was too private to reveal and, besides, it had no objective corroboration. I simply filed it away in my memory. But this kind of experience was to recur in Brazil.

I first heard of Arigó, the Brazilian healer, from an intelligent, articulate doctor named Lauro Neiva, who practiced in Rio de Janeiro. Dr. Neiva told me that Arigó was a man in his early forties who performed major surgery on humans without using any known form of anesthesia, bleeding control (hemostasis), or antisepsis. I was told that Arigó had become a "court of last appeal" for hopeless medical problems in Brazil and that his rate of success was phenomenal. On August 21, 1963, I set out from Rio de Janeiro for Arigó's village, Congonhas do Campo, which was about three hundred kilometers to the north of Rio in the state of Minas Gerais.

Arigó was of medium height with a powerful muscular build. He had a hearty outgoing manner which radiated confidence to all around him. Although I did not understand Portuguese, it was obvious that his speech had a rough peasant quality. I shall not go into details of his background or his present social situation because this material has been adequately covered in other writings.[2]

I was warmly welcomed and given free rein to observe his work, to interview patients, and to ask any questions I wished. On August 22 I observed Arigó handle about two hundred patients over a period of four hours. Arigó worked in a small dilapidated espiritista church. First he addressed the assembled patients and said that he himself was *not* the healer but that he acted only as an agent for a higher power, which, he said, was the spirit of one Adolpho Fritz, who had died in Germany in 1918.

In order to assure the patients that he would not harm anyone, he said he would demonstrate the safety of his work. He took by the shoulder a man standing next to him and without a word plunged a paring knife (a very sharp, four-inch stainless steel blade with a cocobolo wood handle) toward the man's left eyeball.

The knife was skillfully inserted under the upper eyelid, and the sharp point plunged deep into the eye socket. The patient was calm and relaxed, and when queried as to possible pain, he answered that he felt nothing. Arigó then pressed the point of the knife up through the upper chamber of the eye socket so that

[2] John G. Fuller, *Arigó: Surgeon of the Rusty Knife* (New York: T. Y. Crowell, 1974), with an appendix by Andrija Puharich, M.D.

Introduction

the point lifted the skin above the eye (supraorbital forehead area). Arigó asked me to feel the point of the knife through the skin, which I did. I affirmed that I could palpate the sharp tip of the knife. This exercise lasted about twenty seconds. When the knife was withdrawn from the eye socket, I asked the patient how he felt. He replied that he felt normal. Examination of the eye did not reveal any laceration, redness, or other signs of irritation. I was stunned at this demonstration of surgical and medical power.

For the rest of the four hours I watched Arigó's mode of handling patients. The patients stood in a long line waiting to see Arigó. When one stepped up, Arigó looked up at him or her from his desk, asked no questions, and in a few seconds began a definitive treatment, either surgical or medical, on each of the two hundred patients. He sent a dozen patients away, saying that their problems could easily be handled by any medical doctor. He performed eye surgery and ear surgery on ten patients, each operation averaging about thirty seconds. He used the same knife on each patient and wiped it on his shirt after each operation. No attempt was made to give any anesthesia or hypnotic suggestion; no sterile precautions were used; bleeding was minimal; and each patient walked out of the room by himself after surgery. The rest of the patients were given long complicated medical prescriptions which used proprietary pharmaceutical preparations from well-known drug houses. Arigó never charged for his healing services; he worked at a full-time job as a civil servant to earn his living.

I was in a state of shock as I witnessed his apparently successful handling of these patients while violating every rule of medicine and surgery in which I had been indoctrinated. I simply could not believe what I was seeing and experiencing.

At the end of the day of August 22, 1963 I pondered how I could prove to myself and my colleagues that we were not hallucinating. It occurred to me that if I could persuade Arigó to operate on a tumor on my right forearm I could get a personal and realistic evaluation of what he was doing. I approached Arigó with this request on the morning of August 23, and he cheerfully agreed to operate on me. I arranged for Jorge Rizzini to film my operation.

I had a lipoma on the elbow over the right ulnar head which measured by palpation about 0.5 inches×1.2 inches×0.4 inches. It had been there for seven years and had been checked regularly by Sidney Krebs, M.D., of New York City, during the past two years.

We appeared before Arigó at 10 A.M. There were dozens of patients crowding the room. I rolled up my right sleeve. Arigó asked if any of the surrounding patients could lend him a pocket knife. One man offered a knife, but Arigó said it was too dull. Another man offered a Swiss army knife; Arigó said, "This is a good knife."

Arigó told me not to look at the surgery. I turned my head toward Rizzini on my left, who was running the movie camera, and gave Osmar, my translator, some advice about the lighting. At the same time I felt Arigó grasp my arm at the tumor area with his left hand. All I could feel was something like a fingernail being pressed into the skin. Within five seconds Arigó displayed an elongated egg-shaped tumor for all the patients to see and handed it to me with the pocket knife. I had felt no sensation of pain. When I looked at the wound, there was a trickle of blood from the incision, which was about a half inch long.

Arigó then said that Dr. Fritz had told him to make the following statement: "This is a demonstration only—so that people will believe. I think every doctor in Brazil should come here and do what you do. After the legal prosecution against me is over, you must come back, and I will do major surgery for you."

Immediately after the surgery I took black and white pictures of the tumor and the knife. I then asked Altamiro, Arigó's assistant, to place a dressing on the wound. He took some unsterile gauze squares and taped them over the wound.

I felt that my surgery was not adequate for scientific purposes, as I was not able to observe it properly, nor did I experience enough significant data points to evaluate it. However, given the unsterile conditions of the surgery, I would have a real test of

Arigó's powers if the wound did not get infected. Hence I determined not to use any antiseptics on the wound nor to use any antibiotics, in order to test the postoperative course with respect to possible infection.

I therefore changed the bandage once a day so that I could photograph the healing and infective course. By the third day the wound had healed by primary intention, and not one drop of pus had appeared. I did not develop any symptoms of blood poisoning or tetanus. By the fourth day I dispensed with the bandage. With this evidence I was now convinced that Arigó had extraordinary powers in surgery, bacterial control, and anesthesia.

Six days later I visited Jorge Rizzini in São Paulo and saw the developed movies of my surgery. The film clearly proved that there had been an operation, and thus personal and mass hallucinations were ruled out. The film showed that Arigó had made six "sawlike" strokes of the knife through my skin to make the incision. This alone should have been painful. And strangely enough the tumor popped out of my arm without Arigó having dissected it. The entire procedure lasted five seconds.

It is now ten years since the operation. The surgical scar remains; the tumor is still in a bottle of alcohol; there have been no complications.

In September 1967 I went to Brazil to continue my studies of Arigó. I had seen him many times since that operation in 1963, and it had never occurred to me to ask him for personal help. One day as I was working with Arigó, he suddenly turned to me and said, "You have otosclerosis." I replied, "I don't know about that, but I have a chronic infection and drainage in my left ear from a cholesteatoma."

Arigó said, "Yes, you have had that for a long time, but the otosclerosis is new. Check it when you get home. I will give you a prescription that will cure both of your problems."

There is not much need to explain the items in the prescription except to state that the first drug was an ear drop solution, the second was a bile salt, and the third was gabromicina, a primitive form of streptomycin, which had largely been dropped from use by physicians. The prescription involved two successive treatments.

When I returned to the States, I had the audiologist in my own laboratory run a hearing test on me with an audiometer. When the test was done, she volunteered the diagnosis: "You have otosclerosis." I checked the audiogram. Arigó was right; I did have otosclerosis, a hardening of the bony tissue over the stapes in the middle ear chamber. I decided then and there to start Arigó's prescription.

Because of my odd working hours, it was easiest for me to give myself the gabromicina injection just before I went to bed each night. I started the first treatment series on October 7, 1967 —including the injection of the gabromicina once a day. By October 14 I had developed a reaction to this form of streptomycin. I had a swelling and tenderness of my hands and palms and on my feet and toes. Therefore, I had to stop the injections and wait for the allergic reaction to go away. By October 25 I was in good enough shape to begin the second treatment. In my opinion it was too dangerous to try to continue with the streptomycin. Therefore, I never did fully complete the first treatment. I finished the second treatment on January 11, 1968.

I was now free of the ear drainage problem that had plagued me all of my life, and have continued so to this day. Over the next six months my audiograms showed that my otosclerosis had disappeared. My hearing improved. I want to make one other point here, for the record: I never told another human being that I had not finished the first treatment because of an allergic reaction. (See page 159.)

In early 1968 I was busily engaged in preparations to lead a team of medical researchers to Brazil to study Arigó. We arrived in Congonhas do Campo on the afternoon of May 22, 1968. To house our group we had rented a large *fazenda*, or ranch, some two miles out of the village. As the sun set, we all assembled on the huge lawn to observe the incredible brilliance of the wintry stars. The night was cold and the air very dry. At 6 P.M. one of our researchers, John Laurance, noted a bright white light moving across the sky from south to north. He brought it to our attention because, as he explained, it was not a plane or a satellite. John could make this statement with some authority because he worked for the Astroelectronics division of RCA in New Jersey, designing and building satellites for NASA. For about six minutes we watched this light move slowly overhead, resembling a very bright star. It was impossible to determine its distance from us. Then it suddenly winked out in mid-course and was gone. We discussed what it could possibly have been and concluded that it was an unknown type of aerial light. The owner of the fazenda, Walter de Freitas, joined us, and we told him what we had seen and asked for clarification of our observation. He laughed and told us the following story.

"You see, the common folk around here always see what you just saw, mostly between May and August. They call them Rivers of Gold in the sky because they believe that these lights will lead you to gold. I don't believe these superstitions, but I have an idea why they believe such things. One day, two years ago, I was standing where we are now, and I saw one of these lights slowly come down from the sky. It landed about five hundred meters from here, in that direction by the river. It was just after sunset, as it is now. I could see pretty well in the dark, so I started to walk toward the light to see what it was. When I came to within fifty meters, I could clearly see moving figures under what looked like a metal craft, looking like a giant lens. I still am not sure whether the creatures were more like people or more like animals. But I could see and hear that they were digging in the earth. As I got closer, about thirty meters away, three or four of these figures suddenly disappeared into the metal hull which I now saw was standing on legs. The lens hull shot out fire and smoke and rose straight up in the air. When I examined the ground where the metal hull had been, I saw many small fresh holes. I went there the next morning looking to see if there was any gold, but I didn't find any."

We quizzed Walter for a few minutes, and then Dr. Luis Cortes called out, "Hey, there is another one!" Again we saw a very bright white light at an indeterminate distance, going slowly overhead from north to south. It, too, lasted for a long time—twelve minutes—and then winked out.

I immediately set up my Hasselblad camera, but I had only an 80-mm lens. But fortunately I had a Polaroid back for this camera and very fast 3000 ASA black and white film, which allowed me the possibility of getting some pictures. I set my camera on a stable tripod, and we all sat watching the skies. Fortunately, being in the country, there were absolutely no streetlights around to mar either the viewing or the photography.

Soon another light appeared, moving slowly from east to west, and I was able to photograph it, as a streak, through time exposure. Moreover, the film was so sensitive that I was able to get a background star map photo as a reference frame. We set up a night watch, and I was able to get three more photographs that night. After comparing our collective observations we all agreed unanimously that the lights we had seen and photographed were indeed unidentified aerial light effects.

During the next few days we discussed for the first time the theory that Arigó's powers may not be due to a Dr. Fritz, but to some intelligent beings associated with spacecraft of extraterrestrial origin. This seemed to be a perfectly logical hypothesis, but, of course, there was no way to test it. We spoke to Arigó about this possibility, and he just laughed away the question.

For the next three years I made plans to undertake a concentrated study of Arigó's powers, but other work intervened. At about 11 A.M. on January 11, 1971, I was working in my office at Intelectron Corporation in New York City when the telephone rang. Normally my secretary, Lorraine Shaw, would pick up the phone first. But this time, for no reason, I picked it up, and a woman whose name I don't recall blurted out the following: "I am looking for Dr. Puharich."

I replied, "This is he speaking."

"Dr. Puharich, I just got a telephone call from a TV station in Rio de Janeiro, Brazil, asking for you to make a comment on the death of Arigó."

"Would you please repeat that? I don't think I clearly heard what you said," I stuttered.

She repeated her statement. I said, "Are you sure of what you are saying, that Arigó is dead?"

She replied that all she knew was what had been relayed to her. I told her I could not then reply because of my shocked state. If she would give me her name and telephone number, I would call her back. This she did, and I wrote these items down on my desk calendar pad.

I sat back in my chair. It did not seem possible for Arigó—the greatest healer in the world—to be dead! He was too young, too vital. Besides, he was the hope of thousands, perhaps millions, of people who looked to him as the witness for higher powers. "There must be a mistake," I thought. "I will have to check this out myself."

I called the Brazilian consulate in New York, and they had no such news. I called the Brazilian embassy in Washington; they had no such news. I called the various press services; they had no such news. Finally by 4:30 P.M. I called friends in Brazil, who finally confirmed the dread news that Arigó had been killed that very morning in an auto accident.

I proceeded to return the phone call from the woman, and looked at my desk calendar pad. Her name and phone number were not there; the sheet was clean. I thought I had perhaps written the information somewhere else. But I could not find any such paper. I checked with my secretary; she had not heard the phone ring at 11 A.M. nor had she logged any incoming calls at that time. Then I began to worry; had I really received the call as I remembered it? Perhaps she would call me again. But she never did call back.

In any case, I was personally despondent over the loss of Arigó. Humanity had lost its great luminary. It was as though the sun had gone out. The shock was so deep to me that I decided to go on a fourteen-day fast and re-examine all of my life and weigh the meaning of Arigó, both in life and in death.

During my fast my sorrow was lightened by information I received from Dr. Juscelino Kubitschek, the former President of

Brazil. Kubitschek said that he had visited Arigó two weeks before his death, and in the most simple and casual way Arigó had said, "I do not like to say this, Mr. President, but I will soon die a violent death." The former President was shocked and disturbed. "You don't mean that," he said.

Arigó nodded and repeated in a sad, soft tone, "I am sure I will die violently very soon. So I say good-bye to you with sadness. This is the last time we will meet."

Later Arigó said to Gabriel Khater, editor of the local paper, *O Propheto*, "I am afraid, Gabriel, that my mission on earth is finished. I will leave soon."

But two years later I was to learn from John G. Fuller, who wrote a book about Arigó, that he had received a report that Arigó had been killed at exactly 12:15 P.M. in the car crash. Since the time in Congonhas is one hour earlier than New York, he had been killed at 11:15 A.M. New York time. How did I get the news of his death at least fifteen minutes before the event occurred? This mystery was not solved until my experiences with Uri in Israel. But the answer will be given later in this story.

The knowledge of Arigó's foreknowledge of his death helped me a great deal. That his death was not the result of blind chance eased my pain. Near the end of my fast, I came to some strong conclusions. The first was that I had failed both Arigó and humanity by not completing my studies of Arigó's healing work. I realized that I should have dropped my other work in 1963 and concentrated all of my efforts on Arigó. I was sure there would never be another Arigó in my lifetime. But if there were, I would not fail the next time.

I looked back over the ten years since I had moved to New York. I had become a slave to my company, to my inventions, and to a complex and costly way of life. While it was true that I had been issued some fifty patents for my inventions, which promised to help many people with deafness, I could not really make any more creative contributions in this area. Others could carry on what I had started. But most of all I wanted to get into the full-time study of the mysterious powers of the human mind. One day I made my decision. I would resign from all my duties and jobs from foundations, companies, and laboratories and give myself two years in which to find a new place in fulltime research on the mind.

When I informed my family and colleagues of my decision, they tried to talk me out of it. But I was determined in my course. By April 1, 1971, I had freed myself of all these ties and began my new way of life. I had two goals: one was to develop a theoretical base for all of my mind researches, and the other was to find human beings with great psychic talents who would cooperate as research subjects.

CHAPTER ONE

"Uri" Means Light

As far as Itzhaak and Margarete Geller were concerned, the birth of their first son, Uri, on December 20, 1946, in Tel Aviv, was a moment of peace in an unending struggle for survival. Itzhaak had fled from Hungary in 1940 before the holocaust consumed Europe. Upon landing in Palestine he had worked on a kibbutz, happy to be alive and free. When the British finally decided in 1942 to allow Jews to fight in the Allied cause to help defeat Nazi Germany, Itzhaak was one of the first to volunteer. He was trained as a tanker and fought with great courage and ingenuity against Rommel's forces in Africa.

Itzhaak Geller, like so many others, believed that he had a covenant with God by living in the Promised Land until God, in his perfect wisdom, revealed to his chosen ones why they had been chosen. If a man settled on a piece of land in Palestine, and if by sunrise he had established a water supply and a dwelling, Turkish common law gave him the rights of a settler. Itzhaak and his friends purchased a piece of scrub desert from a sheikh near Beersheba. The sheikh felt sure that the land could not be settled because the nearest waterline was a mile away. The planning for this new Jewish settlement went on for months. In pitch-darkness the young men and women practiced assembling their prefabricated huts and laying down a waterline that would not leak. They loaded their new community on six trucks and under cover of darkness arrived at "their" land. When the sun arose the next morning, it saw a brand-new kibbutz complete with huts, fences, watchtowers, and a precious waterline. The weary kibbutzniks proudly patrolled their settlement in the searing heat of that long first day. The Arabs came up with their flocks and tents and just stared at this miracle in the desert. There was no hostility in the air. The ancient law had been honorably fulfilled.

But Itzhaak and his friends learned that if they did not patrol their land twenty-four hours a day, they would be killed by anti-Jewish fanatics. They became a part of the home defense effort called the Haganah. This was a primitive home-guard militia defending land, home and family, and especially children.

Some of Itzhaak's friends who were political-minded joined a secret military group called the Palmach. The Haganah was solely concerned with defense; the Palmach was concerned with pre-emptive attacks, reprisals, and sabotage. Itzhaak was neither bloodthirsty nor war-minded and served only in the Haganah.

By 1949 the local outbreaks of violence had become more dangerous each day, and the little world of Israel had no peace for the baby Uri. Itzhaak found himself spending more and more of his time in soldiering and training others to be soldiers. The stress and strain was beginning to take its toll. Unlike many Jews, he could find no solace and peace in reading the Bible, nor in prayers. He was a man of action, and when he was troubled, he found some release by going to another woman. One day he found a young woman who gave him more peace than did his wife, Margarete. And Margarete was so heartbroken that she took young Uri and left home. Itzhaak, too, was heartbroken, but now it was a matter of personal survival.

Margarete moved to the budding town of Tel Aviv near the old Arab city of Jaffa (biblical Joppa). She found a job as a seamstress, and Uri spent the day in the company of a neighbor and her children. He loved this kindly lady, but she shouted too often and too loudly at her unruly brood. Uri eventually found a place where he could be happy in the midst of all of the bustling humanity around him. Across the street from his apartment was a stately Arab estate. It was fully a square block in size with a gray shuttered villa in one corner. It was surrounded by a high wooden fence that screened it off completely from eyes on the street. One day, Uri, in trying to peek through the fence, found that a vertical board gave way as though it were hinged at the top, and he stepped into what seemed to him a magic world. He saw near him a pool with fish in it. Through the ancient olive trees he saw the shuttered, gray stone house. No one appeared to be near, so he cautiously moved into the garden. The heavy foliage was sweet-smelling, the air was fresh, and the sounds of the street seemed far away and unreal. He dipped his bare feet into the pool and found that the fish were friendly and began to nibble on his toes. For the first time in his life he had a vision of beauty and peace. As this feeling settled down into the heart of a three-year-old boy, he lay down on the grass and fell asleep. At least for one soul in Israel there was peace in December 1949.

Uri awoke from what seemed like a long, long sleep, and he knew by his stomach clock, and by the shadows, that he had missed his noonday meal. He decided to take a trip around this vast scented forest before going home. As he reached the south side of the pool, with the sun at his back, he looked up at the clear sky over the pool. Slowly settling down from the sky was a huge, silent, bowl-shaped object. He stared in fascination: What kind of an airplane was this? All the planes his father had shown him were wonderfully noisy things with bird-like wings. This one was as quiet as his garden. It looked like the bottom of his mother's huge aluminum bowl, which she used to wash vegetables. It gave him a feeling of peace and beauty and of strength like when he was with his father.

Suddenly between himself and the bowl in the sky there was the shadow of a huge figure like the shadow of a man with a long cape, because there were no arms or legs to be seen. As he stared at this figure, a blinding ray of light came from its head and struck Uri so forcibly that he fell over backward and into a deep sleep. Again he slept for several hours to be awakened by the chilling shadows of the setting sun. He leaped up cold and hungry. He looked to the sky for the bowl, but it was gone. He remembered the blinding light of the shadow man, and somehow it made him feel good. He ran to the fence, found his loose board, scuttled through, and ran up the steps to the third-floor apartment. His mother asked him where he had been for so long. He eagerly told the story of the garden, the fish that nibbled, and the bowl in the sky. His mother spanked him for being away and scaring everyone by his absence and then telling such a tall tale. So for many years he did not speak to anyone again about his secret garden or the bowl in the sky. For a while he would return to the gárden and await the bowl. But when it did not reappear after a few months, he forgot all about it.

The only recreation that Uri's mother, Margarete, had was playing cards at the homes of her friends. When she returned, Uri would awaken, tell her how much money she had won or lost, and go back to sleep. Margarete was amazed because he was always accurate down to the last piastre. How did he know this? She didn't think about it too much, but made it into a "guessing game" that she and Uri would play when she came home.

Itzhaak was scarcely aware of this aspect of his son's life, because he saw less and less of him and because it never occurred to Margarete to tell him. Ever since the United Nations resolution of November 29, 1947, to set up the independent Arab and Jewish states in Palestine, he had spent more and more time soldiering. When on May 14, 1948, the leaders of Jewish Palestine declared their independence, and proclaimed the State of Israel, he had given up trying to live as a civilian and had returned to being a professional soldier. When he did see his son Uri, he talked only about his life as a soldier, of raids, guns, and skirmishes. It made Uri proud of his father to know that he was guarding all the people from harm. Uri decided that he wanted to be a soldier when he grew up and guard the people from the ever-lurking dangers. Itzhaak had no idea that his son was developing a reputation as an extraordinary guesser.

Uri continued to play in the garden of his Arab host. In the years that he had this sanctuary he never met anyone else in

"Uri" Means Light

this garden, and he wondered who his host really was. Although he never met his host or discovered anything about him, he instinctively liked him for letting him play in his garden.

In June 1953 Uri Geller was squirming in his seat in the torrid heat of a Tel Aviv summer day. The teacher droned on about the correct formation of Hebrew letters. He looked at his new wristwatch; it said 10:30 A.M. Would noon ever come so that he could get out of this classroom and dip his toes in the pool of his cool garden? He thought for a moment of the metal bowl in the sky. Why didn't it come back? He looked at his watch again. It now said 12 noon. He jumped up and started to leave the room. No one else moved. The teacher stared at him and then at the wall clock. The time on the wall clock was still 10:30. He backed into his seat. He furtively stole a look at his wristwatch: it said 12 noon. He stared at the watch. What could be wrong with it?

When he saw his mother at dinner that evening after his visit to the Arab garden, he said, "Mommy, that watch you gave me for my birthday, something is wrong with it. The hands keep jumping around."

Margarete looked at the watch. It was an hour and a half fast; perhaps it needed to be adjusted. "I'll take it to the jeweler; he'll make it run nicely."

A week later Uri had his watch back. It was another hot, steamy day. He wished school were over. He looked at the wall clock. It was only 10:30 A.M. He looked at his wristwatch. It said 12 noon. He was angry. He thought, "Stupid watch—work right!" He looked at the watch again. It was 11:30 A.M. He looked around to see if any of his classmates were watching him. No one paid any attention. Then he closed his eyes—wished hard that it would be 12 noon and that class would be over! He peeked at his wristwatch and it said 12 noon. He felt his heart leap! But when he looked at the wall clock, it was 10:31 A.M., and his heart sank. He couldn't get out of this classroom. He looked back at his wristwatch, which now read the same as the wall clock, 10:31. Now he was getting angry. He whispered to his friend Mordechai, "Here, take my wristwatch, and tell me what time it is."

Uri concentrated again, hoping that the school day would end. Mordechai whispered excitedly. "It is twelve noon on your watch, but it was ten-thirty one minute ago."

The two boys played this game until recess time at 12 noon. They went into the playground, and Mordechai excitedly asked Uri, "What kind of a trick watch is that? How can I do the same trick?"

"It's not a trick watch! I just wished it to move!"

Mordechai screamed with laughter until a crowd gathered around. Tears ran from Mordechai's eyes as he gasped to the crowding children, "Uri's got a trick watch, and he can move the hands with the trick! But he is trying to fool me by saying that he can make the hands move by wishing! He can't fool me —it's a trick watch."

The children wanted to see the trick. Uri didn't know what to do with all this laughing and jeering. It wasn't a trick watch!

"All right," he blurted out with unexpected authority. "I'll show you. Mordechai, show everyone the time, and then put the watch on the ground so that no one touches it." Mordechai did as he was told, and everyone saw that the time was 12:10 P.M. The watch was placed on the ground face down.

Uri suddenly liked being the center of attention. He dramatically placed his left hand across his forehead and tried to look like he was concentrating. He felt as though he was being watched by everyone. He said to himself, "Watch, please move the way you did in class." The school bell suddenly began to ring. Mordechai picked up the watch. Everyone crowded around him.

The clock hands were at 2 P.M.

"What a great trick!"

"Where did you get the watch?"

"Let's do it to the school clock!" exclaimed the children as they straggled into the classroom.

Uri was very, very quiet. The watch was not a trick watch. Why did it move? He tried once more. He set the watch hands at 12:15 P.M., the same as the wall clock. He closed his eyes and made a wish for the hands to move back to 12 noon. When he looked at the watch, it was 12 noon. It had worked! He was unsuccessful, however, in any attempts to affect other clocks than his own.

Over the next few weeks Uri's classmates never tired of wanting to see his trick watch. He tried to please them, but they only seemed to want to tease him into revealing the trick. When he insisted that it was not a trick watch, they began to jeer at him. Finally he became so hurt that he refused to do it anymore.

But secretly he continued to move the watch hands. He found that he could move the hands only when he was in school. He could never do it at home alone or in his garden. He wondered why it worked only in the midst of his crowded classroom. But because the watch trick did not make him popular with anyone—even Mordechai—he gradually stopped trying to move the hands by "wishing."

In Israel, shortly after Uri had passed his ninth birthday, Margarete had met Ladislas Gero, a pianist who had taken a great interest in her. She wanted very much to be with Ladislas but did not want to offend Uri by having him see her with a man. She solved the problem by arranging to have Uri live on a kibbutz not far from Tel Aviv.

When his mother left him at Kibbutz Hatzor Ashdod, Uri ran away and hid for several hours. Not only was he hurt by being parted from his mother, but he feared having to deal with a lot of new people. He came out of hiding as he got hungry and walked into the communal dining hall. A friendly girl escorted him to the cafeteria and then led him to their quarters. It contained sleeping arrangements for eight children—four boys and four girls—and their teacher. This area also contained their classroom. Since Ashdod was subject to sudden raids from Arabs in the nearby Gaza Strip, the children were thoroughly drilled to be constantly alert to danger, and what to do about it.

Although Uri was now a part of a real family for the first time in his life, and everyone was very good to him, he could not get used to this "public" life. He was always being kidded about being stuck-up and a loner. And, in fact, try as he could to change his attitude, he really was most comfortable when alone. He tried to make friends on his own terms by showing his watch trick to his classmates, but somehow it did not work to make him popular. Nor did his unusual quickness in class endear him to them.

So Uri spent much time out in the orange groves by himself. He was happy only when his mother came to see him on Sabbath. But he was not too happy when she brought Ladislas. Oh, Ladislas was all right, but his mother didn't pay enough attention to him when Ladislas was around.

One day Uri was called out of his class to see a visitor. As he came up out of the stairway into the bright sun, he could scarcely see the figure in front of him. It was his father in full battle dress! Uri jumped on him with joy. His father led him out to the road, where there was a company of eight tanks, each looking like a powerful fortress. Itzhaak said to Uri, "This is my group, and the front tank is the lead tank under Captain Avram. I'm his sergeant major. We are going off on maneuvers to the border. Hop in and I'll give you a ride, and then you can hitch a ride back here."

The excited child climbed into the Sherman tank and found himself in a blazing hot hellhole where the noise was deafening. His father tried to point out where the gun controls were, but he couldn't hear a thing. Before he knew it, the tank lurched to a stop, he was handed up the hatch, and his father was standing in the dust with him.

"Uri, don't say anything to anyone, but war may come any day. This time it looks bad because the Russians have armed the Egyptians to the teeth. Always remember that I love you, and I only go to battle to protect you. Shalom, shalom, son."

And his father was gone down the road in a whirlwind of dust.

Uri stood there for a long time, trying to remember something in a garden when he was three years old. But he could not recall what it was. He placed his hand on his head and prayed to God for his father. He didn't want to hitch back to the kibbutz, so he walked in the dust and heat.

Two weeks later, on October 29, 1956, Itzhaak's tank unit got orders in the early dawn hours that war was on, and to get to the Suez Canal without fail. Itzhaak's unit battened down the tank hatches and raced toward the Mitla Pass. As they entered the Pass, they could clearly see the massive Russian tanks strategically placed on each curve and hillock. Itzhaak thought, "God, how can we survive this gauntlet? Sooner or later they will get us."

There was no further time to think. The first Egyptian tank was coming within gun range. Itzhaak's commander, Captain Avram, then shouted a radio order to all his tanks, "Don't fire—wait!" Everyone thought, "He is mad! We'll be blasted to bits at this point-blank range!" But Captain Avram showed even more madness. He lifted the turret lid and stuck his head out. "The fool," thought Itzhaak. "He wants to be the first to go!"

Strangely enough, all of Captain Avram's men held their fire. An uneasy calm came over each of them as they came up to the first Egyptian tank and saw that the Egyptian soldiers were staring at them as though hypnotized. As the Israeli tankers passed one Egyptian tank after another, it was the same story. The Egyptians stood with hands frozen on the triggers of their guns. Captain Avram's men opened the hatches of their tanks to stare at the Egyptians as they raced on in the eerie silence of Mitla Pass. Unit after unit of the Israeli Tank Corps raced by the paralyzed Egyptian soldiers. Finally, when enough Israeli armor had pierced through the pass, the Egyptians began to surrender voluntarily. To this day, no one has ever explained what happened that day to give the Israeli Army complete victory over superior forces.

When the war started on October 29, 1956, Uri and his friends were kept in their bomb shelter for four days. They listened to the radio and prayed many times each day for their parents and that God would spare Israel as he had in the times of Moses. Uri kept wishing especially for the safety of his father. Two weeks later he received a message that his father was alive and was going to visit Uri on the following day. Uri stood in the road all day where the bus stopped, waiting for his father.

This was the longest day of his life. When he was about to give up, a bearded, dusty soldier leaped from the back of a truck with two rifles. It was his father!

Uri rushed up and got scratched by his father's new beard. He was bear-hugged till it hurt, but he didn't mind. His father stayed at the kibbutz that night and told the marvelous tale of how God had led them through the Mitla Pass, going almost invisibly past the huge Russian-built tanks. Uri slept very soundly that night, knowing that God watched over Israel and that his father was safe.

In the fall of 1957 Uri left the kibbutz and came to live with his mother again. His mother confided that Ladislas had asked her to marry him. What did Uri think? Bravely he replied, "Mother you do need a friend. You are always alone. Does this mean that you would not have to go to work every day?"

"Thank you, Uri. Yes, I would not go to work. You see, Ladislas owns a small hotel in Cyprus, and we would all work together there."

"Where is Cyprus? Is it like the kibbutz? I didn't like it there at all!"

"No, Uri, it is not like the kibbutz at all. Cyprus is an island."

"An island! That sounds great. What's on the island?"

"It is a very civilized place with resorts, mountains, and different people live there, Greeks and Turks."

"Mother, what are Greeks and Turks?"

"Well, you see, we are Jews."

"But, Mother, what are Jews? I thought we were people like everyone else. My father talks about Jews and the covenant with God and the Promised Land and how God helps the Jews when they are in bad trouble. But why should God do this only for the Jews? How do you become a Jew?"

"Stop, Uri. I can't answer all those questions at once! First, you are a Jew because your mother is a Jew. And I am a Jew because my mother was a Jew, and so on all the way back to the beginning of our history, which starts with a man called Abraham. He was not Jewish, but God came to him here in Israel and said, 'Walk in my ways and be blameless. I will establish my covenant between me and you, and I will make you exceedingly numerous.' And God and Abraham entered into an agreement. And all of Abraham's descendants became the Jewish people."

"But, Mother, I don't feel like a Jew. Why is that?"

"Well, you see, your father and I agreed when you were a baby that it was enough for you to be brought up in freedom here in Israel. We didn't want you to have to go to Shule and be told a lot of things about Judaism while you were too young to understand. Because you have not gone to Shule and do not know the synagogue, no one has pounded it into your head that you are a Jew. You are a citizen of Israel. That is enough. When you grow up, you can decide for yourself if you want to be a Jew."

"I understand, Mother," Uri said very gravely, and left the room. From now on he began to notice who was a Jew and who was not. He found that those who were religious Jews spent a lot of time praying and eating special foods and obeying many rules. Those who were not religious spent more time playing and at the beach and were not fussy about food and rules. Both Jewish groups got along well in Israel.

As 1957 came to an end, and his eleventh birthday approached, Uri got more and more unhappy about leaving his cozy apartment and the garden across the street and about the prospect of going to a place where no one spoke Hebrew. Somehow, he could not like Ladislas, although Ladislas was very nice to him. When they finally moved to Cyprus in early 1958, Ladislas bought a beautiful fox terrier for Uri, which the boy named Joker.

The name of the small hotel on number 5 Pantheon Street, in Nicosia, was the Ritz. It was a marvelous place. It had many rooms, and Uri would explore them after each guest left, hoping to find some treasure. He shared his own small attic room with Joker.

Living in Cyprus made him aware for the first time that he was a Jew. He attended the Terra Santa College presided over by Father Massamino, the Catholic priest. Most of the boys in the school were American or English, whose parents were stationed on Cyprus with some military job or other. Uri learned to speak fluent English in two months, much to everyone's surprise. Neither Margarete nor Ladislas ever learned English. Since they spoke Hebrew very poorly, Uri spoke to them in Hungarian, which he had spoken since childhood. In the streets of Nicosia, which were as noisy and dusty as the old quarter of Tel Aviv, his fine ear soon mastered the Greek language. As these four languages flowed easily through his mind, so did the customs and peculiarities of each of these peoples.

In class his teacher, Brother Bernard, told his young students of the life of a Jew who had lived in Nazareth in Israel. Uri's father had once taken him to Nazareth while they were en route from Tel Aviv to Safad near the Sea of Galilee. This man from Nazareth was called Jesus, and considering what a tiny hillside town Nazareth was above the Valley of Jezreel, it was hard for Uri to understand why he should be so revered here in far-off Cyprus. Uri's strongest memory of Nazareth was that as you entered the hot dusty town and went up and down the narrow stone streets, you were flooded with the smell of fish. It was puzzling why Jesus, a Jew, was popular only with these Catholic people, and not with Jews.

When Jesus was born, there appeared a star in the sky that had never been seen before. Brother Bernard chuckled when he told the boys that the star then was a lot like the lit-up spacecraft that people were now seeing all over the world.

"And this star slowly moved in the heavens by day and by night, leading three wise men who were seeking the Messiah. Although Jesus was born in Bethlehem, he grew up in Nazareth. As he grew up, he began to show a wisdom and knowledge unlike that of anyone else around him."

Uri impulsively blurted out, "Brother Bernard, could Jesus move the hands of a watch without touching it?"

Everyone burst out in laughter at this crazy question. Brother Bernard rapped for order and said to Uri gently, "You see, they did not have watches in Jesus' time, so the answer to your question is no. But he could do other things like that. For example, changing water into wine or making many loaves of bread out of one."

Uri was embarrassed by the laughter and didn't really know why he had asked the question. Of course, no one on Cyprus knew that he had once been able to move the hands of a watch. But somehow he liked this man Jesus, especially the boy Jesus. It seemed that he could do things that nobody else could do, and people laughed at him. What's the use of telling people your secrets if they laugh? Besides, all these people in Cyprus who believed in Jesus, and went to church every day, were also out in the streets fighting every day. The great riots between the Greeks and the Turks were heavy in the air and ready to explode at any moment. Why did not the Greeks heed the peaceful words of Jesus and the Turks heed the tolerant wisdom of their prophet, Mohammed?

In the intense emotional heat of Cyprus there was also cool sanctuary. Uri and his dog Joker had found some deep, seemingly endless, cool caves in the hills above Nicosia. Here with his flashlight, the security of Joker, and his tingling sense of excitement, Uri found peace and happiness. People were all right, but to be alone in these cool caves was joy. For Uri, these caves were magical. Somehow, when he was in them, he felt complete security, as when his father's arm was around him. He felt a peace and serenity that he could not understand. It was like the garden of the Arab villa in Tel Aviv.

As Uri reached his twelfth birthday, no one in his family told him that it was time for his Bar Mitzvah ceremony when a boy becomes a man and is formally accepted into the ancient religion of Judaism. But this did not interest him very much. Religion in Cyprus seemed to him very unattractive. The Orthodox Catholic Greeks were forever in riots with the Muslim Turks.

On the street where he lived there was a charming old Muslim scholar, Mustafa Sa'abud. He was called an 'Uluma by his fellow Turks, which meant that he was learned in the Koran and taught the young people from it. He seemed to take an interest in Uri for reasons unknown to Uri. When 'Uluma stopped Uri with a nice Turkish sweet, the two would chat in Greek.

The 'Uluma once asked Uri why he did not wear the Jewish skull cap, the yarmulke, like the other Jewish boys. Uri replied, "Wearing a cap will not make me a better Jew. Being a Jew is like being anyone else. All you have to do is believe in God. I believe in God."

'Uluma gently replied. "You are wise. To be a Muslim means the same thing. 'Muslim' means to 'submit to the will of Allah,' and 'Allah' is our word for God. This is the same as to believe in God. You know we Muslims and you Jews believe in the same God."

Uri hastily interrupted, "Then why are the Jews and the Arabs, who are Muslims, always fighting? My father has to fight with the Arabs all the time because they want to take our land and homes away from us!"

"My son," said 'Uluma with a tear welling in his eye, "your El and our Allah are one and the same. He always spoke to his people through his prophets. Our common ancestor and prophet is Abraham, and so is Moses. Jesus, whom the Greeks here in Cyprus worship, was a Jew who was rejected as a prophet by his own people. We Muslims accept Jesus, but not all the doctrine that Christians have added to his name. The next prophet that God spoke to was our Mohammed, who is not accepted by either the Christians or the Jews. You see, over the centuries these three faiths have at times fought each other, and at times have known peace. Did you know that the Jews, the Christians, and the Muslims all consider Jerusalem to be a holy place?"

"No, I didn't. Tell me why this is so." Uri replied with an intensity that surprised the old man.

The 'Uluma slowly leaned back and lit his pipe as he got ready to tell a story.

"It all started with Abraham (whose name was Abram then), who was brought up in the very ancient city of Ur in what is now Iraq. Did you know that Ur is the most ancient word that we have for 'light' and that your name, 'Uri,' also means 'light' in Hebrew? Well, God came to Abraham and told him to leave his home in Haran, to carry out a job for God in the land that is now Palestine."

"What kind of a job could an ordinary man do for God?" interrupted Uri. "After all, God can do everything!"

"We don't know for sure what kind of a job, but our books, the Bible and the Koran, tell us that it was something very difficult and not easy to explain. God asked Abraham to enter into a covenant in which he would believe in Him and worship Him. If Abraham did all this and passed this covenant on to his descendants, there would eventually come the perfected man. Abraham entered into this covenant at Hebron, which is in Palestine between the Mediterranean Sea and the Dead Sea.

"My son, I believe that it is the will and the compassion of Allah that all men love him, and love one another. I believe that another prophet shall arise whose task will be to lead all men back to the true love, the only God, for there is but one God. It is man who has made so many gods. My son, I am a Muslim, and you were born a Jew. Let us agree that there is one God who made man and that it is wrong for us to hate or to fight."

Uri looked at him thoughtfully. "Yes, I agree to try not to hate, or to fight, and I believe in God." Uri turned away and walked up the cobbled street to get Joker and to go to the caves.

One day about a year later Uri was in his attic room doing his homework when he heard a noise in the attic part that no one used.

He thought that maybe a bird had gotten trapped. He took a flashlight and gingerly stepped over the open rafters of the rooms below, seeking to find the bird. When he got to the far end, the sound had ceased, and he stood still for several minutes to listen for a bird. Suddenly, a door slammed in the room below. He heard voices. Light was coming up through the attic floor from the room below, right at his feet. Slowly he lay down on the rafters, put his eyes to the crack, and listened.

The man doing most of the talking was a Jewish grain buyer, Joav Shacham, who stayed at the Ritz when he was in Cyprus. The other men were strangers to Uri. They were speaking in Hebrew. Joav was telling a man he called Amnon, "You will leave for the Sudan in two days. All of your credentials are prepared as Klaus Sachs. You will set up your agricultural equipment business in Khartoum. Send all of your orders to Joel in Essen, Germany. He will ship out whatever you request. Max here will listen for all of your radio messages in Ethiopia. Remember, you have about six months in which to infiltrate the Egyptian Army through the Sudanese."

At these last words, Uri's heart began to pound. Were they talking about a spy operation, just like in the movies? The meeting lasted for another hour, and Uri heard more and more details of the spies' plans.

He figured out that these men were Israeli agents and they were using his stepfather's hotel as a base. He waited until the men had left Joav's room, and then he tiptoed back to his room.

He told no one of his discovery. But every time Joav came to Nicosia, which was quite often, Uri hung around him in the dining room. They got to be friends. Uri was puzzled because Joav didn't look like a spy. He was husky, about six feet two inches tall, and very powerful in build. He wore scholarly-looking glasses and had thick unruly hair. His clothes always looked rumpled. He looked like a grain buyer, but definitely not a spy. Uri got very clever about spying on the spy from the attic peephole. He did this for about six months. One day just he and Joav were playing basketball. Seeing that no one was around, Uri decided to broach the subject of spying to Joav.

"By the way, Joav," Uri started out casually, "how is Amnon doing in the agricultural equipment business in Khartoum?"

Joav stopped dribbling the ball he was getting ready to shoot. He looked around to see if anybody was within earshot. "Where did you learn about Amnon?" he asked grimly.

Uri laughed, "You would be surprised what I know, and how I know it!"

"Listen, Uri, let's take a walk to the hills. I want to talk to you."

They walked to the hills, not saying much.

Finally, when they sat on a hilltop looking down at Nicosia, Joav said, "All right, tell me how you know about Amnon."

Uri proudly told him how he had first accidentally overheard Joav's meeting and then how he had regularly spied on the spies. Joav listened thoughtfully and then addressed Uri. "Yes, I am a spy for Israel. But it is not what you think it is. It is a plain dirty hard job and no pay. Let me tell you why I do it, and hundreds of others risk their lives every day. You see, Uri, Israel is surrounded by enemies who boast every day that they will turn the sea red with Jewish blood. They mean what they say. We Jews will no longer wait, as we did in Europe, to be slaughtered like sheep. Our only hope of survival is to know every move that our enemy makes against us. If we find out that our enemy is going to strike, we must strike first in order to survive. That is why we were able to win the war in 1956. We knew the Egyptians were going to strike, and we caught them off balance by striking first. You, too, are a young Jew, and in a couple of years you will be in the Israeli Army. Your survival will depend on what our agents are doing in remote places scattered all over the world.

"Uri, I beg you, please keep what you know about my activities a secret. In fact, you have been so clever that I would like to have you work for me!"

Uri was really taken aback by Joav's offer. How could he be a spy? He was only sixteen years old. "But," he thought, "maybe if I find out something really big, I can help my father who is stuck in the Army in Israel. Father doesn't really know what the enemy is planning."

"Okay, Joav, I'll join you. What can I do? Should I have a code name?"

Joav smiled in relief at Uri's questions. "Well, I will have to work out a careful plan. But there is one job that is very important. You see, I get my mail from a postal box at the post office. The more I go there, the more likely it is that I will be spotted by enemy agents. So if you will go to the post office for me, you will save me from possible detection. I will see how well you do before I give you more dangerous jobs."

"Gee, that's exciting," said Uri. "How can I tell who are the enemy agents who are watching at the post office?"

"Well, I'll teach you how to do all that, and what to do if somebody tries to steal my mail, and how to steam open letters, and things like that."

Thus it was that Uri became a courier for an Israeli spy ring on Cyprus when he was sixteen years old. About a year later, after he had seen Joav come and go from the island many times, he was complimented by Joav for doing a good job. One of the things that Uri had to do was to deliver the letters he picked up to the Israeli consulate when Joav was not on the island. Joav said, "In about a year you will be old enough to serve in the Army. Men of your abilities are hard to find. I would like you to apply to the paratroopers when you enter the Army. I am sure that you will be accepted. When you finish your basic training, apply for the Officer's Candidate Training School. If you have any problems, look me up. You can always locate me through the Army."

This was an exciting prospect for Uri, and in his mind it became a commitment. He knew that if he did what Joav had suggested, he would be helping Joav as well as his country.

During his sixteenth year another event occurred that left a deep impression on Uri. It was true that he did not like his stepfather, although Ladislas was good to him. Sometimes in his boyish way, Uri would pout when Ladislas disciplined him. Then Ladislas unexpectedly died of a heart attack. The burden on Margarete was suddenly increased. Uri had mixed feelings. Partly guilt and partly relief. But he had to work harder and harder to help his mother run the small hotel. As his eighteenth birthday approached, there was heavy pressure on Jews to leave the island as the new government moved toward independence for Cyprus. Under these various pressures Margarete sold the small hotel at a sacrifice price, and she and Uri moved back to Tel Aviv.

By the fall of 1965 Uri was a soldier in the Israeli Army. He was now six feet two inches tall and weighed 180 pounds. He was quick, alert, and powerful. He volunteered for the paratroopers, passed all the qualifying tests, and began his rigorous training. After the eleventh month of his training and his acceptance into the class for Officer's Training, personal tragedy struck him. He picked up a newspaper and read that Major Joav Shacham had been killed in action during a border raid on the Jordanian frontier near a town called Es-Samu', just south of Hebron. He was deeply depressed. He had lost one of his best friends. Suddenly there was no meaning in his going on to Officer's Training School. He lost all interest in being proficient. And then another blow fell upon him. His dog Joker, who was living with his mother, was getting old and very ill. Uri took him to several veterinarians. They all told him that nothing could be done, that it would be best to put him away. Uri sadly left Joker with a veterinarian, and as he left the premises, he leaned against a fence and cried for both Joker and Joav.

Uri deliberately failed his final tests for officer's candidacy. He returned to paratrooper training in the desert. He pushed himself without mercy, sleeping on the ground in the sun, in the rain, in the freezing nights. He jumped out of planes, gathered up his chute, and went into mock battle. His bones ached, his muscles were sore, his skin was parched, his feet pained him, and his ears rang with gunfire. And always the paratroopers were told that next to the fighter pilots, they were the elite on whom the safety of Israel depended. They would be the first to be dropped into the hottest point of battle.

Two years later, by May 1967, Uri was as tough as Damascus steel. He was a sergeant, and he was so proud when he met with his father, who was a sergeant major, in different army camps, and they would swagger around together. But in May the paralyzing grip of a war threat settled over all of Israel. The tension for the Israeli civilians—mothers, wives, oldsters, and youngsters—became unbearable. A song, "Jerusalem of Gold," appeared on the radio and became the morale builder of the nation. War and war clouds hung over the Middle East once again.

Uri and his fellow soldiers got fidgety. Guns were cleaned and recleaned. Ammunition was counted, checked, packed, and unpacked. Parachutes were always being packed and then checked and rechecked. To relieve the tension all leaves to soldiers were continued as though an emergency did not exist.

Finally, at the predawn hour on June 5 the Israeli military machine acted on intelligence that the Egyptians were going to attack. The handful of Israeli fighter planes struck at every known Egyptian air base and in three hours destroyed the entire

Egyptian Air Force. In the Sinai Desert there exploded one of the largest tank battles in human history. The Israelis attacked like a swarm of hornets sweeping enemy tanks out of the way.

When the war started, Uri was on leave in Tel Aviv visiting his mother. At 6 A.M. June 5 he hitchhiked to join his unit, which was held up for hours while a decision was being made as to where they should be thrown into battle. Finally, in the afternoon at 2 P.M. the order came that they were to join in the battle for Jerusalem led by Colonel Mordechai Gur.

Uri was relieved to know where they were going. As his truck roared toward Jerusalem, Uri thought of his father. Where was his unit? Did it go to the Sinai? Was his father going to the attack on Syria? What if he were sent to Jerusalem? It would be a miracle if he and his father could fight side by side, helping each other. If his father was hit, he would save his life! He prayed to God to save his father. He didn't need a yarmulke—he had a steel helmet on. Somehow it never occurred to him that anything would happen to him. His only concern was that his mother at home must be kept safe. He knew that his friend Joav had risked and lost his life so that Israel would know when to strike to protect itself.

The truck slowed down as the traffic got dense to the north of Jerusalem. Finally they were there. Heavy mortar fire was just ahead. The staccato machine-gun fire echoed all over the Jerusalem hills. The sun was going down, and Jerusalem lit up with a golden glow. It was the magical blush of the bride of God. The word was tersely whispered from soldier to soldier, "This year—Jerusalem!" It had been nineteen centuries since Israel had been dispossessed of its Holy of Holies.

Uri had a squad of eight men under him. The Arab Legion was fortressed in concrete pillboxes in this area north of Jerusalem. Every pillbox had to be assaulted by hand grenade, machine gun, and human bodies. Signals were worked out for spotting mortar and artillery fire.

During his first long night of battle, Uri never saw the enemy; it was a kind of impersonal fighting, with these holes in concrete staring out of walls. But as the day and the battle heated up, it was no longer impersonal. When they hit a pillbox, blood would splatter out of it. A voice would scream in anguish and keep screaming out of the bunker.

As the fever got stronger, the men became more reckless, and everyone was doing heroic deeds without notice or attention. By the next morning Uri had lost five of the eight men in his platoon. The replacements were slow in coming in. Uri pushed himself and his men. Ahead lay three bunkers, with the center one deeply protected by the two flankers. A combined assault was made on the three. Uri's group was to take the heavily protected center bunker. The bunker to Uri's right was being assaulted so heavily that the fire came out of it sporadically, and Uri was emboldened to move ahead more rapidly, firing his machine gun in bursts at those slits ahead. Suddenly there was a searing flame in both his arms. He looked down and saw the blood spurting. He got angry and rushed ahead, blazing at the bunker slits, while his men surged after him and crept under the bunker and silenced it with their grenades. As the realization of victory was certain to Uri, he slowly fell and pitched against the cold concrete wall.

Uri awoke the next day in a hospital. The doctor told him that machine-gun bullets had gone through both forearms, but no vital nerves or blood vessels had been seriously damaged. He would be back on duty within a few months. Uri went back to sleep. He awoke to find his father standing by his bed.

As Uri recovered from his arm wounds, he was sent to a rehabilitation center. Here the young people of Israel came each day to entertain and help the wounded. A young girl of sixteen, Hannah, came twice a week to the center; Uri was shyly attracted to her. She was a slender, medium-sized girl with flashing blue eyes and honey-blond hair. Joy seemed to bubble out of her, and she was always laughing. Uri began to date her.

Part of Uri's rehabilitation program was serving as a counselor at a summer camp for teen-age boys. One of his charges was a twelve-year-old boy whose name was Shimshon, but everyone called him Shipi. Shipi was tall and thin with an intense storklike head. His mother called him Gandhi with affection. He always seemed to be sniffing and sensing the air around him. He was powerfully attracted to the tall lean paratrooper with the bandaged arms. He hung around Uri so much that Uri could not ignore him. One evening after dinner Uri discovered that Hannah was Shipi's sister!

What these three had in common was an endless round of practical jokes. The laughter never ceased when they were together. When they were apart, each one noticed how quiet it was, because no one else stimulated them to laughter. Uri looked upon Shipi and Hannah as the brother and sister he had never had. One day Uri was moved to tell Shipi about the watch hands. He showed Shipi how he could move a watch's hands without touching the watch. Shipi did not laugh; he believed Uri implicitly. Uri had not done the watch "trick" for years. He noticed that he didn't need a lot of kids around now. He wondered why it was so easy to do when Shipi was around.

The summer ended, Shipi and Hannah had to return to school. Uri was assigned to duty tracing army deserters all over Israel. By the end of 1968 he was honorably discharged from active duty and now faced civilian life, but all he knew were some languages and soldiering.

Uri found a job as an export manager for a textile firm in Tel Aviv. This fancy title meant that he got the purchase orders from abroad written in English, Greek, or Hungarian, and filled the orders. Life was dull. He saw Hannah and Shipi when their school time permitted. He was restless. To make some more money, he found he could take assignments as a photographer's model.

In October 1969 Shipi begged Uri to come to his school and do his "tricks" for his class. Uri reluctantly agreed when the teacher also invited him and promised to pay him fifteen pounds. Uri appeared in the small school auditorium for his first public appearance. He had watched entertainers in the Army, and he had a feeling for what to say. Once on the stage, he pretended that he was addressing Shipi, and everything then proceeded smoothly. He had children draw pictures and numbers on the blackboard, and while blindfolded he would guess what they had written. Once he got started, it just seemed to go on and on without effort. He went on doing his "tricks" for three hours. Everyone was enchanted, including the teacher. Uri had no idea of how he did his "tricks." They just came forth spontaneously and naturally without his ever having done them or practiced them before.

But Shipi was the one who was the most proud. He kept telling Uri how great he was and that he should go on the stage. In the next few months Shipi went around the neighborhood telling everyone what a "genius" Uri was. So now in addition to his job as export manager, Uri was doing modeling work and demonstrating in homes and at private parties. During the shows he enjoyed being in front of people, but as soon as his show was over, he had to retreat. He couldn't enjoy being close to people, except for Hannah and Shipi. By January 1970 he was getting small notices in the newspapers for his telepathic and mind-over-matter feats.

In March 1970 he was approached by a theatrical manager who advised him to quit his job and become a full-time entertainer. The manager was persuasive, and Uri did his first professional stage show in a movie theater, Kolno'ah, in Bat Yam. In two months he had become a sensation in Israel. In June 1970 he did his first college show for some of the graduating class of the Technion Institute in Haifa.

CHAPTER TWO

The Gordian Knot

By early February 1972 the events to be described in this book had resulted in my being in a state of continual, severe pressure, and I was in need of a good rest. It was for this reason that on the morning of February 13, Uri Geller drove me to Lod International Airport where I was to catch a plane for Rome.

As Uri and I parted at the escalator going up to the Immigration Section, a customs official came up to me and insisted on escorting me. I waved good-bye to Uri as I ascended, little knowing that I was walking into a trap. The official took me into an office where, without saying a word, he carefully checked my passport. Then he asked me to follow him; we went right through Immigration and Inspection without being stopped. Suddenly I realized I was in trouble. I was led into a small room, where waiting for me were four tough-looking men in their forties.

They identified themselves as Israeli Army Counterintelligence (Shin Beth) officers. One of them politely requested my permission to search me and all of my effects. I protested vigorously and asked to see their search warrant. One of them said they were exercising normal wartime powers. I asked for permission to call one of my many acquaintances in the Israeli Army. They refused. So I consented to the search, feeling secure in the knowledge that they would find no evidence that I was any kind of

The Gordian Knot

"spy." However, they not only thoroughly searched my person, camera bag, and briefcase but also took possession of almost all of the contents. I became furious when they confiscated my three volumes of research journals containing data on Uri. Again I protested vigorously. One of the men look at me grimly and said, "I hope, for your sake, that we do not find what we are looking for."

After he had taken my research journals, movie films, telephone book, and letters, the leader of the group said that this material would eventually be returned to me. "Where shall we send it?" he asked. I gave him a close friend's address in Tel Aviv. He gave me a receipt for my property, and I was escorted by two men aboard the waiting plane.

As the plane took off from the soil of Israel, I looked down at the Holy Land and wondered if I would ever be permitted to return. I was suddenly aware that I was alone, all alone, for the first time in several months.

When I arrived in Rome, I telephoned friends in New York and discovered that an immense rumor mill had been started which said that I had gone mad. Many even believed that Uri was a Mephistophelian character and that I had made some kind of pact with this "devil." I was able to reach Uri in Israel by phone, and he told me that all hell had broken loose there. The Army was constantly interrogating him, in order to get more information about me. He told me that they were convinced I was a master spy and that they were now trying to figure out what country I worked for. They had also come to his apartment where I had stored my research equipment, tapes, and film documentation and seized them all for intelligence analysis. Uri told me to plan to stay away for a long time, but to keep in touch. After four days in Rome, I assessed my situation and found it to be one where I was not welcome either at home or in Israel, and I decided to take a long rest.

I left Rome by a devious route, checking to see if I was being followed. When I was sure that I was not being followed, I found my way to the Italian Dolomite Alps and the town of Cortina. I scouted around and found a small, totally isolated hotel, the Tre Croci, on the top of a mountain pass. It was the essence of Old World charm presided over by Signor Menardi and his wife.

Realizing that I might never see my confiscated journals again, I decided to try to reconstruct from memory those events that led me to be suspected as a threat to the security of a nation. On February 19, 1972, on my fifty-fourth birthday, I sat down at my desk in the Tre Croci Hotel to begin this task.

My first trip to Israel was in March 1970 to train a research group at the Tel Aviv University Medical School in my technique of electrostimulation of hearing for the deaf. I would lecture a few hours a day to the staff at the Tel H'ashomer Communications Research Unit and then rush off to see the sights of Israel. One of the places I wanted to see was the Qumran site, near the Dead Sea, where the Dead Sea scrolls had been discovered in 1947. I was fascinated by the doctrines and writings of the Essenes who had lived there.

I rented a car and drove from Tel H'ashomer to Qumran. It was a warm, balmy day, and the scent of spring was very much in the desert air. There were no tourists at Qumran, only one Arab boy as a tour guide. He volunteered to take me into each of the caves where the scrolls had been found. This was a great thrill for me, since I am an amateur archaeologist. Finally the boy left me alone, and I sat on the rocks of the community site, drinking in the smell of the Dead Sea and the sights of the Jordan Valley to the north. For me it was a happy and exhilarating hour in the sun. When it was 5 P.M., I reluctantly moved toward my car to drive back to Tel Aviv.

As I started to drive, I felt a heaviness come over me that was like anesthesia. I reasoned that it must be due to all the fresh spring air and the altitude, which was about three hundred meters below sea level. But, then, why had I felt so good a few moments earlier? I checked the car's exhaust system for leaks, but it was all right. My health was perfect, and I had not used any medicines or drugs. I could not account for the sleepiness.

I had great difficulty getting through Jerusalem. Something

was putting me to sleep, and I was fighting it like a punch-drunk boxer who doesn't know when to quit. I have never had to fight sleep so hard in my life. In another hour of slow, sleepy driving, I reached the town of Ramla and finally succumbed to sleep in the car. I woke up an hour later, drank a lot of coffee, got into the car, and barely made it to my hotel room in Tel Aviv, where I fell asleep on my bed fully clothed, with all the lights on. I slept for twelve hours.

When I awakened, I tried to analyze what had happened. I could only conclude that some external force had had this hypnotic effect on me. It might have been a positive ion effect in the air, but it was not the *hamsin* season, when the hot wind blows through the desert. But one thing was clear: I had never, in any other part of the world, experienced this sensation. It was not until eighteen months later that I was to know the reason for my sleepiness.

On my return to New York from Israel, I was offered the opportunity of being the chairman of an international conference, "Exploring the Energy Fields of Man." The purpose of this conference was to explore the energies involved in certain psychic phenomena. I welcomed the opportunity to bring together a distinguished group of scientists to evaluate these problems so close to my work. At the conference, Itzhaak Bentov, an Israeli researcher from Boston, gave a report on a young man named Uri Geller, who had recently done some amazing psychic feats in Israel. Bentov read a letter from a friend in Israel, whose son had recently graduated from the Technion. The letter said in summary: "His son saw Uri Geller, a 23 year old stage performer, do some amazing things for a group of students and their professors. He made it clear that his son does not believe in these things as being paranormal. His son thinks some kind of a trick is involved, but nobody knows the trick, not even the magicians."

His son's friend had held a gold ring clenched in his hand while Geller held his left hand over this hand for about thirty seconds. When his son's friend opened his hand, the ring was split. Geller also held his hand over the face of a wristwatch belonging to a student, and when he moved his hand away, the watch hands were displaced two hours forward. The third thing Geller did was to drive through Haifa traffic while blindfolded, with the windshield of the car on the driver's side masked with cardboard. It seems that someone was required to be in the car with Geller so that Geller could "see" through this person's eyes.

This report was greeted with both incredulity and skepticism by the conference scientists. I made contact with Uri Geller in Israel by letter. Geller agreed to see me in August 1971 and to give me an opportunity to test his alleged talents. I planned to see him the week before I was to go to a conference in France.

Two weeks before I was to leave for Israel, I was suddenly faced with a catastrophic series of events much too complex and personal to report here. There were grave family problems, financial difficulties, and severe illness. For two weeks I felt stressed and stretched to the limits. I felt that I was under some kind of test, that I had to choose between my self-imposed duty to get to Israel and my personal health and comfort. Against all advice I went on to Israel on August 17, 1971. Curiously enough, as soon as I got on the plane, my illness improved, and by the time I landed in Israel I felt healthy again.

I was met at Lod Airport by the father of the boy who had witnessed Uri Geller's feats (I shall call him Jacov, since he does not wish to be identified). Jacov was a balding, sandy-haired, freckle-faced man of deep calm and quiet dignity. He explained at some length that he had arranged for the use of a friend's apartment for me in Tel Aviv. He brought me up to date on his further investigations of Uri Geller. He was frankly skeptical of Geller's powers because there had not been a decent opportunity for satisfactory private demonstrations. He welcomed my presence, just to resolve the nagging question as to whether or not these were genuine powers.

Jacov told me that Geller was performing at 11 P.M. that night at a discotheque called the Zorba in Jaffa. Would I like to go and see Geller or get some rest? In spite of my recent illness, I could not think of conserving myself; I had to go and meet

Geller. After dinner, we arrived at the Zorba. It was a huge barn of a place, put together out of crepe and tinsel for the tourist trade. While waiting in the foyer for the show to start, a young man who recognized Jacov came up to us. It was Uri Geller. He introduced himself in perfect English, welcomed me to Israel, and apologized for our having to meet under the squalid roof of the Zorba.

I greeted him in return by saying I had waited for a year to meet him. I was surprised at his healthy appearance. I had expected to find some kind of a strange nebbish somehow not related to this world. Instead he was tall and very handsome, with a quick, sharp, here-and-now sense of presence. His manner was easy, even gentle. He didn't look like a man who broke metal rings by sheer willpower.

Uri soon excused himself to get ready to go on stage. Jacov and I got ringside seats and suffered through a series of rock numbers, jugglers, clowns, and comedians. Uri was the last to appear, since he was the star of this show.

He was simply introduced as Uri Geller as he appeared on stage. The crowd of youngsters went wild with applause. He was evidently very popular. He announced, "With the cooperation of the audience, I am going to try to demonstrate simple telepathy and psychokinesis. I hope I will succeed."

He then did a series of telepathic demonstrations wherein members of the audience wrote numbers, the names of cities, and the names of colors on a blackboard. Blindfolded, he would try to guess what they had written. He was correct on every attempt. I was not impressed, because any magician could do the same thing in a number of different ways by trickery, mostly by having collaborators in the audience. However, I reserved judgment on this subject because I could easily test this talent when we met privately.

Finally he came to the big event of his demonstration. He said that if anyone would volunteer a ring, he would attempt to break it. A lady sitting near us volunteered her costume jewelry ring for the test. She went up on stage, took the ring off her hand, and held it up for all to see; it appeared intact. Uri then told her to clutch the ring in her hand and to make sure that he could not touch it. This she did. Uri then placed his left palm over the lady's clenched fist for about thirty seconds. He asked her to open her hand and to examine the ring. She gasped, "The ring is broken." She held it up for all to see. There was wild applause as Uri ended his demonstration. The lady returned to her seat, and Jacov asked her in Hebrew if we could inspect the ring. She handed it over to us. It was split in two pieces, with no signs of any tool marks. The lady assured Jacov that she was not in collusion with Geller. All this was intriguing, but not convincing, since a magician with the assistance of a confederate could do the same thing.

We met Geller after the show. He was very boyish in his eagerness to find out if I liked his show. I assured him that I enjoyed his part of the show, but would have to work with him privately to assess what he was doing. He readily agreed to meet me at my apartment the next day at 1 P.M. to discuss my research interests and find out what I wanted to do.

I did not realize then how lucky I was. Later I found out that Uri had steadfastly resisted all offers by research people to do experiments. He, too, was surprised at how readily he had consented, especially since I was a total stranger.

By the time Uri arrived at the apartment the next afternoon, all of my equipment was operative and in place. Two of my Israeli friends were present, Jacov and Ms. Shifra Mor. I began by asking Uri to show me those talents of his that he felt the most sure of and to do them in his own way. Uri said he would like to do some simple telepathy for me. He said, "Think of one number from one to nine. Don't tell anyone, just keep it in mind. Got it?"

"Yes," I said. I had thought of the number four.

"Now think of another number."

"I have it," said I, having thought of the number three.

"Now the last number," Uri said.

I had selected two for this number.

Uri looked at me intently as though he were checking his own impressions. Then he said very abruptly to me, "Pick up the pad on the table before you, the one I wrote on before you selected your first number. Did you notice that I had written on it then and haven't touched it since?"

"Yes, Uri, I noticed what you had done and that you haven't touched it since or tried to switch it. After all, that is part of my business as an investigator."

I picked up the pad, which was face down, turned it over, and read what Uri had written down before I had thought of my first number. It read, "4 3 2."

Uri laughed, obviously pleased with his coup.

I responded with some admiration. "That's pretty clever; you told me this would be telepathy, and I, of course, thought you were going to be the receiver. But you pulled a switch on me."

"Ah, you got it quick!" interrupted Uri. "I wanted to send you the numbers, but I knew that if I told you to try to receive the numbers, you would fight me. In this way you participated in the experiment without prejudice, and proved that you have telepathy, when I send or pass to you."

I realized now that Uri had an unusual power of influencing others' thoughts. At this point I asked Uri's permission to use my tape recorder and movie camera.

"Of course, if it is easier for you," he replied quickly. "But you probably think that since I sent those numbers to you so easily, I might also hypnotize you to see and do things that are not really there!"

"You are so right, Uri," I laughingly replied. "I can see that we're going to get along just fine."

Now that we had tested each other's mettle, we were able to settle down to some serious work. I then asked Uri to do some more telepathy with my Israeli friends. I might say that these two people were highly trained observers.

After an hour of doing Uri's telepathy with simple units of information such as numbers, letters, colors, and single words, we stopped for a break. We openly discussed our opinion of Uri's demonstration. I led off by stating without equivocation that this was genuine telepathy and I would state so anywhere.

Shifra and Jacov concurred in this opinion. They asked if

Uri could get or give more complex information by telepathic means. He replied, "I can't do things like that. I stick to the simplest bits of things, so that it is like two times two equals four. Then people have to say I am right or I am wrong. If I do whole stories, it's hard to score what I do. This way it is either zero, or a hundred, and no in-between."

"Now what would you like to do?" I asked Uri.

"Does anyone happen to have a watch that does not work? I will try to fix it," said Uri.

Shifra replied first. "I have a watch that is not broken; it is not working because I haven't wound it in a few days. Can you start it without touching it?"

"Well, I'll try," said Uri. I interrupted, "Shifra, first let me inspect the watch before anything is done." She handed me the watch. It was a well-known Swiss-brand watch. I listened to it. I shook it. This made it tick a few cycles and then it stopped. I then took a motion picture of the face.

Uri said, "I don't want to touch it. Let Shifra hold it in her clenched fist."

I placed the watch in Shifra's open palm. She closed it, and then Uri placed his left hand palm down over her hand without touching it. After thirty seconds Uri said, "Okay, check it. I think it's running."

I took the watch from Shifra and inspected it. The watch ticked now and continued to do so. The hands moved for several minutes normally. Shifra agreed to let me keep the watch to see how long it would run. The watch ran for thirty minutes before it stopped.

Uri then asked if I would take my watch off and just hold it in my hand. I noted the time. It was 2:32 P.M. I placed the watch in my right hand. Uri placed his hand over mine without touching it. He concentrated for about ten seconds, then said, "Check it."

I looked at the watch. The hands now stood at 3:04 P.M., an advance of thirty-two minutes. My watch is a Universal Geneve Chronometer, with additional dials to add up stopwatch time. I noticed that two of these dials had also shown an advance of thirty-two minutes. But the stopwatch sweep-second hand should have been running for thirty-two minutes, but the stopwatch sweep-second hand was motionless. There is no known way to advance these two dials thirty-two minutes except to run the stopwatch for thirty-two minutes. This complex feat of psychokinesis was unparalleled in my experience, or in the literature, for that matter.

This ended our research session for the first day. I had only one reservation: I must wait until my motion pictures were developed to make sure that my companions and I were not hallucinating. One month later when the film was developed I had my confirmation; the film had seen the same thing as had my eyes.

The next day I repeated the telepathy tests and found the same positive results. Then I asked Uri to concentrate on a pair of identical thermometers of the bimetal type. He was able to raise selectively the temperature of one thermometer six to eight degrees Fahrenheit, while the other one remained at the room temperature. I found that he could do this equally well from across the room as when near the thermometer.

There was now no question in my mind that Uri Geller's powers of telepathy and psychokinesis were extraordinary. I now wanted to know more about him as a person: What were his interests and his motivation?

"Uri, you must have thought a great deal about your powers. What is your idea about where they come from? Or how do you think it works?"

"Yes, I have thought about them. You see, my ideas may seem funny to you because I have only had a high school education. I don't read books. But my ideas are my own, and I don't like to discuss them. I believe that in telepathy I am passing the light speed. I feel that telepathic waves travel at a speed of light or faster. Every object gives off radiation which moves out into the universe. When we pass the light barrier, we can see into the past or into the future, and we can transmute materials one into the other. Everything is based on the light speed, and once beyond that there is no end to what can be done. But as yet, we cannot find the particles beyond the light speed because they are too small. I also believe that there is no limit to the smallness of particles. This is the way I think, but let us not get into theories that we cannot work with."

I was quite taken with the depth of Uri's ideas, especially since they were so unexpected. "Someday," I said, "when we have time, I would like to tell you about Dr. Vinod, a man from India who taught me many things. One of them had to do with superconscious states of mind being due to, or related to, velocities near to the speed of light. What you say about telepathy strikes a responsive chord in me."

"There is an interesting thing I have noticed, Dr. Puharich," Uri interrupted. "Sometimes when I break a ring, it loses some of its material. With the breaking of a chain, sometimes a link disappears."

"Uri, I saw you break metals with your willpower at the Zorba. Would you try to show me that?" I asked.

"Yes, I would like to do that for you, but a little later," he said.

I asked Uri when he had first decided to show his powers in public.

"It slowly started in late 1969 when I did some small things for a friend of mine, Shipi Strang. But I really had my first show, with promotion and advertising and all that, in March 1970, because an agent said I could make a lot of money. It was in a movie house in Bat Yam. After a week of this I knew it was easy and I enjoyed it. Then I found that I really need the stimulation of working in front of people in order to do these things. When I am by myself, nothing happens. Now, there are also many people who are opposed to me. They say it is all a fraud and a trick and that I should admit it. But I don't really care whether they believe or don't believe; as you see, I have two things going for me. First, there is my plain, naïve appearance. Second, I am a showman and I do have powers."

To this candid immodesty, I had to add my honest opinion about Uri. "You have not realized your full powers yet. You are just at the beginning."

The Gordian Knot

"Thank you, Dr. Puharich, but what else is there for me to do? Everything is written. If we go out of the route, and we leave the third or fourth dimension, we go on into another dimension and another form of life. I believe there is life everywhere in the universe. There are advanced beings who can pass the light barrier, who can travel millions of light-years in an instant. They can transfer themselves to different dimensions; they can change themselves into any form they wish, and appear as ants, birds, people, or even UFOs. These space people now know that earth people are finally advanced enough so that they can show newer forms than they used to take in biblical times. That is, they take different forms now."

"Uri, did you ever see these things that you are talking about?" I asked.

"No, to tell you the truth, I never have. I just believe in these things, but I don't know why I do."

Uri went on. "I'm talking about these things because I see them in my mind. I believe them. I believe that we live other lives. When our energy runs out in this life, it goes into another dimension. You see, I believe that if you have telepathy, you pass the light barrier, and you go into other dimensions. People ask me, 'Why do you have powers, and I don't?' I have an explanation, and I suppose you can say it comes out of four theories, or any one of them.

"Maybe on our own earth before the Ice Age, there was a civilization, very advanced. All that I do now, they once did. Somehow they have remained, not incorporated in a body, and I somehow have their powers.

"Then maybe I am a descendant; my ancestors were people not from earth. They landed in a flying saucer. They had these powers, and somehow they came up in me. This is like a science fiction theory, that I was planted on earth.

"Or somehow while growing up, my mind split. Basically it appears okay, but something turned a little away, a little sharper. There is a warp in its makeup.

"The last one, I don't even want to say it. They are somewhere out there. They have their reasons. This is related to my second idea.

"Now I will try to split a ring for you," Uri announced in the face of our silence. Jacov's wife, Sara, had joined us. She offered her gold wedding band. I think she felt that it was perfectly safe; no one could break a ring without touching it. Uri asked her to clench the ring in her fist. He held his left hand, palm open and down, over Sara's fist.

Uri said, "I know this ring is precious to you. I won't break it badly; I'll just crack it lightly. Tell me, do you feel anything?"

Sara said after about thirty seconds, "I feel some tingling in my palm."

"Okay, I think it is broken. Open your fist," said Uri.

We all crowded around Sara. I picked up the ring first. There, clearly across the yellow gold, was a crack in the metal! Now I felt the full impact of Uri's powers. The Gordian Knot had been cut! (Several months later I got a report on the ring from the metallurgist at the Stanford University Department of Materials Science. It stated that there was no known way to cause this kind of fracture and that the electron microscope pictures were unique.)

I spent my remaining few days repeating each of the tests with Uri that I had already done, just to make sure that I was not being fooled. I wanted to make arrangements for future research with Uri. He was quite willing to work with me. I decided that the preliminary research should be done right in Israel, and Uri concurred. Before I left Israel, Uri proudly showed me his scrapbook of news clippings. One story from Israel's leading newspaper, *Ma'Ariv*, of February 19, 1971, caught my eye. It was about "Captain Edgar D. Mitchell, the Uri Geller of the astronauts." I told Uri that I would be talking to Captain Mitchell on my return to the States.

Since I had to be in France on August 24, I did not have much time. I had to reach key figures in the government to make sure that I would have their cooperation. Jacov understood totally what had to be done in Israel, and he undertook to be my emissary. I left for France on the understanding that if he could

The Gordian Knot

arrange a meeting for me with certain key figures, I would return to Israel.

At the International Conference in St. Paul de Vence, I was especially interested in a report by Dr. Hans Bender on a phenomenon that involved recording on a tape recorder voices whose origin was unknown. Dr. Bender told me of a man in Germany, Dr. Konstantin Raudive, who was doing such work. I decided to go see Dr. Raudive right after the conference.

At the conference I met a young parapsychologist from the University of Wisconsin, Ila Ziebell, who impressed me very much with her quick wit and good judgment. But more of her later, when she enters this story as a principal. I did not report on my work with Geller at the conference, since I felt it was premature to say anything about his startling powers. I knew that, paradoxically, the bigger his powers, the more proof it would take to be convincing.

From the conference I flew to Zurich, where I met my friend and assistant of many years, Melanie Toyofuku, to do some work with Dr. Raudive. I phoned Dr. Raudive and found that he was able to see me for the coming week. Since I had all my research equipment with me from the work in Israel, I was prepared to join Dr. Raudive immediately.

Melanie and I drove down along the Rhine to Bad Krozingen where Dr. Raudive lived and worked. Bad Krozingen is a spa built for chronically ill people, and I did not like its atmosphere. Therefore, as was my habit, I simply drove around the area looking for an inn that suited my mood. At sunset I drove into a small town which was guarded by a castle high on a hill. It had a warm rustic atmosphere. I found an inn that had rooms free, and Melanie and I settled in. The next morning we were having breakfast at a sidewalk café in the village square when we inquired as to the name of the town. The waiter informed us that it was Staufen and was famous as the place in which Dr. Johannes Faustus had lived in the sixteenth century.

Dr. Konstantin Raudive was a Latvian philosopher living in Bad Krozingen because of his wife's disability. Although he spoke many languages, English did not come easily to him, so we settled on French for our discussions with Melanie serving as the interpreter. Dr. Raudive explained how he was able to record the "voices" of people who had died. He used an ordinary tape recorder with a diode placed in series with the input jack. Sometimes he used the tape recorder with an ordinary microphone input, but this created too much noise in the recording, with the result that the "voices" were buried in the noise level of the electronic system. Therefore, one had to train oneself to hear the signal in the noise. It took me about twelve hours of such training to hear the voices that Dr. Raudive said were there. At last Melanie and I were able to hear the voices without any help from Dr. Raudive.

On August 31, 1971, Dr. Raudive conducted an experimental session in which we would try to record "spirit" voices on my Sony TC 120 tape recorder. The procedure was simple: The tape recorder was placed on a coffee table, and we sat around it. The recorder was started, and Dr. Raudive simply said, "We would like to have a message for Miss Melanie." We waited two minutes and then played back the tape recording. All of us distinctly heard the words "Melanie," "yes," following Dr. Raudive's last words. Melanie said the two words had the voice quality of her deceased Japanese grandmother who had never learned to speak English properly.

Following this attempt, the tape recorder was started again, and I asked for my mother, Rose, who had died in 1956, but I spoke in Croatian, the language in which she and I had spoken so often. When the tape was played back, we heard the phrase in Croatian "To Rosalija," and to my ear it had the voice quality of my mother as I remembered it. The phrase meant "This is Rose."

We went on working in this fashion for two more days with similar results. I was totally convinced that the effect was genuine. However, I was forced to the conclusion that in order for the effect to occur, Dr. Raudive's presence was required. This meant that we were dealing with a two-termed process in which one term was an instrument, the tape recorder, and the other term was a human being, Dr. Raudive. For example, the same effect did not occur with me at this time. A person who has such a special effect is called a medium. A medium serves as a bridge between this material world and the world of the unknown, from which the voices came. The fact that one needed a medium did not make the effect less valid; it just introduced the factor of special human dependency.

After our final sessions with Dr. Raudive, I left for London and from there drove to Cambridge University to discuss my findings on Uri Geller with a group of friends whom I considered to be on the "cutting edge" of knowledge advancement. I met with Ted Bastin, a physicist; Chris Clarke, a cosmologist; Margaret Masterman, a philosopher and linguist; and Richard Braithwaite, a philosopher; and others. My data on the Geller effects were received with great interest as a possible contribution to a fundamental revision in philosophy and in science. We began to make plans for the kind of research that we would have to do in future years, just to build a new data base for the new science to come.

On September 12 I got a phone call in London from Jacov, who was in Israel. He said he had made contact with the right Israeli authorities and that I should return immediately for a discussion. On September 13 I had extensive discussions with a key government figure in Tel Aviv about research with Uri. He told me that there was a consensus among his colleagues that the kind of things Uri Geller was doing should be taken seriously from a scholarly point of view and that I could count on cooperation in my program from his government. I was encouraged to return to Israel, to try to organize a research program on my own.

On September 14 I picked up a copy of the *Herald Tribune* in Tel Aviv and read a story by Walter Sullivan. It said that some American and Soviet scientists had called an international conference "to consider the possibility of communicating with life on other worlds." The meeting had been held in Byurakan in the Soviet Union. Many distinguished scientists were in attendance, including Dr. Charles Townes, Nobel Laureate from the University of California, Berkeley. This was the first time that such a conference had ever been held at so high a level.

I did not try to do any research with Uri on this trip, but spent our time together simply trying to get to know him better. I also met his two closest friends, Hannah and Shipi Strang. It was easy to see that a tight bond held these three together, and I knew that any plans for work with Uri in the future would necessarily have to include Hannah and Shipi.

By September 20 I was back in my home in Ossining. The next two months were a blur of activity in which I saw people all over the United States and Canada, trying to enlist their interest and support for the Geller research in Israel. Most of my professional colleagues simply did not accept my data on Geller, even after viewing my films of his effects on watches, metal breakage, etc. I soon discovered the reason: they were threatened. If Geller were true, then the very foundations of science would have to be questioned.

One of the more open minds was that of Captain Edgar D. Mitchell, who had just completed the *Apollo 14* mission to the moon in February. He and I met for the first time in Houston, where he told me that he had completed the first moon:earth telepathy experiment. He had been the sender in space to four human receivers based on earth. He told me that the results had been just as I had predicted ten years earlier in my book *Beyond Telepathy*. He was most enthusiastic about the prospects of doing research with Uri, and we made some plans to do so.

By November 17 I had completed all the complex tasks necessary to launch a long-term research effort in Israel with Uri, and was on my way back to Israel. My goals were now quite clear. I had to make arrangements with the institutes of higher learning in Israel to get them to work with Uri. It was essential that others participate in the process of validating Uri's powers; and Uri had to become accustomed to working with scientists.

By 7:30 P.M. November 19, 1971, I was settled in Reuven's apartment in Tel Aviv. The next day I was scheduled to start a series of meetings with Uri, Jacov, Reuven, and others to plan how to accomplish all the goals I had set. Little did I know at this moment as I settled into bed that my lifelong quest for true knowledge was about to commence.

CHAPTER THREE

Dakashem

I met with Uri on November 20, 1971, and outlined to him my plans for research. I explained that I would need him for three to four hours every day. He agreed to make this time available if I could tolerate odd hours that he would salvage around his public demonstrations. I agreed to this if I could also attend all of his public demonstrations, which was acceptable to him. We decided on the compensation for his demonstrations for me.

Then I explained to him the rules of being a research subject. First, it was not to be a game between us. Since we were both interested in the truth, we had to be brutally honest with each other. On my part I would not pull any surprises on him; I would state my goals for each experiment and what I expected him to do. If he could not do it, or did not feel like doing a test, he was to tell me immediately. Experiments would have to be repeated until I felt I had enough data, and of such quality as to be fit to introduce into any court as evidence. This meant that he would have to submit to my testing conditions and not to break them during a test.

Uri said, "I understand what scientists have to do, but I don't know if I can do it. You see, I can only do what I feel I am able to do. If I don't feel like it, I can't do it."

"Fine," I replied. "That is why I want to make my goals clear to you before each test so that there is no misunderstanding. Let me show you by example how I work. The last time we worked I let you determine the conditions under which you demonstrated. Now we will do the same kind of telepathy test, but I will control the conditions. We will do a telepathy test in which I will think of a three-digit number, and you will try to guess what these numerals are. You take this blank pad and pencil and go into the next room. I will stay here with a pad and pencil. When I say 'Go,' I will write down three digits, and at the same time you will write down the first three digits that come to your mind. Is this clear?"

"Yes, I understand," said Uri, as he took the pad and pencil and went to the next room. I shouted "Go" and without thinking, wrote down "6 3 1" on my pad. Uri came out of the room a minute later and said, "That is very fast; I usually work much slower. But here is my paper."

I laid his paper alongside my paper: Mine: 6 3 1; Uri's: 6 3 1.

"This is a hit," I said. "No one could question the results, except to accuse us of being in collusion. But even that possible weakness in the test can be eliminated by bringing in a third party. Besides that, I will document each test with recordings, both audio and video tape. I am going to rent an apartment in Herzliyyah Heights, and it will take me two days to set it up as a laboratory."

"All right. Let's have dinner tomorrow evening and start research on the twenty-second," he offered.

I agreed on the time and place, and Uri was off. I rented a car and went to look at the apartment that Jacov had located. I liked it. It was a new high-rise apartment called the Herzliyyah Heights Apartment, and I sublet apartment 61 on the sixth floor. This apartment had a striking night view of Tel Aviv ten kilometers to the south and a day view of the Mediterranean a kilometer to the west. In two days I converted the large living room into a laboratory.

On the evening of the twenty-first we met for dinner. Uri had brought along Iris Davidesceu, an eighteen-year-old fashion model who was his girl friend and for whom he had a very tender affection. Jacov's friend, Reuven, joined us in Jacov's stead and brought along Gedda Ornstein, a woman who had healing and psychic powers. Gedda had been born in Russia, was brought up in China, then married and moved to Chile. She had been imbued with something of each culture before coming to Israel three years before. At dinner in a restaurant, Uri had Gedda hold her gold ring in her clenched fist while he concentrated on it. When she opened her fist thirty seconds later, the ring was bent. Gedda, who did not know such powers of the mind existed, was most impressed. She was quite frank in revealing that she lived on the same street that Uri had lived during these past two years, and that she had heard the local gossip about him. The gossip dismissed Uri as a clever magician; nobody took him seriously. Uri said that he knew this, and he really did not care what people said as long as he could make money at it.

After dinner we went to my new apartment so that Uri could see where we were going to work. Uri and Iris left at midnight. Reuven and Gedda stayed on, and we talked for several hours. I was curious about Israel and Israelis, and they were curious about psychic phenomena and my experiences in this field. Reuven and Gedda left my apartment about 2 A.M. Shortly thereafter, Gedda phoned and said she had an unpleasant premonition about my health, and felt I was in danger. I assured her that I was well. She persisted, and asked if she could return, in case I did need help. I agreed to this, but insisted that I felt well. Reuven brought Gedda back to the apartment. At about 3:15 A.M. I suffered the sudden onset of a racing heart, or what is called paroxysmal tachycardia. I have had these attacks once or twice a year in the past and know how to handle the problem. But in addition, I suffered an excruciating stabbing pain in my right hip joint area somewhere near the sciatic nerve. Between the tachycardia and the hip pain, I was in a very precarious condition. Gedda had worked as a healer and tried to help. I massaged the carotid sinus in my neck and eventually stopped the tachycardia. Finally I suggested that Gedda call New York and talk to a Chilean friend of mine, Carmen, who had treated me before for this condition, and see what her diagnosis would be. Gedda liked this idea and talked to Carmen for a long time in their Chilean Spanish. She informed me that she and Carmen understood each other perfectly and that they had agreed on the diagnosis. They both believed that I was being attacked by black magic. I, of course, laughed at this suggestion, having been trained in Mexico, Hawaii, and Brazil in how to prevent any such psychic invasion. However, Gedda was firm in her opinion and offered to stay with me and nurse me through this illness. I welcomed her help, and she began to work on my afflicted hip and massaged it all through the night. By morning my tachycardia had totally disappeared, and my hip pain was all but gone. I insisted on going ahead with my work of getting the laboratory finished. Gedda was kind enough to help me all that day. By evening all was ready for my first real experiment with Uri.

My first experiment was to see if Uri had the power to move a magnetic compass needle solely by mental effort. I had two liquid-filled compasses as the test instruments. Uri had never before tried to move a compass needle, so he was very unsure of himself. Before the tests began he gave me permission to search his body for any hidden devices; I found nothing.

On the first try, after some seven minutes of concentration, Uri was able to move a compass needle sixteen degrees clockwise. We both felt that this was not impressive, but that he did have potential in this area.

On the second try he asked my permission to place some rubber bands on his left hand, which acted as a tourniquet, the better to occlude the venous return from his hand. I agreed to this, since it could not compromise the test conditions. He was now able with great mental effort to move the compass needle ninety degrees clockwise. This ended the first day's work. Uri was thoroughly exhausted by these new tasks. He complained that he had never worked so hard before and that it would be a lot easier for him if there was a crowd of people watching. He felt as though he actually drew some kind of energy from a crowd of people.

The next day, the twenty-third, we again worked at the magnetic compass experiments. This time I began to vary some of the conditions. I had him place his left hand in a rubber glove filled with water. He then held his hand over the compass and tried to move the needle as he had yesterday. Under these conditions he could not move the compass needle. He felt as though his "energy" were being trapped in the water.

When we went back to the previous day's tests with his hand bound with rubber bands, he was again able with great effort to move the compass needle as much as ninety degrees.

Then I tested his power to "bend" a thin stream of water falling from a water tap when his hand was brought near it. This is purely an electrostatic effect, which anyone can bring about with an electrically charged plastic comb, but very few people accomplish it solely with a finger. Uri was able to bend the water stream when he brought his dry finger near the stream of water. But he could not bend it when his finger or hand was wet with water; wetting his skin seemed to neutralize the electrical charge on his skin.

On the twenty-fourth I started an additional series of tests. I was interested to find out whether Uri could control his mind energy in a narrow beam, or whether he used his energy in a kind of shotgun "scatter beam." My experiment was a simple one. I prepared five wooden matches of equal length and weight and placed them in a long row, end to end. The matches were on a glass plate monitored by a movie camera. Uri's task was to concentrate on the five matches and then try to move any match or group of matches that I selected.

On the first try Uri was able to make the match that I selected move forward some thirty-two millimeters. On succeeding tries he was able to move any match that I selected while the others remained stationary. When moved by his mind power, the matches always moved by jumping forward like a frog jumps. I concluded from these tests that Uri could in fact control the beam spread of his mental energy.

On November 25 I was joined in my research by Itzhaak Bentov, who had attended the Life Energies Conference of November 1970 and who had introduced me to his friends Jacov and Reuven. Itzhaak, Reuven, and Jacov had all been engineering students at the Technion in the late 1940s following the War of Independence. Their life together as students formed the basis of their camaraderie some twenty-five years later. Itzhaak was an inventive and disciplined lab worker, and I welcomed his help in the research with Uri. Since Itzhaak had never seen Uri work before, I repeated much of the former work for his benefit. Both Itzhaak and I were impressed with Uri's accuracy; he never missed. As these tests progressed, we developed more and more confidence in the reliability of Uri's powers. But as we repeated the same kind of tests over and over, it became more and more boring for Uri.

By November 28 we had reached a crisis in our relations with Uri. Uri wanted to know what our long-term plans were for him; how much money we had to support this work; and what we really could do for him. He felt it essential for us to hear his life story and to know what he wanted out of life.

"I want to be very frank and open with you," he said. "May I call you Andrija?"

"Please do," I replied. "I regret that we've kept up this formalism so long."

"Good," said Uri. "Andrija, I have been studying you, just like you have been studying me. I have never known any professors before, so I don't know what is important to them and what makes them tick. As I listen to you, I can't figure out what you're up to. You talk about research, the soul, evolution, and all these things, and I don't get the point. Why is it important to learn about the soul and these powers that I have? All I am interested in is how to make enough money so that no one can tell me what to do. I want to be free. I want to have a car so that I can travel when I want to. I want to have my own apartment so that I know where I will sleep at night. Maybe you don't understand how important these things are to someone who doesn't have them. You have to understand my life. My father, God bless him, never had a piastre in his life. He has always been a soldier, a sergeant major in the Army. When I was little, he left my mother and me. My mother had to work for years just to keep us in food and a roof over our head. She had nothing in life except to suffer for me. Now I can make some money, and she doesn't have to work anymore. Then she met a man when I was about eleven; she got married and we moved to Cyprus. Her husband owned a little hotel, and my mother had to work very hard just to keep it running. But I never liked her husband because when she first met him I was sent away to Kibbutz Hatzor for a year—it was just like being in a concentration camp. I hated being away from my mother, and my real father was far away. I learned in that year on the kibbutz that I just can't stand a lot of people around.

"I really blamed my stepfather for a lot of my problems. In Cyprus I was sent to a boarding school for two years. Again I felt trapped and in a concentration camp. I hated my stepfather so much at one point that I honestly wished he would die. This was right after my sixteenth birthday. I remember so well. When he died of a heart attack a month later, I was sure that I had done it; because it was a feeling just like moving the hands of a watch."

I interrupted. "How could you be sure that you had anything to do with his death? Men are known to be prone to dying of heart attacks, especially at the age of your stepfather."

"Well, I can't be sure. All I know is that I was lonely and frustrated and I wanted him to be dead. And then he died and my mother couldn't afford to keep me in boarding school. I was happy again when I was home with her, even though I had to work very hard to help run the hotel. When I was about sixteen, I was very impressed by the freedom of the people who stayed at the hotel. Some were show people, some were businessmen, and some were even spies. I always wanted to have the kind of freedom and excitement that they had. But the fighting between the Turks and Greeks on Cyprus was very depressing to me. Eventually these troubles forced my mother to sell the hotel for about a thousand pounds, and we moved back to Israel just in time for me to go into the Army.

"Even in the Army I was frustrated again. I volunteered for the paratroopers because I wanted to have the freedom of the skies. But I found that I was spending all of my time on long forced marches in the Negev. I got to hate marching, the crowded life in barracks, and the never-ending discipline. I tried to get to Officer's School in the paratroopers by finding the man who was a spy on Cyprus, whose name was Joav. Joav was now a major in the Army, and he recommended me for Officer's School. The officer's training was even more difficult than being a paratrooper, and I got to hate it, too, after I heard that Joav had been killed. I now realized that I probably did not want to be an officer. In our final tests we had a mock battle and I was on the blue team. I looked around the desert and I couldn't see any of the red army. So I told my men to take it easy and to take a nap. We woke up with the guns of the red army in our faces. We were all captured. When we had the final exams, I found out that three of the generals had voted against me as an officer candidate.

"I disliked them, too, and wished that all three were dead. I know it sounds strange, but a year later all three were dead. Of course, they were all killed in battle during the Six Day War in 1967. That is why I think I may be responsible for my stepfather's death. But things like this scare me, so I never wish anyone any bad, like I used to. If I get angry at people now, which I still do all too easily, I fight to control myself and think only good thoughts about people.

"Then in the Six Day War, I was a paratrooper sergeant, and I got wounded in the battle for Jerusalem. I was in a hospital for two months. There I met some girls who changed my life a lot. One was Hannah Strang, and her brother, Shipi. We became the best of friends, and you met them. But I also met a girl who was the daughter of Schleuss, who was chief of the Israeli secret military police in the Jordan border area. I really liked this girl, but I went with her mostly to be able to meet her father. You see, I wanted to get into intelligence, police and spy work, because Joav in Cyprus had impressed me so much. You see, I knew all this was dishonest, but again I felt trapped and wanted to get some personal freedom while I had to stay in the Army. I did get to meet Schleuss, and he suggested that I go to school and learn to be a military policeman and later go to the

Shin Beth. All I had to do was to go to school for six months and learn Arabic, and I would be paid six hundred pounds a month. This sounded like good pay, and if I could sweat out the schooling, it might become exciting, and fun. There was a waiting period to enter the school, so Schleuss had me assigned to duty, looking for deserters. Andrija, I finally had it made. I had my own motorcycle. I rode the desert alone, looking for suspicious-looking men. I had the freedom I had always wanted. I had plenty of danger and excitement, I feared no man, and I had enough money. For the first time in my life I was happy. I was so happy that I stalled going to school to learn Arabic. By the time my three-year service was near an end, I met a man who offered me a job in a textile plant at nine hundred pounds a month.

"I was so hungry for money that I took his offer and forgot all about the excitement of going to a spy school. I gave up my army life with an honorable discharge and forgot all about Schleuss and his daughter.

"But I soon learned that the nine hundred pounds a month was a curse of dullness and boredom. I just wrote letters all day in the export department in English, Greek, Hungarian, and Turkish. How I longed for those days in the desert on my motorcycle chasing down deserters. I knew that I had to get out of this new jail quickly. But having earned nine hundred pounds a month, I could not go back to six hundred pounds a month. Besides, something else had happened to me. Being in a textile firm had put me in touch with the advertising business, and I had an offer to make an extra thirty pounds an evening as a photographer's model. My first assignment was a photograph for a beer ad. I'll never forget my excitement and happiness at having my picture in the papers. People actually recognized me on the streets! Me, who had always been a nobody, someone else knew me!

"Once this happened, I knew I could not go back to military police work, no matter how much I liked the freedom of being alone on a motorcycle. In police work there is no publicity; no one would know who I was. So I took more and more jobs as a photographer's model. I worked for a man named Norbert, who said I was a good model. All this happened in 1969. My young friend Shipi, who was then fourteen years old, talked me into my first public demonstration of my powers. I don't really know what happened, but I showed things for three hours, and everyone, teachers and students, kept saying how fantastic my "tricks" were and that I was a "genius." This was the first time in my life that I was really applauded and liked by a crowd of people. I felt even better than when I saw that first beer ad in the paper. Also, for the first time in my life, I didn't feel lonely. My shyness was not so painful in front of this crowd of youngsters.

"Then another thing happened—this was in early 1970. I began to feel a compulsion to show everyone my powers. I don't think that I was showing off. I felt more like a teacher, more like you, Andrija and Itzhaak, feel about your research; you're really doing it not for yourself, but for someone else. Then in March 1970 I met this manager, Mickey, who said I could earn a thousand pounds a week if I would let him manage me. So I signed a three-year contract, and I opened with my first really professional show in Bat Yam in a movie house that same month. From then until now, life has been what I needed. I have money, I bought a car, my mother doesn't have to work anymore. People recognize me on the street. I am finally somebody. And I like it. Now I get to the point.

"I don't want to work just in research. That would be like secret work for the military police. I want to be known; I want to be successful. If you want to work with me, you will have to deal with my need for fame and fortune. That's it!"

Uri finished his long speech and waited to see what we would say. Itzhaak and I looked at each other trying to frame a reply to this unabashed egomaniac. Our problem with Uri was complex. We both liked him personally because of his honesty and boyish charm, but we both felt saddened by his small-minded approach to life, an almost desperate hunger for security and recognition. It was too ticklish to try to frame any adequate response to his position. So I suggested that we all take a break and go to Jaffa for dinner. We did relax somewhat at dinner, but everyone knew that we had to face the questions posed by Uri. After dinner, Uri insisted that he be allowed to demonstrate his blindfold driving. We were reluctant to indulge in such hazardous experimentation at this midnight hour, but Uri was insistent. So we went along with his wishes. Years ago I had done research on Kuda Bux, the famous blindfold driver, and so knew the trick involved. Kuda Bux always managed to get a line-of-sight vision from his left eye to the tip of his nose, no matter what kind of a blindfold was used. The only way to prevent this trick being used was to black out the windshield.

I insisted that the windshield be covered on the inside with paper to prevent any tricks. Uri readily agreed to this precaution as long as the person sitting in the front with him could see the road. Uri claimed that he saw the road only through someone else's eyes, and therefore that person had to be able to see. However, since we did not have the proper materials—thick paper and masking tape—we could not cover the windshield. So we settled for a blindfold over Uri's head which he was not allowed to touch or to manipulate in any way.

I offered to sit next to Uri. In the back seat of the car sat Iris and Itzhaak. Uri started forward with a lurch and rapidly accelerated to eighty kilometers per hour. He drove nervously but well. He stayed on his side of the road without crossing the center stripe. He saw every traffic light accurately and crossed each intersection describing what was on each side. One of the most interesting things he did was to call out that a red Peugeot sedan was coming toward us down the road from around an approaching curve. About a minute later, a red Peugeot sedan did emerge out of the darkness as it rounded a curve ahead of us. His perceptions in the dark were astounding as to detail. For example, he saw a girl to the right and described the color and shape of her dress. But this kind of driving was nerve-racking, and we begged Uri to cease, after some three kilometers. Uri was as pleased as we were relieved, when it was over.

On our return to the apartment, Itzhaak started to give Uri a long lecture about the evolution of the soul through eons of living. After a half hour of polite listening Uri said, "But what is the point of all this soul business at this time?"

Itzhaak patiently replied, "The point is that whatever you do in any lifetime, you will have to pay back at some time. If you cut off someone's arm, for example, at some time your arm will get cut off. The purpose of life and living is to develop one's soul to a higher state. You should be more concerned with your soul than with your body and all its material needs."

"That may be all right for you, Itzhaak, but all I know is my body. I don't know anything about my soul, or if I even have one," replied Uri.

I interrupted here. "It's getting very late for all this heavy talk. But I do have one suggestion. We really feel, Uri, that you have more potentialities for evolution than anyone we know. But you have become so brainwashed by the ugly side of poverty that you have lost perspective. Just remember that you are handsome, attractive, intelligent, and gifted. With these four advantages you don't have to think and act so selfishly. But you must learn to know yourself by looking at your soul. I can help you do this."

Uri seemed interested. "How can I find out about my soul?"

"It is so easy," I replied. "Allow me to hypnotize you. Nothing will happen to you that will violate even the slightest of your wishes. I want to separate your soul from your body so that you will clearly be able to know which is which."

"That's easier said than done," replied Uri. "I'm in show business, and many hypnotists have tried to hypnotize me and nobody can. So I know what it is all about; it just won't work."

"Well, that's very safe for you then. But if you allow me to try, there is a chance that you may know your soul. Think about it, and give me your decision tomorrow."

Uri said he would think about it, and we all parted for the night. As Reuven was leaving, he said to me, "You know we have a word in Hebrew for a kid like Uri; *puscht*, which means "a punk" in English. He is really insufferable. I don't know how you can be so patient with him."

"Reuven, I feel he is so extraordinary that he is worth almost any effort," I replied.

"Good luck, Andrija. I think it is a mission impossible, but I'll try to help you if I can. Shalom!"

The next morning was November 29. Uri was not scheduled to come over until 8:30 P.M. At 11 A.M. Itzhaak and I decided impulsively to leave the apartment and to walk to the beach, about a kilometer away. We enjoyed the exercise while we talked about how to handle Uri. No one knew where we were going, including ourselves. We dropped in at the Accadia Hotel and had breakfast. There we framed the problem. We agreed that Uri had the psychic talents required for sustained scientific research, but he did not have any motive for sustained scientific work. We could not make commitments on Uri's behalf at major research institutions knowing that he might walk out on us at any time. There was no one in the world like Uri, so we would have to try to help him find his true self, and if he did, we could only hope that this true self would be interested in the same goals as we were.

We left the Accadia Hotel and walked a half mile to the village square of Herzliyyah-by-the-Sea. We stopped in to look at the Tiran Hotel and then headed back to our apartment via back streets. At 1:30 P.M. a car drove up to us; it was Uri and a friend, Itamar Serlin. Uri jumped out and said he had gotten very much tuned to us, and on impulse he had set out from Tel Aviv to see us. Finding no one at the apartment, he had the idea that he could find us. So he searched for us telepathically and here he was! Then he looked at me and blurted it out, "Andrija, something keeps telling me to let you hypnotize me. I personally don't want to do it. But something pushes me, and I'm scared. Andrija, will you do it tomorrow night?"

I was really surprised at his intensity of feeling. I had never seen him so deeply moved before. "Of course I'll do it. What time?" I replied.

"Tomorrow I have a show right near here in the discotheque at the Tiran Hotel at ten. I should be through by eleven, and we can do it then."

"It's a date," I said. Uri jumped into his car and was off as quickly as he had appeared.

Itzhaak and I trudged back to the apartment wrapped in silent thought. What if the hypnosis failed on the following night? What could we do then? These questions weighed on me as I prepared for this evening's research session with Uri, which would begin within hours.

At 8:30 P.M. all of our friends assembled for the research session with Uri. This was to be strictly a work session in which there was a minimum of conversation.

We started out with a series of telepathy tests in which Uri received numbers, colors, and symbols from each of the people present. He was 100 per cent correct in twenty attempts.

Then Itzhaak gave his watch to Gedda, who covered it with her hands. The watch was filmed before she covered it, and the hands read 9:25 P.M. Uri placed his hand over Gedda's without touching it. Gedda said she "felt a thin streak of energy going through my hand." The watch was examined in one minute; the hands now read 8:13 P.M. Under Uri's influence the hands had moved back seventy-two minutes.

Next my watch, which then had a stainless steel spring watch band, was placed on a table. Uri asked that some pieces of metal knives, spoons, etc., be placed around it. Uri placed his left hand over my watch without touching it. He took his hand away in twenty seconds. The steel band of my watch was twisted where it joined the body of the watch with a half twist. This was most impressive.

Next Uri worked on the "five matches" test with his hand underneath the glass-plate platform. He was able selectively to move one of the five matches for a distance of one centimeter. All this was recorded on film.

The next test was to see if Uri could break a steel chain furnished by Itzhaak. I covered the chain with my left hand. Uri placed his left hand over mine without touching me. The chain broke in half after twenty seconds of concentration by Uri.

We all felt pleased with Uri's efforts and with the sound

method of documentation by witnesses and instruments. Even Uri was pleased.

After everyone had left the apartment that night, I sat down and made the following summary about my research to date with Uri:

> The results of the "five matches" test are conclusive: they show that psychic energy can be "localized." The results of the compass test and the watch test show that the "beamed energy" has a torque which operates both clockwise and counterclockwise. This energy can be used at one time to break metals, and at other times to exert a torque on watch hands without breaking the plastic or metal. Thus I conclude that psychic energy can act in a discrete volume of space. We can now make some hypotheses about psychic energy, as it acts on materials (Ψ=psychic):
>
> I. Ψ energy interacts with matter.
> II. Ψ energy can be modulated by the mind.
> III. Ψ energy writes information on the screen of the mind like a moving finger of energy.
> IV. Ψ energy appears to be quantal, pulsed, and vortical in nature, and can be directionally beamed.

The next day, Tuesday, November 30, 1971, Reuven, Gedda, Itzhaak, and I met for dinner at Reuven's apartment and discussed how best to deal with Uri. We were all concerned about how to help Uri become the kind of strong leader who could make the best use of his talents. No matter what proposal was made, it was turned down as inoperable because it did not include Uri's own knowledge of his pattern of self-realization. It was clear that until Uri came to a conversion experience through his own inner timing, no progress could be made. After dinner we went to the Tiran Hotel to meet Uri.

The discotheque was in the basement of the hotel. It was painted all in black. It was dimly lit and not easy to move around in. The place was filled with beautiful young Israeli boys and girls, all between sixteen and eighteen years old. The youngsters above eighteen were in the Army or had outgrown the discotheque syndrome. There was obvious intense excitement about Uri's show. The music was pumped out of speaker systems that radiated hundreds of watts of power each second. This electronic sound pulsed through one's body like a wave going through jelly. At times the sound would hit nodal points in a bone, an organ, or a cavity, creating a massagelike thrill. However, when the colored strobe lights started flashing, the cacophony was overpowering. My friends and I looked at each other in dismay. We felt as if we were trapped in a Dantean circle of hell and were so sorry that Uri, with all his vast potential, was similarly trapped here, and did not even know it. When Uri's act came on, it was at least a relief, because the electronic music and lights stilled. The youngsters came out of their "rock" stupor and seemed to come to life when Uri did telepathy and psychokinesis demonstrations for them.

I began to feel during this show as if I were on the wrong trip and would do better to leave Israel and Uri and do something more scientific and less complicated. We left the Tiran about 11:30 P.M., quite depressed about the prospects of research with Uri.

It was just past midnight when Uri lay down on the living room couch of apartment 61 to cooperate in an attempt at hypnosis. It was now the morning of December 1, 1971. Reuven, Gedda, Itzhaak, and Iris quietly gathered around to see how I would fare in trying to hypnotize the "unhypnotizable" Uri.

When all was quiet, I explained to Uri that even though he was going to be hypnotized, he would remember everything that happened in this first session. We would only explore things of interest to Uri that had happened in this lifetime.

We started. I simply had Uri count backward from twenty-five. He said, "Twenty-five, twenty-four, twenty-three, twenty-two, twenty-one, twenty, nineteen, eighteen," and he was in a deep hypnotic trance. I asked him to look around and tell me where he was. He said he was in a cave in Cyprus just above Nicosia with his dog, Joker. I asked him what he was doing here. He said, "I come here for learning. I just sit here in the dark with Joker. I learn and learn, but I don't know who is doing the teaching."

"What are you learning?"

"It is things like I told you last August when we first met. It is about people who come from space. But I am not to talk about these things yet."

"Is it secret?" I asked.

"Yes, but someday you too, will know."

"All right, Uri, now let us go back to the time before you moved to Cyprus. Where are you now?"

Suddenly Uri began to talk in Hebrew. I quickly realized that Uri had not learned English until he moved to Cyprus. I did not want to disturb Uri now, so I asked his permission to allow Itzhaak Bentov to take over the interview in Hebrew. Uri gave his consent, I turned him over to Itzhaak.

Uri recounted in Hebrew a number of childhood episodes that are not of any importance here. Then he told of when, just after his third birthday, he was playing one day in a garden across the street from his home at Rehov Betsalel Yafe 13 in Tel Aviv. Uri looked up from his playing and saw a large shining bowl-shaped light in the sky above him. The day was December 25, 1949. Then there was a huge, very bright shining figure in front of him in the garden. The shining figure had no face that could be seen, only a radiant countenance. Uri gazed at this radiance in total hypnotism. Then he became aware of arms slowly moving out from the side of the body of the radiance. The arms were raised over the "head" of the radiance, and then Uri saw that held between the hands was the sun. It was so blazing in its brightness that Uri passed out from the power of its rays, with the pain of blindness.

Now there appeared a voice in the room speaking in English that was not Uri's voice. I am not sure where the voice came from, but all of us in the room heard it. It may have come from the air above Uri. It may have come from Uri. I do not remember exactly what this voice said, and there is no record of its words. I will shortly try to reconstruct as best I can what was said.

When the hypnosis session ended, Uri awakened. He could scarcely believe that he had been under hypnosis for an hour and a half. He had no memory of what had occurred, so we started to tell him of the unearthly, almost mechanical voice that had occurred near him. It was quite obvious that he did not believe what we were saying. So I proceeded to play back portions of the tape where he could hear his own voice. When we reached the part where he was a three-year-old in the garden, he began to show signs of fear and terror. He kept muttering, "I don't remember any of this." When we reached the part that said, "This is the voice—," Uri deftly ejected the tape cassette and held it in his left hand. He paused momentarily, looking at the cassette, closed his fist over it, and I believe that I saw the cassette disappear from his hand. Then he rushed out of the apartment door, heading toward the elevators. We searched the building, top to bottom, inside and out. He was not to be found.

Uri had truly vanished. We assembled in apartment 61 in a half hour to go over the event. We decided that we had better call the police, because if Uri had slipped out of the building past the door guard somehow, and if he was still in trance, he could endanger himself. We also decided to make one last search of the building before calling the police. As I pressed the button on the sixth floor and opened the swinging door to the elevator there was Uri with his back to the far wall like a standing mummy! He didn't seem to be conscious, so I addressed him gently. He suddenly awakened and said, "Where am I?"

I simply said, "You are all right. Come back to the apartment with me."

He meekly followed me and sat down on the couch in a daze. He had no memory of where he had been for the past half hour. He was still in a state of emotional shock. I decided that he had better go home to bed. Iris offered to drive him home and to look after him. After Iris and Uri left, we sat down to try to reconstruct what the voice had said. This is what we remembered, but none of us was certain of the exact wording:

It was us[1] who found Uri in the garden when he was three. He is our helper sent to help man. We programmed him in the garden for many years to come, but he was also programmed not to remember. On this day his work begins. Andrija, you are to take care of him.

We reveal ourselves because we believe that man may be on the threshold of a world war. Plans for war have been made by Egypt, and if Israel loses, the entire world will explode into war.

There will be one last round of negotiations that may not avert war. America is the problem. The negotiations will not succeed. The Egyptians have as of now no fixed date to start the war. The critical dates as are figured by Israel are correct as of now. The critical dates as seen by us are: December 12, 15, 20, 25, 26, 1971: or nothing at all.

Now the reader must be reminded that the rumors of a new war were always in the air in Israel, so that there was no particular novelty to the statement that "plans for war" had been made. Plans for war were in continuous existence in the Middle East; the real question always was when and where would war be triggered? Our real problem was to find out more about the when and where and to have more certainty about the information.

There were more things said, but I dare not write them down because I might not be accurate. My Israeli friends were linked to the Israeli Army Command, and they pondered all night long what to do with this information. One of their difficulties was that they didn't know how much credence to place on this kind of utterance. They were prepared to believe that we had all hallucinated the entire scene. I was the only one who was sure that I had seen the tape cassette vanish in Uri's hand. When dawn came, we had not reached any conclusion as to what to do.

---

[1] Here and elsewhere the reader will note grammatical errors in the speech of the extraterrestrial beings. This is how the messages were delivered; no attempt has been made to alter their words in any way.

Dakashem

Uri appeared at the apartment at 2 P.M. December 1. He didn't seem to remember anything of the events of the previous night. I decided that the best policy was not to go into it all again, to wait and see what would happen. If there was a real war threat, I felt that we would be contacted again. As it happened, I was alone with Uri, since both Reuven and Itzhaak had to keep prior appointments.

One of the first things that I noticed about Uri was that he seemed very relaxed and full of quiet self-confidence. He walked by one of the magnetic compasses on the test platform and absentmindedly put his hand over it. It immediately turned thirty degrees. He had never been able to get this effect before so easily or quickly. I could sense that something had changed for the better.

At 3:30 P.M. I placed a coded machined steel ring inside a wooden microscope box. The ring had been specially prepared by Bentov in his machine shop, to see if Uri could bend it. Uri said, "Why did you put the ring in the box?" I said I really didn't know. Uri in a very authoritative way said, "Take a movie of putting the ring in the box, and I will make it vanish." His sudden self-confidence was new to me. I did as he requested. He placed his hand on the closed wooden box for about two minutes, then said, "I think the ring has vanished. Check the box!"

I cautiously opened the box lid. The ring had vanished! This is the first time I had experienced an object vanishing where I was certain there had been no deception involved. I had to stop routine experimental work now and talk to Uri about the previous night. I repeated what had happened. I could see that he felt that I was making up the whole story to fool him. He could not remember anything. So I did not press the matter.

Uri then got very excited and asked me to buy him a Polaroid camera. I said, "Uri, I have a Polaroid back for my Hasselblad camera. I can take any pictures you wish."

"Well, that's not it, Andrija. I need the camera for myself. Besides, I can't learn to use your complicated camera. Please trust me. Buy me the camera—you'll never regret it."

"Okay, let's go to Tel Aviv and see if we can buy you a simple Polaroid camera, and I'll teach you how to use it."

I purchased the Polaroid camera and color, and black and white film packs. Uri learned how to take pictures after a dozen tries. He was so happy with the camera that he stopped in the middle of the street and said he would "move" my watch. He put his hand casually over my wristwatch, and the hands moved from 6:55 P.M. to 7:55 P.M. Then, for good measure, he waved his hand over an apartment key that I held, and it bent about thirty degrees.

We drove back to the apartment to find Itzhaak awaiting us. He urged me to do another hypnosis session with Uri, just to verify the previous night's happenings. Uri got involved in the discussion, saying that he couldn't remember what had happened but was now getting curious about it. He suggested that we might ask for some kind of a sign as to what to do. I suggested what I considered to be an impossible sign. "If Uri can bring back the coded steel ring that vanished this afternoon, I'll concede that we may be dealing with a superintelligence and that we ought to follow 'their' suggestions. The reason I say this is that returning a steel ring takes us personally out of the class of mass hallucination, or of fraud on Uri's part."

This suggestion was accepted, and Itzhaak examined the microscope box where the steel ring had vanished earlier that day. Finding it to be devoid of any ring, and with no possibility of deception being used, we went ahead with the test. Uri held his hand over the box for some fifteen minutes without any result. Then he asked me to place my finger on the side of the box facing north. This I did while everyone hovered near the box. Suddenly we all simultaneously heard the sound of a metal object falling inside the closed box and settling down with a clatter on the bottom. We looked at each other; it was silently agreed that I should open the box. When I did, there was the steel ring that had vanished six hours earlier!

This was a clear "mandate from heaven," if I may borrow the Chinese expression. I went right ahead and hypnotized Uri. This time the "voice" appeared in the room as soon as Uri was in a deep trance state. I recorded the entire session, which lasted for sixty minutes. When Uri awoke, he looked at the clock and said, "I have a show in Tel Aviv at midnight. I must leave here in ten minutes." So I quickly spot-checked the tape. It had recorded properly, and we all heard that it had. I would not let Uri drive to Tel Aviv so soon after a hypnosis session and insisted that I take him there.

On the road to Tel Aviv, as we passed the area just south of Herzliyyah, Uri complained of a sudden pain in the forehead area between the eyes. He asked me to stop the car because he felt sick. I did this. I also took out my Sony TC 120 tape recorder, which still had the tape in it from the second (most recent) hypnosis session. I could see that Uri was going to say something, so I tried to make the tape recorder work. I found that the tape cassette was okay, but the start and record buttons were jammed and would not engage. Then Uri suddenly said:

"Remember every word I said to you because the evidence is gone."

I again looked into the tape recorder. The cassette that had been there moments before had vanished!

Uri came to, his headache eased off, and he was able to do his show in Tel Aviv. We returned to the apartment in Herzliyyah Heights at 2 A.M. to find Itzhaak waiting for us. He grimly informed me that after hearing the voice speak the second time, he felt a moral obligation to report it to the Israeli Army.

I then told him how the tape recording of this second session with Uri had vanished. This meant that we had to sit up all night again to reconstruct what had been said. Uri then informed us that he had a show scheduled in the Sinai Desert for the Army and he could not be with us the next day. With apologies to Itzhaak, he begged me to go along with him. He felt I must be there. Itzhaak consented, and I agreed. Uri bade us good night and left.

We now tried to reconstruct what had happened earlier that evening. This is what we remembered:

Uri said, "I am flying out of my body somewhere on earth. It is a flat wide place with no vegetation, and there are some mountains in the background. There I see two figures. One is Andrija looking very young with all black hair and no gray. Itzhaak is there, too. He is not bald and has full black hair. Then I flew to another place. It is the place where Andrija served in the Army." All this was said in Uri's voice. (I had worked as a civilian in the U.S.A. Hospital at Fort Ord, California, in 1959.)

Then Uri's voice stopped, and the voice appeared. Again we were not sure where it came from. It said:

I am now looking over the flat place in the Sinai where there are enormous numbers of tanks. Attack first! Don't wait! In Khartoum and in Egypt there may be many dead. Sadat will be taken by his officers. Syria will attack. Jordan will not intervene. There will be many Egyptian soldiers in Jordan. You, you are the only one to save mankind. The earth will be exploded by man himself, not by us. Uri, you have been given enormous powers, you can do everything and anything. Uri, you are very powerful. I will call you when I want you.

The session ended. Other things were said, but they are not directly related to the suggested immediate war threat. They had to do with what would happen if Israel took the initiative and either won the war or averted a war. If Israel entered into a pre-emptive war, there was the danger of escalation to world war. If Israel prevented a war now, she would still have to face a major war in the future with her Arab neighbors, but in this latter scenario there was no danger of escalation into a world war. I omit all the ramifications of these contingencies because they do not bear directly on the immediate threat of war.

My Israeli friends now decided to seek an appointment with a key figure in the Army for December 3 on my return from the Sinai. However, they insisted that I go with them in order to lend credence to all the psychic aspects of the information.

At 6 P.M. December 2 Uri and I arrived at the military section of Lod Airport on our way to Uri's show in the Sinai Desert. Uri made it clear that only personnel cleared by the Israeli Army were allowed to go to the war zone in the Sinai. He told me to sit down in the terminal and keep my mouth shut; he would try to get me on the plane. First he went to the military ticket agent, who refused to give tickets for my passage because I did not have the proper papers. Uri then went to Sergeant Major Aaron; no tickets because of no clearance papers. In a half hour Uri had the entire airport in an uproar, insisting that if I, his friend, did not go to the Sinai, there would be grave international repercussions. Although it looked impossible for me to go on this flight to the Sinai, I secretly knew that if I had to go, some miracle would happen and I would go. As 7 P.M. approached and the plane was ready to depart, Uri unexpectedly got clearance for me to get aboard the plane. However, it was stated that my security clearance would be checked. To this day we do not know why I was allowed to go. We both had wide grins of satisfaction as the Viscount lifted off the runway and we were off to some unknown air base in the middle of the Sinai Desert. The pilot received word by radio thirty-five minutes out of Tel Aviv that my security status was okay.

We landed in the midst of the cold, wintry desert on an airstrip without any buildings. Several trucks met the plane as it rolled to a stop, and an officer rushed up to Uri to welcome him. The first words from the officer were that some Egyptian commandos had infiltrated the area and that a battle alert was on. The second words were the passwords for the night. We were in the war zone.

After a cold and bumpy ride to a base camp, we were fed in the mess hall. As we ate, we were surrounded by officers and soldiers who showed an unabashed hero worship for Uri. Here on the war front, the normal reserve of civilian life in Israel was dropped. Everyone was alert with electric excitement. There was no discernible gap between the officers and the rank-and-file soldiers. The big excitement in the air was not that the Egyptian commandos were lurking somewhere in the dark, but that Uri's show was scheduled for eleven that evening. As an American I was fascinated by this cavalier spirit.

Uri turned their interest in the show around by first asking for, and then demanding, a Jeep. He insisted that he must go into the desert immediately, and alone. The officers did their best to talk Uri out of taking a Jeep into the desert night. They insisted that it was dangerous but if he must go, he had to be driven under escort by armed guards. Finally a compromise was reached. Uri and I could have a Jeep, a driver, and an armed soldier; if the driver or guard sensed danger, we would have to abide by their orders. Uri accepted this, and we went out into the frigid desert night to a waiting Jeep. The driver said that he and the guard had to make a stop at their barrack to pick up a rifle and a machine gun.

We pulled up to the barrack, and the driver remained in the Jeep with Uri and me while the other soldier went in to get the guns. I noticed that when the young soldier returned, he was bareheaded. I thought it was strange. If there was so much danger, why did he not wear a steel helmet?

At exactly 9 P.M. we drove past the gate sentries out of the camp. All of us, except Avram, the young soldier, buckled on our helmets, and the Jeep roared out into the night. Now, I must confess that I had no idea where we were in the Sinai, or even where the cardinal points of the compass were. My disorientation was such that I could have been on the moon.

At 9:02 P.M. Uri leaned over to me in the dark and whispered, "Now I'm getting a message, 'thirty K,' what does it mean? 'Thirty K'—ah, now I get it! It means thirty kilometers. We must drive thirty kilometers to be met by the red light."

We noted the speedometer reading. Every time we reached a fork or intersection in the road, Uri insisted that I make the decision as to whether to turn left or right. I did this purely in a random fashion.

Uri then whispered to me, "Our teacher said to us that he is going to appear to us as a red light that will look like a UFO." Now I finally knew why Uri wanted me to go to the Sinai Desert with him. By now I had located the constellations and the stars in the sky which gave me the cardinal points of the compass.

The excitement built up in us as the speedometer moved up to the thirty-kilometer mark. Just as it turned from twenty-nine to thirty km, I spotted a red light in the sky to the northwest, at about a 315° bearing and an elevation of about 18° above the horizon. I silently pointed it out to Uri. He dismissed it by saying, "That's just a radio tower light." But then he immediately ordered the driver to stop the Jeep and turn it around so that the headlights would face away from the red light in the sky. We both jumped out of the Jeep, and the driver and guard got out to keep an eye on us. Neither Uri nor I said a word. We looked at the red light from a spot about thirty meters from the road.

Uri kept whispering, "It can't be *our* red light." I took out an American penny, held it at arm's length in the direction of the red light, and judged the light to be about ten times the diameter of the brightest star in the heavens (this is a common technique used by star watchers). The red light was motionless in the sky above a mountain peak. I later identified this peak as Mount Ugrat El Ayadi, which has an elevation of 1,791 meters. Since the night was quite bright, it soon became obvious that there was no tower below the light, so we abandoned the idea that it was a radio tower light. It was the quality of the red light that intrigued me. It was like the clearest of claret wine. It didn't seem to shine or sparkle like the stars, but it seemed to me as if one could look into it, and through it, as if looking into a human eye.

Then Uri and I decided that we were probably hallucinating. I asked Uri to go to the driver and the guard and to point to where the light was and see if they saw what we saw. Uri walked over to them and spoke in Hebrew, since they did not speak English. He returned in a few minutes. He reported the following sequence: He approached the two men and, pointing to the red light, asked them what they saw. They said they saw the outline of the mountain. He said, "I don't mean the mountain, I mean above it."

They said, "Stars, just stars."

"Well, isn't there supposed to be a radio tower on that mountain?" Uri pressed.

"Not to our knowledge," they replied.

"Well, I would have sworn I saw a red light on that mountain," Uri said while looking directly at the light.

They looked at the mountain again. "There's no tower, and no red light," they replied.

Then Uri said to me, "They don't see what we see."

I stated rather flatly, "Then you and I must be imagining the red light, because we want to fulfill our wishes."

Uri said weakly, "For the past day I have been pushing to get you to the Sinai. I got you here; now we don't even know what we are seeing." So we stood in the cold night stillness, staring at what now felt like a red eye in the star-studded sky. How could we be sure of what we were experiencing?

Uri broke the silence. "Quick, move five feet to the left." I paced off this distance and looked around. Nothing. Then my foot touched something soft. I reached down; it was a soldier's fatigue cap. I picked it up and showed it to Uri. "That's it, that's it," he said. "That's the sign!"

"What do you mean, 'That's it'?" I replied, annoyed. "That's just some soldier's cap that blew off his head as he was driving by."

"No, no. It's a sign! Take it. Take it." Reluctantly, I rolled up the cap and stuffed it into my pocket. I just couldn't understand why Uri attached any importance to this rag. We stood there another ten minutes looking at the red eye in the sky, which now seemed to have a sharp disklike edge. Its red clarity seemed to pull my gaze into it and through it. But I did not know what I was seeing, nor if I was seeing anything at all. Now I was beginning to feel cold, and Uri and I walked back to the Jeep.

Uri tried once more to elicit a response out of the two soldiers about the red light, but they simply did not see it. I regretted that cameras were forbidden in the war zone. One time-exposure would have settled all of our doubts. We climbed back into the Jeep. With the night air blowing, it was now colder than ever. I took off my steel helmet and absentmindedly put on the soldier's cap I had found in the desert. I was sitting in front, alongside Avram, who was now driving. The red light was still in the sky to our left, and I strained toward the driver to get a better view. Uri and I both saw that the red light was moving and was, in fact, following us. But our two soldiers, while they kept looking in the direction we were staring at, did not see what we saw. Suddenly the driver flipped on the map light and stared closely at my cap.

"Where did you get my cap?" he asked in puzzlement. A big excited discussion started in Hebrew in which we learned the following facts: When Avram had gone into his barrack to get the guns, he had tossed his fatigue cap on his bunk just as he walked out of the barrack. Now he pointed out that I was wearing his cap with his name written on it in his own handwriting. He wanted to know what trick I had used to obtain his cap, since I had not been out of his sight at all. Uri tried to explain in Hebrew that we had really found the hat where we had stopped. Neither soldier would accept this explanation.

While the three young men argued in Hebrew about this "trick," I buried myself in thought. I already had proof that Uri could make objects vanish and then to make them reappear. So it was possible that Avram's cap had disappeared from the barrack by the same kind of power and appeared at our feet in the desert. But Uri had already said to me that he had not "willed" this event. He had only sensed a message "to look for something." Uri had been obsessed with getting me to the desert.

Why did Uri and I see the red light and the soldiers not see it? Were our minds being controlled? If so, *whose* minds? The soldiers? Or Uri's and mine? Did this red light have something to do with the voice? And what was the voice? A fragment of Uri's mind? A spirit? A god? Did the voice have any relationship to the Nine that had reached me so many years ago? The red light that followed our Jeep now seemed to be totally unlike what I had seen in the sky in Ossining, New York, in 1963 or in Brazil in 1968.

My mind wandered to a memory I had of the prophet Mohammed and of his experience of a "star" in these very deserts. Before God revealed himself, Mohammed had the practice of retiring for one month each year to meditate on Mount Hira. Here he saw a "star" descend toward him. Of this experience the Koran says: "By the star, when it descends, your brother is not dismayed. It was at the highest horizon; then it descended and remained suspended. It was two bows lengths away, or thereabout."[2] But after that first visit from the star, the Prophet had to wait three years before it came again.

I wondered whether Mohammed's star was related to what I was looking at now. Would I ever see it again? As we turned into the base camp, the red light just winked out.

Avram made one last attempt to find out how I had "stolen" his cap. I could only repeat what I had said earlier. We entered the brightly lit entertainment hall for the show. The soldiers went wild with cheers for Uri. In fact, the sergeant major had to address them three times before they quieted down. I sat as a guest of honor with the officers in the front row. Although I did not know a word of Hebrew, it was easy to follow Uri's show. He did some telepathy by correctly "guessing" numbers, colors, and cities. The soldiers cheered wildly with each success by Uri. He ended the show by "repairing" a dozen wristwatches by simply waving his hand over them.

The officers requested of Uri the opportunity of a private demonstration after the show. We went to the commanding general's office, and Uri introduced me to the group. They asked what was my interest in Uri, so I gave them a ten-minute lecture on the importance and meaning of Uri's phenomena for science in particular and mankind in general. Then Uri worked with each of them to show that what he was doing was genuine and not a trick. It is no exaggeration to say that they were all deeply moved by their experience that night with Uri.

At 2 A.M. Uri and I were ushered into a small boxlike barrack that was more like a walk-in deep freeze than a bedroom. It was frigid. There were two iron cots along one wall, and Uri and I each crawled into the cots in such a way that we were feet-to-feet to each other. I went to bed with all of my clothes on and mountains of blankets on top of me. I was still cold. Eventually, since I could not sleep, I decided to sit up and work on my notes of the day's events. Just as I started writing, Uri asked me to

---

[2] Quoted in Paul Thomas, *Flying Saucers Through the Ages* (London: Neville Spearman Ltd., 1965), p. 175.

turn out the light, to stop my writing, and to meditate. He insisted that I would get an important message from the voice. So I complied. But Uri broke the depth of my meditation every ten minutes by asking, "What did you get?" I kept saying, "Nothing," for the next two hours, until finally Uri fell asleep and I could really concentrate.

By now the full moon was just past the top of the sky and was shining directly into my face from the window to my right. There were a few high clouds in the sky to brighten the night. I looked at my wristwatch, and it was 4 A.M. Friday, December 3, 1971. I decided to stare into the moon, and as I did so, I suddenly got a vision.

The vision started with the appearance of a single chain link of stainless steel of about three-eighths-inch stock and two-inch diameter. Each chain link popped into my vision like a single water drop and hooked into the previous link. The links spelled out the following message, link by link:

THE WAR WILL START ON DECEMBER 26, 1971, AT DAKASHEM THE EGYPTIANS

This was a breathtaking vision on the screen of my mind. Somehow I did not try to rationalize and explain away this vision and its message. It all seemed to fit in with the events of the past three days. I had never had an experience like this before, nor have I had one since. However, all this war business was getting on my nerves, and I made the decision then and there that I would join my Israeli friends that day at their tentative meeting at the army headquarters. I did not sleep that night.

When Uri awoke at 6 A.M., I told him of my vision. He didn't seem to be particularly interested or impressed. He rather sleepily said, "I think there are spacecraft overhead. I think that's what the red light was last night. I want you to make a note that I will get a photograph for you by tomorrow of a spacecraft. Now I know that that is why I wanted the Polaroid camera."

When we arrived at the airstrip at 7 A.M., our soldier guard,

Avram, was there waiting for us. He insisted that I keep his cap and still wanted to know our "trick" in stealing it. Uri and I were back in Tel Aviv at 9:20 A.M. I dropped him off at his apartment after getting him two fresh packs of film.

At noon I returned to my apartment. I showered, shaved, and ate. My Israeli friends joined me at 1 P.M. They said that they had had further discussions with the army chief of staff, and he had made an appointment for them with an officer from military intelligence at 3 P.M. that day. Itzhaak and Jacov had prepared a document that summarized all the military information that had developed in Uri's presence over the past three days. We agreed, as a matter of strategy, to state that all the material in the document had come from Uri's psychic powers, and not to mention the "voice" phenomenon.

Although our appointment was at three, it was three-twenty before we were ushered into the general's office to meet him and his staff. I felt that it had been fortuitous that I had met this gentleman the previous September. It made it easier to discuss our business. The first ten minutes of the meeting were somewhat stiff and formal. When Jacov mentioned that Uri's information said that the Egyptian attack was planned for December 26, 1971, the atmosphere suddenly became electrified in the room. One of the generals tipped his hand when he said, "Yes, we know, but exactly what time and where?" Of course, none of us knew, but we said that we would press Uri to work on this problem.

The meeting ended very cordially at three-forty. When we left the army headquarters building, I inquired if anyone had told Uri about our meeting. It was then that we suddenly realized that nobody had told him that an appointment had been made and a meeting held. We realized that we had committed him to do some work for the Army without his consent. It was a serious breach of confidence. I offered to try to straighten things out with Uri.

When I got back to the apartment, I called Uri to have a private meeting with him that evening. As soon as he recognized my voice, he kept me from speaking by telling me a breathless tale. "Listen to what happened to me today," he gushed forth. "After you left me, I took a shower, had lunch, and made a lot of phone calls. Then at exactly 3 P.M., I got a phone call. It was not a human voice, but it spoke in perfect English. It sounded like the kind of voice that robots use in movies, very mechanical. It said, 'Take the camera that Andrija gave you. Use color film. Go to Arlosoroff Street on the other side of the Ayalon River. Take Shipi. Watch the sky. You will see our craft. Take a picture.'

"I was so shocked by the power of this voice that I grabbed the Polaroid camera and the film and drove to Shipi's house. We went to the indicated street which is actually Petah Tikvah Road and waited on the corner. At 3:32 P.M. someone shouted to us that there was a UFO over the Israeli army headquarters. A bunch of people gathered, and I pointed the camera at this dark egg-shaped thing in the sky. By the time I developed the picture, the thing was gone. Everybody crowded around to see the picture. Remember yesterday in the Sinai, how badly you wanted a picture of the red light? Well, we have it now."

"Calm down, Uri, I'll be right over. I want to see that picture," I said.

I drove the fifteen kilometers to Uri's apartment in record time. When I saw the photograph, I knew it was genuine. The shape on the picture was that of a flattened ovoid, totally dark brown, with no reflections on it. I now realized why our meeting with the general had been so easy and so fruitful. When I explained to Uri about our meeting, he was furious with me. He said he did not want the military mixed in with his powers, that he would not do any further work for the Army. But when I explained to him that not only Israel but all of mankind might now be endangered, he relented a bit. But I think his own photograph of the spacecraft had the strongest positive influence on him.

Before I left Uri at 7 P.M. a reporter had tracked him down by phone. The reporter said that several witnesses had claimed to see a UFO that day and that one of them had recognized Uri at the scene. Uri quickly clamped his hand on the phone and asked me, "What should I say to this reporter?"

I said in no uncertain terms, "Uri, you must deny any knowledge of a UFO sighting immediately, before the story gets out of hand."

I hated to do this, but Uri complied with my wishes. I explained to him later that if we affirmed the UFO story, I could not carry on my research with the privacy we now had. "Besides," I said, "the best way to get yourself discredited is to claim that you have seen a UFO."

CHAPTER FOUR

Spectra

On December 4, 1971, a Saturday, we discussed the events that were crowding us and how we could best proceed toward the truth. It seemed to us that the most important line to pursue was the phenomenon of objects that disappeared and reappeared instantly. If we could be certain that the power of vanishing objects resided solely in Uri, it would simplify our problem. However, if this power was controlled by an extraterrestrial intelligence, we would be faced with one of the most momentous revelations in human history.

When Uri appeared at 3 P.M. for his laboratory session, Itzhaak and I explained our position to him as we had summarized it. Uri also made it quite clear to us that he had never been able consciously to control the appearance and disappearance of objects in this way prior to the December 1 hypnosis session.

In a sense he was quite dejected because he had always assumed that his powers were truly his own. Now he was beginning to feel more and more the presence of an outside intelligence in his mental and emotional life. But, as he admitted, all this was only a suspicion—none of the evidence thus far gave a clear-cut answer. In view of his uncertainties and our probing he agreed quite readily to our suggestion to try to make objects vanish and reappear.

I asked Uri what kind of test material he would like to work with. I told him that he had a choice of metals, plastics, glasses, organic material, etc. He thought about this for a long time and said, "Give me five pens." I collected five ball-point pens and offered them to him. Uri said, "Why don't you pick one of the five pens yourself?"

I picked a Parker ball-point pen that had three main parts, and I proceeded to scratch code numbers on each part as follows: plastic body, ※36; metal clip case, ※145; brass filler cartridge, ※367299.

I assembled the pen after this procedure and placed it in a wooden cigar box. Uri sat down, very seriously, near the box, and placed his left hand over it, without touching it, for nine minutes. "Okay, I think something happened, Andrija. Open the box and see." He said this very quietly.

I opened the box. The Parker pen was exactly where I had placed it. The experiment had failed. I reached in the box and picked up the pen; I knew instantly that the pen felt lighter. I pressed the metal cap to spring out the ball point. There was no spring action and no point. I unscrewed the metal clip case from the plastic body. There was no brass filler cartridge! I don't think that I have ever been so amazed in my life. Bentov and I discussed the question of how this brass filler cartridge got out of its plastic-metal housing and out of the cigar box, without affecting any of those fragile materials. In order for this brass filler cartridge to disappear without damaging these housings, it would have to be taken apart atom by atom. To do this required enormous intelligent energies, unknown to man today.

I asked Uri if he had any feelings during this disappearance. "Well, I don't think I did it. I didn't know whether or not it would disappear. I certainly had no knowledge that only a part of the pen would disappear. I have no special feelings when this happens. It's just like breaking metal; I wish very much for it to happen. I have no idea where that cartridge went to. All I can say is that it will come back as some kind of a proof."

Uri then had to leave for a social engagement and said he would return about midnight. Itzhaak and I sat down to talk. He said he had to leave the next day for Europe and then was heading back to the United States. Itzhaak felt very strongly that what was happening to Uri was very much in the Old Testament prophetic tradition, and we were catching him in an early stage of development. He was also fully convinced by now that there was an intelligent power behind Uri, although I was not fully convinced. I needed more evidence. But Itzhaak had gone one stage beyond me. He was worried about whether the power was "good" or "evil." He was so concerned that he wanted to call up his guru, Maharishi Mahesh Yogi, the Transcendental Meditation teacher, and get a "ruling" on the problem. The reason that we were in a quandary about these things was that when the "voice" appeared, we had little or no opportunity to ask questions, and if we did, they were not answered. Itzhaak and I decided that since he was leaving, we would try to have another hypnosis session and see if some of our questions could be answered.

Uri returned to the apartment at 1 A.M. December 5, 1971, and agreed to the plan for hypnosis. At 1:30 A.M. the hypnotic induction was begun by me.

Uri said, "Somebody is talking through a big loudspeaker."

Then the "voice" was heard. The tape recorder was disabled by some invisible power. We could not tell where the voice came from. It was not Uri's voice.

Here I am. I am ready. Ask.

Itzhaak asked: "I would like to have your permission to tell my teacher, Maharishi, about you. May I do this?"

No. He has no interest. But you must await further information in the U.S. You shall receive instructions from us. You have to meditate by yourself on the fourteenth of December, 8 P.M., New York time. The day will be raining. That is your power, the rain. Do not repeat this to anyone.

Andrija, you shall take care of Uri. Take good care of him. He is in a very delicate situation. He is the only one for the next fifty years to come. We are going to be very, very far away. Spectra, Spectra, Spectra: That is our spacecraft.

Andrija: "How far away is it?"

It is fifty-three thousand sixty-nine light-ages away.

Andrija: "How far is a light-age?"
There are some books on your planet left by our people. Uri will find them in the years to come. Your questions will be answered. Keep them, keep them, keep them. They will materialize themselves away after they have done their work. Do not ask any questions about the Israel situation. It will come out of him [Uri] alone. Do not worry. Do not worry. Do not worry. By the way, your little toy—the pen part—is right by me; I will return it to you in time to come. I am sending Uri back to you now. Farewell!

Uri woke up with a headache and was very much dazed. I told him what had happened. He didn't remember a word of it. I told him that the tape recorder had jammed and we could not record. He placed his hand over the tape recorder, and it immediately began to work perfectly. Since Uri was still dazed, I drove him home.

At 2 A.M. December 6, 1971, I was talking to Uri about the above session, but he could not remember anything. While I talked, he kept doodling unconsciously. When he was finished, I saw that he had made a drawing of a big room, which he felt he had been in. As we went over the drawing, he suddenly began to remember the details and said that this was a spacecraft from "Spectra."

On the morning of December 6, 1971, Itzhaak left for Lod Airport to go to Europe and the United States. I spent the morning logging tapes and notes and getting camera and tape recorders in order. At ten-thirty I went into the bathroom to bathe and shave. I turned on a small battery-operated Sony AM radio. I was shocked to find that every radio station but one was blocked out by a tone signal. I assumed that this was some radio alert system such as the Conelrad system in the United States. One station at dial 860 kc setting continued to play American music with Hebrew commentary. After about ten minutes of this I called up Uri to ask him what was going on. He checked his radio and reported that all stations were operating normally. He suggested, half in jest, that maybe Spectra was teaching me some lessons in science. After about fifteen minutes of this strange radio effect, all the radio stations came through with their regular programs. Although I was not aware of it then, I was to learn in time that this was, indeed, a science lesson, the first of many.

At noon I went over to Uri's apartment, and his mother made a great Hungarian meal for us. There I again met Uri's best friend, sixteen-year-old Shipi Strang. I soon discovered that Shipi was a precocious lad. We set up a game among the three of us in which two of us would try to guess what the other was thinking. It turned out that I could receive telepathic signals perfectly from Uri when Shipi was with him. We tried numbers (one-digit, two-digit sets, three-digit sets); colors; and words in English, Hebrew, and Greek. I was truly prodigious in my telepathic abilities! I tried to figure out why. When Uri and I had done such tests before, I could not perform this well. Uri confided to me that when Shipi was around he had extra "power." Somehow the two of them, Uri and Shipi, were doing something for me as well. Shipi went home at 6 P.M.

Uri and I were invited to Iris's home for dinner. The three of us decided to go to old Jaffa for the evening, and en route we had to pass the area where Uri had lived as a child, where he had enjoyed his Arab garden. As we reached the corner where Uri had lived, he slowed the car, then stopped at the intersection and waited. Suddenly a round, white, luminous spacecraft with side fins (or wing stubs) flashed across the north-south street heading from west to east. This was seen by the three of us. It was very low and moved without a sound. I checked my watch. It was exactly 9 P.M. The sighting lasted about two seconds. The sky was overcast with low heavy clouds, and the light from the craft reflected brightly from the cloud cover. We drove on in silence. No one felt like going to Jaffa anymore. Instead we decided to go to the Dizengoff to have coffee.

About 10 P.M. a heavy downpour started with a high wind of some fifty miles per hour. We abandoned our sidewalk café and entered a covered shopping arcade. Finally we tired of this and made a run through the driving rain to get to my car parked on the street.

I drove Iris, then Uri, to their homes, then returned through the blinding rainstorm to my apartment in Herzliyyah. As I drove, I realized that something was happening to me. I was experiencing a budding talent for telepathy and clairvoyance. The thing that bothered me about it was that it was as if I had no part in it. I hadn't earned it; it was a "gift." I could now sympathize with Uri when he said, "But it's not me that's doing it!"

The apartment looked toward Tel Aviv over the Haifa Road. The rain lashed at windows blurring all vision. I sat there for a couple of hours. Perhaps I was hoping to see another luminous craft flash by. But nothing happened. Finally I went to bed, fully awake, thinking thoughts I had never dared think before. Was there really some kind of civilized life out there in space, nursing mankind along in secrecy? While I could muse on these possibilities as an exercise in imagination, the problem of scientific proof seemed insoluble.

On the morning of December 7, 1971, I had an excited call from Jacov. He had some information to deliver in person. Uri and I drove to the Hilton Hotel to meet him at 12:45 P.M. Jacov told us with intense excitement that Israeli scholars had cracked the meaning of the word "Dakashem." It was the name of a town in Egypt that had not been used in this form for some four thousand years. The modern name of the town was Khashem El Galala. On a military map of Egypt its coordinates were 892 891. It was believed that "Dakashem" was the code name for the Egyptian invasion plan. Jacov informed us that enough details of the information we had submitted were verified so that it was now being taken seriously. A request was made for Uri to meet and talk with some of the staff officers who were working on the problem. None of this pleased Uri, as he did not want to get deeply involved in this military exercise. As we parted with Jacov, Uri said he had reservations about a meeting with the army people.

I wanted to go and see the spot from which Uri and Shipi had obtained the picture of the spacecraft hovering over the army headquarters building on Friday, December 3. Just before we reached this area we had to cross the Joppa-Haifa Road at Arlosoroff Street. At the Joppa-Haifa Road we were stopped by the traffic signal. While waiting for the light to change, Uri asked for my wristwatch, the Universal Geneve Chronometer. The time was 1:32 P.M. He pulled out the stem to reset the watch hands to 1200 hours. He requested that I say out loud to him three numbers. I said "4, 6, and 9."

He then gave me the watch and asked me to place it face down on my left knee and to place my right index finger over it. This I did. He then asked that I pick one of the three numbers that I had selected earlier. I said "9." The traffic light changed, and Uri drove onto the Ayalon Bridge. As we crossed under the power lines on the bridge, Uri said, "Now turn the watch over and see if anything happened."

I turned the watch over. It was set exactly at 0900 hours! I asked Uri what he thought this meant. He said he had a strong feeling that this was a rendezvous time for a meeting with a spacecraft. I must confess that the mere thought of a bonafide sighting or a meeting with an extraterrestrial being sent shivers running through me. Uri and I inspected the street corner where they had taken the picture. The view of the Israel army headquarters was perfect. This area made Uri rather nervous, so we did not linger very long. We made arrangements to have dinner with Iris that evening. I drove Uri back to his apartment and then returned to my apartment at Herzliyyah. I lay down to nap for a couple of hours.

I got up about four o'clock feeling very refreshed. Suspecting that I had better be ready for anything that evening, I packed my equipment carefully for portability and easy access. I checked out my Super 8 Nizo Braun movie camera and loaded it with a fast-film cartridge, Ekta 160. Then I loaded my Hasselblad camera with 3000 ASA Polaroid film for any night sky pictures such as I had taken in Brazil. But this time I had a Sonnar 250-mm telephoto lens. I put a fresh Hitachi 120 minute cassette for audio recording in my TC 120 tape recorder. I also attached a supersensitive microphone and preamplifier for recording very low level sound. By six-thirty I was finished with all my technical preparations.

I phoned Uri at seven to tell him I was ready. It was then that Uri told me that Iris was with him and that something unusual had happened. He reported that both he and Iris were wearing wristwatches. While waiting for my call, each of the watches had had the hands advanced exactly one hour by some unknown and invisible agency.

All these manipulations that had occurred on this day seemed like the portents of a coming storm. I asked Uri what he thought the advancement of the clock hands meant. He felt that instead of encountering a spacecraft at 9 P.M., as he had predicted earlier, it would now occur at 10 P.M. that night. We ended this phone conversation by agreeing to meet at Iris's apartment in Tel Aviv at 8:30.

When we met at Iris's apartment, it seemed that Uri had not yet eaten dinner. Iris asked Uri what he would like to eat, something that was easy and quick to make. Uri asked for three hard-boiled eggs. We all went into the kitchen to help make the meal more quickly. Iris took three fresh cold eggs out of the refrigerator and placed them on a counter top. Then she walked over to get a pot, filled it with water, and placed it on the stove. She then walked back to the counter to pick up the eggs and screamed with fright. The three eggs were boiling hot, and inspection proved that they were now hard-boiled! After some confused discussion we agreed that this was a sign that we had better hurry up. But, of course, none of us had any idea as to where we were supposed to hurry.

Uri ate his three eggs while Iris had some tea and I drank some coffee. We sat around the table looking at each other. No one knew what to do. Then Uri jumped up and said, "We must leave now!" Iris started to clean up the kitchen. Uri shouted, "There is not time! Let's go!" He led the way out, and I followed. Iris fumbled with the door lock. As she turned to go down the stairs, she felt an invisible presence give her a shove. She frankly confessed that she was getting nervous.

As soon as we got into Uri's car, and I had made sure that all of my equipment was secure, Uri drove away from the curb with a screaming acceleration and drove out of Tel Aviv madly. He would reach an intersection and insist that I choose the direction in which to turn. This drive was very much like the ride in the Jeep in the Sinai a few days before. By this method of navigation we stayed on secondary roads and back roads. I had no idea where we were going or where we were. I sensed that we were generally heading through the suburbs of Tel Aviv toward the east in the direction of Lod Airport.

Just before 10 P.M. we were driving past an open area that looked like a dump, surrounded by new high-rise apartments. Suddenly I commanded Uri to stop. All three of us simultaneously heard a sound like one cricket continuously chirping. Uri stopped the car. I led the way toward the dump, and we climbed up an embankment that looked like a levee. As we reached the top, we all saw, in the direction of the chirping sound, a blue stroboscopic light pulsing at about three flashes per second. We kept walking toward the blue light and the cricket sound, over a wet muddy area freshly bulldozed. We stopped about a hundred yards from the source of the light and sound and whispered to one another.

Uri forbade Iris and me to take another step forward. He said, "Only I am allowed to approach it." I asked if it was permissible to take a movie film. Uri said, "Go ahead and shoot but don't move." Uri then moved forward alone and disappeared from view as he went down into a hollow. I started to take a movie of this strange night scene, knowing that I would be lucky if I could record the blue light. Then Iris began to tremble and cry next to me, so I stopped filming to give her support. As I held an arm around her, I saw the luminous dial of my watch glowing in the night. I thought it said 10 P.M.

Iris calmed down. We stood and watched the powerful blue light flashing; the cricket sound had ceased. Now we heard only the *pock-pock-pock* sound of the stroboscopic flash. I looked around. There was no one in sight in this vast dark field. Would Uri ever return?

Then about thirty yards away I saw Uri coming out of the

hollow. He was slowly walking toward us as though he were carrying a book in his upturned palms. I picked from his palms the brass filler cartridge that had vanished from the inside of my Parker pen three days before! I quickly flashed a pocket light on it, and there I saw my code: ⚙367299. I was overwhelmed by the meaning, the immense meaning, of this small object. But I quickly put it into my pocket and tended to Uri. He seemed to be in a trance, in a sleepwalker's state. Otherwise, he appeared pretty much as he was when he had left us. I asked him what he had seen. He looked at me in anguish; he could not speak.

Iris and I led Uri over the bumpy mud field to the car. Finally Uri spoke: "Andrija, please let's get away from here." I drove the car to a quiet area about a mile away. Uri asked me to park. He was still in a daze, but I just had to persist in finding out what had happened. He told me the following story, which I tape-recorded on my TC 120.

"When I left you, I climbed down and then up a slope, where I saw this light clearly. There was a large cypress tree behind it. I also saw the blue light clearly against the tree. The light was pure blue. Then I went into a hollow and lost sight of the light. As I climbed out of the hollow, the light loomed over me. I walked without any thought or feeling. Then I put out my hands, and in them there appeared your pen cartridge. I don't know what happened next. My mind was blank. The next thing I know I saw you and Iris. How long was it?"

"You were out there about four minutes," I reported.

"It seemed like hours," Uri replied.

Iris had been very quiet; I asked her what she had seen. She reported that she had seen and heard the same thing as I had. She was very sure of the blue light and the cricket sound, but was not sure of what was below the blue light. We dared not state what we suspected, but were not sure of—the possibility of there being a hull under the blue light.

We decided to return to Tel Aviv to go to a coffee shop and talk it all over. Uri insisted on driving. Iris talked to Uri in Hebrew, trying to get him to recall what had happened. I sat in the back seat, going over all the events of the day. But the almost preposterous thought kept coming back to me: "That was not anything supernormal that we saw in the field. It was all some kind of hallucination. Maybe that blue light was all hallucinated. Uri had fooled me. He palmed that cartridge off on me by buying a duplicate. But then how did he know my own serial number?" So my thoughts went on in circles. Since Uri and Iris were in a loud animated conversation in the front seat, I thought that I would tape-record some of my thoughts. I was sure they would not notice me. I reached in the dark for my tape recorder and pressed the forward and record buttons. They were jammed. I turned on my penlight and looked at the recorder. The cassette on which I had recorded Uri's impressions of the experience in the field had vanished! I felt this was an object lesson to my doubting Thomas attitude. I showed this effect to Iris, and she confirmed that I had indeed tape-recorded my interview with Uri some twenty minutes earlier.

We went to the coffee shop and ordered some snacks. We tried to make some sense out of our experience. Skeptical though we were, we seemed to agree on all the details I have recorded up to the point where Uri left Iris and me and walked toward the blue light. But none of us could really accept the possibility that the blue light might be associated with a UFO. Uri could not clearly remember what he had seen in the field after he walked toward the blue light. But I could see that something was gnawing away at him. He told Iris that he was very tired and upset by the evening and wanted to retire. Iris was very understanding and agreed that he should get some rest. We drove Iris to her home. As soon as she was gone, Uri said that "we must work some more tonight. I remember much more than I let on before Iris. I just don't want her to take all this seriously. I want her to forget it. You and I will have to keep this matter secret until we can get some sign that others can know. But I tell you I know it is real. When I was out in that field, I realized for the first time in my life where my powers come from. Now I know for sure they are not my powers. Oh, I know that I have a little bit of telepathy and psychokinesis—everybody has some. But making things vanish, and having things come back, and the red light in the sky in the Sinai, the blue light tonight, that is the power of some superior being. Maybe it is what man always thought of as being God."

We drove back to apartment 61 in Herzliyyah Heights. Somehow the shock of Uri articulating his real feelings wiped out my doubts; it also gave me a strange sense of helplessness.

When we got back to the apartment, Uri asked me to bring out my very large steel camera trunk. He took my Nizo movie camera encased in a plastic bag, which still contained the film cartridge with which I had filmed the event in the field; he locked the camera in the trunk. He asked me to open the trunk in fifteen seconds, which I did. There was the Nizo camera in the intact plastic bag, but when I opened the camera, the Ekta 160 film cartridge was not there. It had vanished.

To a research man the idea of losing data was unthinkable, but to have it vanish was sickening. As I write these lines long after the event, I have in my possession but very few bits of evidence. There are the photographs taken in Brazil of the lights in the night sky. There is Uri's photograph of the UFO in daylight over the Israel army headquarters. And there is a photograph taken over West Germany from an airplane of three spacecraft. (This latter photo will be described later.)

However, every magnetic tape cassette on which was recorded the "voice of Spectra" (and the voices of other beings later recorded) has vanished. With such sparse evidence it was apparent to me that I could never try to convince another human being of my experiences. The secret of Spectra was safe because they had leaked out just enough information to convince me of their reality, but not enough for me to ever convince any other human being.

CHAPTER FIVE

When Time Stood Still

Now that Uri and I had come to accept the reality of this mysterious being as well as its power, we were naturally intensely curious as to whom we were dealing with. We felt very much like people in prison who hear tapping on the other side of the wall and who must try to guess who the tappers are and the meaning of their message.

Every session that we had had to date was a one-way affair, in which we were subject to seeing or hearing a brief message and then it was cut! We tried to figure out some way of opening up a dialogue that was meaningful to us within our human framework. We came to the conclusion that we must try once again the proven technique of trance induction, and try to make the contact, and then ask our questions. Uri had the evening of December 9 free, and we attempted to make our contact then.

At 10:59 P.M. Uri was in hypnotic trance.

AP: "Please ask if I can use the tape recorder."

Uri: "I am alone here. There is no one to ask the question of." Then I heard a voice, not from Uri, for he was asleep. The voice had no source.

Andrija, I have told Uri to come to me now.

AP: "May I use the tape recorder?"

If you do not want to lose the fourth cassette, you will not record. (The tape recorder was placed aside.) *Take this, Uri;*

hand it over to Andrija. (I opened Uri's clenched left hand. There was my missing earphone from my Sony ICR-100 radio in its leather case. It had been translocated from wherever I had lost it weeks ago—most probably New York City.)

The voice in the room went on: *You have done everything. Do as Uri says. How are you feeling? How is your energy?*

AP: "My energy is tops. I feel as though I am in my twenties again. May I ask some questions purely for my own needs?"

Yes, proceed.

AP: "Are you of the Nine Principles that once spoke through Dr. Vinod?"

Yes.

AP: "Are you behind the UFO sightings that started in the United States when Kenneth Arnold saw nine flying saucers on June 24, 1947?"

Yes.

AP: "When did you first notice me?"

In 1946.

AP: "Why was I noticed?"

Our computers studied everyone on earth. You were noticed for your abilities as the ideal and perfect man for this mission.

AP: "What is this mission?"

Do not ask. It will be revealed.

Uri, be prepared. Be wise. Be calm. Calm down. There is a very, very heavy task on your shoulders for the next coming fifty years. There is a lot to be done to help the universe. The cosmic brain will be sent to you. Andrija, I am sending Uri back to you now. Do whatever he wants. Take care of him.

AP: "May I ask one more question?"

Yes.

AP: "Do you have a name?"

Yes, but it is not to be revealed to you yet.[1]

AP: "How can we communicate with you?"

You cannot. We will reach you. We can command any communication system man has devised to reach you. Be alert. We

---

[1] This answer made me realize that "Spectra" was not the name of the being with whom I was speaking.

will use your tape, phone, radio, television, telegram, letters, computors, and so on. Farewell.

The communication ended at 11:09 P.M.

When Uri awoke, I repeated to him from my notes what was said. He did not seem interested. He said, "Andrija, I do not like to think all these heavy things. I am here to *do* things for people. You are here to think and speak. I would rather not hear about these things. I have to remain simple like a child. I really get depressed if I have to think hard about anything, for any length of time."

"I understand," I replied. "Uri, it is a heavy burden we have taken on. But we must do it joyfully, like servants who sing at their work. We must not take ourselves too seriously."

"You're right, Andrija," Uri replied. "God can do anything he wishes. We have seen enough already to know this. Then why does he need us? You know, in the battle for the Golan Heights, we had fighter aircraft, helicopters, tanks, and all kinds of complex machines. But do you know the only creature or thing that could go up the steep mountains was the donkey? You and I are donkeys. If we keep that in mind, we will carry our burden lightly."

The idea of Uri and I being donkeys seemed to describe our role perfectly. Uri went home just after midnight.

Before going to bed I checked my tape recorder, because I wanted to rewind it to the beginning. I tried but found that it would not rewind. I tried to eject the cassette, but the ejector mechanism would not work. Since I could neither rewind nor eject, I got curious and decided to see if anything had been done to the tape. So I pressed the forward key and it worked. To my utter surprise I found that the entire session with Uri had been recorded. This was amazing in that I had set aside the recorder. Furthermore, after the audible communication had ended at 11:09 P.M., there was a further message which said, *Andrija, on the twentieth hypnotize Uri. We will place any messages to you on this machine. Present war is the important thing. Pray. Peace.*

The last message was in a voice totally new to me. It was in

English but had the mechanical quality of synthesized speech. There was no signature. This was to be the first of many messages that appeared to me or to Uri in this totally impersonal medium. When I had finished playing and transcribing this tape, a hall light that had been inoperative for four days suddenly switched on and off by some invisible hand. Somehow I knew that this meant "Wipe out the tape, or it will vanish." Reluctantly I wiped the tape clean of the recorded material.

The events of this day, December 9, 1971, finally brought my lifetime quest into sharp focus. What had made it all fall into place was that last message that had appeared on the tape independently of Uri's presence. There was no use trying to go to sleep that night. I sat down to write out my thoughts about the greater mysteries.

I had always been puzzled by man's use of the word "God." When the Bible says that "God spoke to" or "He spoke to God," I had always assumed it was a figure of speech. It never occurred to me that humans could speak to God, and even now I could not accept the idea. But if humans were reached by beings from space who were so superior that man in his ignorance identified them with gods (the Elohim of the Bible), or God, then the literary allusions became clear. If I had had my experiences with Uri in the time of Moses, I would have leaped to the conclusion that I was dealing with God.

In addition to the confused record with respect to God and gods, I now felt that the role of prophets and sages in human affairs became more understandable. In biblical times an Uri Geller would eventually be honored as a prophet in local religious lore. Today he was a show freak and a guinea pig for science.

The elements of this prophetic strain in human affairs now seemed to be quite simple. First there must exist a local cosmic being of superior intelligence who has been assigned by an even more superior being to a task on earth. Somehow the cosmic being has control of intelligent energy (or "inergy," for brevity) by means of which it can create any form of matter-energy it desires. Thus the local cosmic being can assume any form it wishes to suit its purpose. For example, if it wishes to appear to some earth person, it chooses a form suitable to the local taste. In ancient Egypt the sun god, Ra, for example, was said to appear in the form of a hawk called Hor, or as corrupted by the Greeks, Horus.

Another aspect of inergy as used by the cosmic brain is to imitate any local language that is appropriate for getting a message across. Still another is the power to de-create thoughts or matter forms, as I have already reported. This aspect of inergy would account for all the sudden appearances and vanishings of mythological lore, as well as modern UFO reports. It could also take the form of matter-energy being transported, stored invisibly, or recalled to and from different places on earth (or in the universe).

I had the very strong feeling that the cosmic being does not normally exist in our space-time framework, except when it is necessary for it to interact with humans. Through these principles I have just cited, I believe that a prophet, an Uri Geller, if you wish, is specifically created to serve as an intermediary between a "divine" intelligence and man. The same idea would hold for living beings existing anywhere on any planet in the universe. I now fully believe that life exists anywhere and everywhere in the universe as divine intelligence dictates. I was prepared to believe that life exists in forms and states beyond the imagination of man to conceive.

Now I was totally convinced that Uri and I had been contacted by such a local cosmic being; by this I mean some representative or extension of the Nine Principles. In this sense I believe that a cosmic being is superior to any life that exists on any planet in a material form. But for this I did not have any proof. I am well aware that any clever race of beings from another planet who were reconnoitering earth could easily fool me to think that I was dealing with Elohim, gods, or even God. I could only know the answer to this possibility if open communication were to be established someday. Whatever the final verdict would be, I was now convinced that a contact had been made with a superior form of intelligence. But being realistic as to the atavistic nature of man, I knew that to disclose what I now knew would be to ask for martyrdom. Besides, it had been requested that Uri and I keep their secret.

One of the mysteries of the cosmic being was its use of the biconvex disk shape (the flying saucer) to manifest on earth to man and his instruments. I have no idea why this shape is used. This is a matter for future scientific study.

I further believed now that if small and insignificant people like Uri and me were contacted and used as ambassadors to other people, there must be a large number of men and women on earth serving as we were. I was determined to find others like Uri and me in the future.

Uri and I both felt the personal solicitude of the cosmic being's interest in our welfare, feelings, health, thoughts, and actions. Also, why was there such concern about mankind's future as the result of a potential war conflagration between Egypt and Israel, which might escalate into world war? I wondered where else in human history there had been this kind of covert intervention in the interests of man's long-term welfare.

I also chose to believe now that the cosmic being was essentially omniscient and omnipotent. If this were so, I wondered why it had to work through Uri and me. Was this because, as stated by the Nine, they never interfere with an individual's will? Were we therefore being "persuaded" to exert our own human will to help mankind within a purely human framework of action? Then there was the more basic question as to how many degrees of freedom we really could exercise in what we were now doing. I wanted to find out eventually when and why the cosmic being chose to intervene in earth affairs.

And how many cosmic beings existed with respect to earth? Was there just one, with multiple manifestations, or were there many?

As far as humankind was concerned, much of the mystery of the inergy of the cosmic being could be resolved by knowing the laws of "creation" and "de-creation" of living forms, matter forms, and energy forms. Such laws are not known to contemporary science. In fact, man cannot even begin to guess at the nature of inergy and its many manifestations. But the solution of this mystery could form the agenda of science for generations to come if it would take this problem seriously.

My thoughts on this long night were more in the nature of wonderment and questions than convictions. They were more in the nature of an agenda for my future work as it existed in reference to Uri, the cosmic being, and myself. My night of thought ended as the sun broke over the Judean Hills in the direction of Jerusalem.

The next few days passed without any notable events. On December 12 I decided to give up my apartment in the Herzliyyah Heights. I wanted to be right on the seashore, where I could enjoy a greater sweep of sky and sea. It was with great sadness that I closed the door on apartment 61, where the most momentous experiences of my life had occurred. I moved to the Sharon Hotel Towers right on the beach in Herzliyyah-by-the-Sea. I had a room that was high above the sea on the eleventh floor.

Since this was the Hannukah festival season in Israel, Uri had many shows scheduled, sometimes as many as four in one day. We spent a great deal of time on the road, going to Haifa and to small towns in Galilee, as well as Safad, Jerusalem, etc.

On December 13 I picked up a copy of *Time* magazine, which had a bold cover-story caption that caught my eye: "Looking for Life Out There." The cover showed a man standing on planet earth looking out into the deep space of planets and stars. The story was written by Los Angeles correspondent John Wilhelm.

As I finished reading the last line of Wilhelm's article, I realized that its timing was truly prophetic: *"Perhaps it would teach that secret of survival to man."* Perhaps this was my immediate task. And I felt incredibly helpless—how could I, a donkey, do anything to stop the huge juggernauts of war of many nations at this last hour? What I heard on the radio and read in the papers was chilling. The war between India and Pakistan over Bangladesh was polarizing the great powers of the world into dangerous positions. Russia had lined up her support behind India. The United States was supporting Pakistan. China, already in a border war with India, put her support behind Pakistan.

And over and through all this tension the Arab radio stations repeated day and night the threat of President Anwar Sadat that by January 1, 1972, the Egyptians would conclude the "final solution" to the Israel problem. That is, that the State of Israel and the Israelis would be liquidated.

My concern for world peace was profound. I could not forget the voice and the words of December 1, 1971. But they made no further contact with us, although I repeatedly tried to invite a communication by hypnotic induction of Uri and the use of the tape recorder. It seemed that we were not only left alone but abandoned. We simply had to wait for the promised contact on the twentieth.

On December 19 Uri and Iris came over to the Hotel Sharon to have lunch with me. As long as Uri was with me, I set up the TC 120 tape recorder and routinely asked the same questions: "What can Uri and I do toward preventing war?"

As I asked this question, Uri and Iris simply sat with me and looked out over the sea. A few minutes after I asked my question, I noticed that the tape was running on "record" and the VU meter was oscillating with the familiar pattern of speech recording. I said nothing to Uri and Iris but pulled the microphone out of the microphone jack to see what would happen. The VU meter kept on with its oscillations. I knew then that I was getting some kind of a recording. This went on for some three minutes. Then it stopped. I didn't want to play the tape in front of Iris, so I stopped the recording process and waited to hear what had last "recorded" after they left. Uri and Iris left around 2:45 P.M.

As soon as they had left, I started to rewind the tape back to the starting point. As I was getting ready to play the tape, I happened to glance at my wristwatch, which had been lying on a table. It had stopped at 2:45 and 45 seconds. (I have already pointed out that my watch was a Universal Geneve Chronometer, with three extra dial faces as well as a large sweep-second hand.) The hour hand had stopped at 2; the minute hand had stopped at 9; and one of the small dial's second hand had stopped at 45 seconds, making 2:45:45, or 1445:45 hours. I wound the stem; it would not start. I listened to the watch; it was silent. I shook it; it would not start. It had really stopped, and I could not tell why. Then I played the tape. There was a message on the tape, recorded in English by a mechanical-sounding voice:

Stay away from Israel Army. Do not interfere. Pray for peace. Pray when your watch is stopped.

Then the tape message ended. Five minutes later the cassette vanished. I now knew at last, what the stopped watch meant. I put the watch on and went out on the balcony over the sea facing Egypt. I prayed for peace. At 3:21 P.M., by local time, my watch began to run by itself. It had been stopped by an invisible hand for thirty-six minutes. The nature of my prayer seemed so sacred to me that I did not tell anyone about it.

The next day, Monday, December 20, 1971, we had planned an outing for Uri's twenty-fifth birthday. Uri wanted only Shipi and Hannah and myself to go. For reason's that I did not fully understand Uri wanted to spend this day in the Judean Hills with his three closest friends. We left Tel Aviv at 7:30 A.M. and arrived in Jerusalem by 9 A.M. We had no particular plan as to where we were going; we just decided as we went along. In Jerusalem Uri wanted to go to the area where he had been wounded in the Six Day War. We went to the area north of Jerusalem, and Uri remembered spot after spot where this or that action occurred. Shipi, Hannah, and I could only faintly imagine what was going through Uri's mind. But thoughts of the evils of war were heavy on all of us.

Uri decided that we must go on to the Dead Sea. On the way there we cheered our somber hearts with loud singing. As we neared the Dead Sea, I told my friends the story of how I had come here almost two years ago and first felt the magic of Israel. To reinforce the story we went to the area of Qumran. I then told them the story of the Teacher of Righteousness who was also Jewish, but more in the tradition of one of the orthodox sects that they knew. The idea of the war between the Sons of Light and the Sons of Darkness touched Uri. He said, "Doesn't 'Spectra' mean light, like my name means light?"

I said, "Yes, it does. Maybe this is what the Essenes were doing here in the desert—watching for signs from a Spectra."

This thought with its depth in antiquity chilled our spines. Were we just the latest in a long line of recipients of light and knowledge? I then told them of my great sleepiness here in 1970, and that I now felt it was caused by one of the spacecraft that we were seeing. (See page 62.)

We drove on down the western shore of the Dead Sea beneath the stark cliffs to our right and the deceptive blue sparkle of the sea on our left. We stopped frequently to take pictures and to run around like wild goats. It was like springtime for me to be out in the wilds with these three carefree children. At one time as I took movies, I lightly grumbled because I did not have my leather case for my NIZO Super 8 movie camera. I was afraid of dust from the desert wind getting into my camera and ruining the shutter mechanism. Uri took notice of what I said. "Where is your camera case?" he asked.

"I was trying to save on weight, so I left all excess-weight items in my home in Ossining," I replied.

We drove on down the seacoast to Ein Bokek, to Sedom, and then turned inland. As we went through Arad, Uri suddenly announced that he had always wanted to see Abraham's Oak in Hebron. Would we like to go? We all said "great idea" and headed north. Only Shipi, in addition to myself, had studied the Bible, so between us we reconstructed the story of Abraham and the Angels for Uri's benefit.

This is how we remembered it at the time: Abraham was living near Hebron at Mamre. He was lying in his tent in the heat of the day when three men appeared before him. They seemed to be real men. Abraham treated them hospitably with food and drink as though they were real men. Then one of them predicted that Sarah, who was around ninety years old, would have a child. She, of course, laughed this off as blarney. The three men indicated that they were on a serious mission for the Lord. Then the

Lord stood out from the men and told Abraham that he was going to pass judgment on Sodom and Gomorrah. Of course, we had just been to the area now called Sedom, which was now only a wasteland, but believed to be the biblical site of Sodom.

The Lord revealed to Abraham his plan to destroy these two cities because of their wickedness. Abraham found himself pleading with the Lord to spare the cities for the sake of the righteous people who were there. The Lord finally acceded to Abraham, saying he would spare Sodom and Gomorrah if there were only ten righteous men there. Of course, we know the end of the story—Sodom and Gomorrah were destroyed, and only Lot escaped.

Uri was very moved by our poor rendering of this great story. He said, "You know, this is just like today. We are told by some invisible power that mankind is close to destroying itself. Somehow we get involved and are trying to help, but we are not really doing much. I really want to know if the Lord talked to Abraham. Were those men that Abraham saw actually from a spacecraft? Are the ones we talk to, the same ones that Abraham talked to?"

"Uri, why don't we ask for a sign when we get there? Maybe we can get an answer to these questions," Shipi interjected.

When we got to the Oak of Mamre, we found it guarded by Arabs, and near it there was an Arab mosque and school. We walked up to the iron fence surrounding this mighty stump of an oak with only a few green branches on it and stood there in silence. Uri tried to feel the vibes from the oak, but nothing happened. Then he said to me, "I know what we must do! We will ask if Spectra visited Abraham here four thousand years ago, just yes or no. Let's go up on that hill away from these people."

We went up the hill and we got out of our car. Uri asked me for my Universal Geneve watch, and I handed it to him. He then said, "Believe me, this is very sacred. I have never done this before. I am going to turn your watch face up to the sky. We will all look at the face of the watch. Andrija, you ask the question like I told you, then we will see what happens to the watch. If nothing happens, the answer is no; if something happens, the answer is yes."

The four of us stared at the watch. I asked the question, "Did you, Spectra, appear to Abraham here?"

At one moment as we stared at the watch it read 4:06 P.M. In the next moment it read 4:35 P.M. The hands had "moved" forward twenty-nine minutes.

Uri was very solemn. "I finally believe that what we are doing today has been going on for thousands of years. It is an old story." We all breathed a quiet amen.

As we got in the car and drove on, we all agreed on one point. The hands of my watch had not moved in the usual sense. We had the impression that they had vanished from the first position and reappeared in the second position. Uri was now sure that this was the process.

I recount this incident in some detail because it was the prelude to my own experience with the war problem for the coming six days. But I must confess that I did not know it as it happened; I see the pattern only now in hindsight.

We drove north past Bethlehem, past Jerusalem, and then west toward Tel Aviv. As we approached the town of Ramla, with the setting sun ahead, we saw the clear outline of a disk-shaped craft in the sky with a red light on the top. It was too far away to see any detail. It did not move. It just winked out about five minutes later. As the light of the craft winked out, the headlights on our car also went out. I pulled over to the shoulder just to watch if the craft would reappear. In a minute the car headlights went on by themselves.

We drove on for five minutes, and then the engine was mysteriously cut off. No one panicked. We all knew it was "they" making us aware of their presence. Now, this was the first time that Shipi had been with Uri and me when unusual physical things were happening. I was quite impressed with how naturally Hannah and Shipi accepted these signs. Uri calmly explained to them in Hebrew what was going on and said we would always be together to do this kind of work. The engine started in five minutes.

I dropped Hannah and Shipi off at their home in Givataim about 7 P.M. and Uri at his apartment shortly thereafter. I drove at a hundred-kilometer-per-hour speed to the Sharon Hotel; my car now worked perfectly.

I had just finished taking a bath at 7:45 P.M. when my phone rang; it was Uri. He sounded awestruck as though he had just seen the angel of Abraham.

"Andrija, listen to what happened. At about 7:40 P.M. I went into my small bedroom to turn on the electric heater. My bed was empty of anything. I went out and closed the door so that the room would heat up. Then I went to the bathroom to take a shower. I entered my bedroom at 7:45 P.M., and there upon my bed was a black leather camera case labeled with printed letters "Braun NIZO." I have never seen such a case before. I asked my mother what she knew, and she said she was in a chair in the living room all the time. Andrija, could this be the camera case you talked about today while we were at the Dead Sea?"

I asked him to identify certain marks in the interior of the case, which I had once made. He verified that they were there.

I said, "Uri, that fits the description of the camera case I put in a locked closet in Ossining, New York, on November 17, 1971, which is over six thousand miles away! How did it get here?"

"I don't know," he said. "Are you playing a joke on me?"

"I wouldn't play such a joke. Bring it over tonight when you come here after your show," I said.

After this call I began to get ready for the evening session with Uri. I synchronized my wristwatch and an electric digital clock to the radio at 8 P.M. Then I tested my tape recorder for the evening's work. At 8:57 P.M. (by the electric clock) I happened to glance at my wristwatch: it had stopped at precisely 8:45:45.

Remembering my instructions, I prayed for peace to enter Sadat's heart. I glanced at the watch from time to time. At 10:07 P.M. (by the electric clock) exactly, I happened to be looking at my wristwatch and saw the small second hand starting to move. The watch had stopped for eighty-two minutes. I realized that I was abnormally drained of energy from the effort of praying.

That evening when he came to see me, Uri handed me the black leather camera bag. I inspected it carefully. There was no question about it; it was my own bag which I had left some six thousand miles away. The only possible conventional explanation was that somebody was playing a trick on us; for example, the Israeli Army might conceivably have obtained the camera bag by normal means from Ossining and then planted it on Uri. Uri told me there were no windows in his bedroom, and there was only one door from the bedroom into the living room; his mother was sitting near this door all the time Uri was in the bedroom. Uri assured me that his mother was not in collusion with anyone. We felt certain then that this camera bag was translocated by means and agencies unknown.

We went ahead with preparations to keep our rendezvous at 11:20 P.M. This time Uri went into hypnotic trance easily and began to speak:

"Andrija, I am in a flat place. Noises!"

Then a powerful resonant voice sounded in the room:

Listen, listen, Andrija. Present war—important thing. We have shown you personally, without Uri, how we contact you through your watch. When it stops, pray. Put your movie camera in its original case. We sent it over. Pray peace.

There were many other things said during this session which I am not yet permitted to reveal. The session ended at 11:30 P.M., December 20, 1971. Now, my watch had been stopped at 10:45:45 P.M. and had remained stopped until 12:11 A.M. (December 21), when Uri had placed his hand over it, and it started running again. The watch was now ninety minutes behind the electric clock. As I was writing up the notes of the session (before the tape vanished), I noticed at 1:32 A.M. (electric clock time) that my watch had stopped again at 11:45:45 P.M. This time it remained stopped for exactly twelve hours. It self-started at 11:45 A.M. on December 21. During those twelve hours I sat on my balcony praying for peace as I faced

Egypt. This was an ordeal I was not prepared for. I am sure that I must have dozed off at times during this vigil.

I realize that it may be tedious for the reader to follow all the details of the various times when the watch stopped. However, to my knowledge, this phenomenon has never before been reported on earth, and however boring it may be, a full historical account is warranted, which will be found in Appendix Three.

After the watch started up at 11:45 A.M. on December 21, I had to go to see Reuven on business. I told him what was happening with my watch, and since 12:45 P.M. was approaching, we both looked at my watch while the hands reached this critical angle. I saw the watch stop, of its own accord, at exactly 12:45:45 P.M., and pointed it out to Reuven as it happened.

I then called Uri from Reuven's apartment, and he told me the following story. A few minutes earlier, at 12:20 P.M. to be exact, Uri had walked into his bedroom and there, at the foot of his bed, was a large (three feet by two feet) brown suitcase. He inspected it, read the brand label, "Taperlite," opened it, and found it to be empty. Then it vanished in front of his eyes. The entire episode lasted about three minutes. I left Reuven to go to see Uri.

As Christmas Eve approached, my thoughts turned more and more to the Prince of Peace, and as the zero hour for possible war approached, I knew that I would have to pray longer and harder. What better place, I thought, than to go to Bethlehem where Jesus was born. As I prayed during the night and on the morning of December 24, I must have nodded off to sleep at one point because I was awakened at 8:18 A.M. I showered, shaved, ate breakfast, and got in my car to go to Bethlehem.

This was one day when I really wished to be alone, just to be able to continue my prayer for peace. It was a beautiful sunny day, this December 24, in the Holy Land. One could never guess by looking at the countryside that within a few days this could be the site of the start of a global holocaust. As I drove through Ramla, a largely Arab town, it was obvious that it was the Muslim Holy Day. Tonight at sundown it would be the Jewish Holy Day, Shabbat. And Saturday, December 25, was the

Christian Holy Day of Jesus' birth. For me, brought up in the slums of Chicago in the Catholic faith, it was a profound experience to be here on the road to life, and perhaps mankind's life.

I chose the back roads to Bethlehem which wound through the ancient hills of Judah. When I left Beit Shemesh, I got on winding gravel back roads of the Ha'ela Valley, feeling as if I had slipped back several thousands of years into time.

As I passed through the Arab villages of El Khada and Beit Jala, I could see that there were more and more Israeli soldiers and military police. At the edge of Bethlehem I was stopped and told that no cars were allowed beyond this point. So I parked my car where I could and walked over to where the soldiers stood. They said that no one was permitted to enter the inner area of Bethlehem without a pass. The pass had to be applied for a week in advance in order that a security check could be done. There were no exceptions, because the authorities feared an incident by one of the extremist organizations. I was determined to get to the Grotto of the Nativity—I had to complete my prayers. Yet I knew how tough Israeli security was. So I prayed as I walked toward the inspection barrier.

A young lady sabra lieutenant sternly asked me, in perfect English, for my pass. I said, "Lieutenant, I come in peace from a far-off land. I did not have time to apply for a pass. Look at me. I am honest, open, and have only love for man. Please, Lieutenant, let me pass that I may pray for the peace of the world."

I don't know what this officer thought of my plea. But she inspected my passport, gave me a searching look, and stamped a pass, which she handed to me. I thanked her openly, blessed her in my heart, and made my way into Manger Square. I also thanked my friends on high.

Although the crowds were large, I was able to enter into the depths of the Grotto of the Nativity and pray on my knees at the very spot where legend has it that Jesus was born. Somehow in the presence of the vast throngs my prayers seemed to gain in meaning and in power. By 3:30 P.M. I felt I had completed my mission to Bethlehem.

When Time Stood Still

I moved on to the old city of Jerusalem. As sundown approached, and Shabbat neared, the shops started closing and the streets emptied. By sundown the old city was quite deserted, and I walked its quiet streets alone. It was hard to believe that the very pavements I walked on had once been known by David, his paramour Bathsheba, and their son, the glorious Solomon. This was the city holy to the Muslims, the Jews, and the Christians. I walked over to the Mosque of Omar, built over the Dome of the Rock where Mohammed had ascended directly to heaven on his white horse. Under this platform surrounding the mosque was the ruin of the Temple of Solomon.

I looked at the watch on my left wrist; the Geneve was still stopped at 11:45:45. As a reference standard I had another watch, the Certina on my right wrist that told me that the local time was 5 P.M. The time on the Geneve portended the approach of the crisis as it had now been stopped for over eighteen hours. I walked back to my car, which was near the Joppa Gate.

I don't know how it happened, but I missed the road to Tel Aviv, and instead made the circumferential drive going north around the old city. I came back to my starting point up the Valley of Kidron along the Jericho Road. Passing through the small Arab villages along this valley, I was once again transported to biblical times. The sun had already gone down; Shabbat had begun. The roads were empty as I headed for Tel Aviv, my heart was full of prayer for the knowledge of the richness of life.

As I crossed the Israel Road (Sardi Yisrael), I saw ahead on the deserted road a small figure dressed in white, hitchhiking. I stopped and saw that it was a girl. I asked her where she was going after sundown. She smiled and said, Tel Aviv, and that sundown was not important to her. Her English was excellent, and she spoke freely. Her name was Miriam El, which translates into English as "Miriam of God."

I asked her what the name Miriam meant in Hebrew. She said, "Miriam means 'strong.' Your English name for this is

Mary. But did you know that Miriam was the elder sister of Moses and Aaron?"

I was truly startled by this reply. "Why did you tell me about Moses and Aaron now?"

She shyly replied, "Are you Jewish?"

I said, "No, I was brought up as a Catholic, but I do not practice in that faith now."

"Well, it would help my explanation if you were. But I shall try. You see, in the back streets of Jerusalem there are many quiet discussions going on about the fate of Israel and of the Jewish people. There is an uneasy feeling about the threat of war now. And when this feeling arises, people talk about Moses, who saved us from slavery in Egypt. But more than that, you can hear it being whispered in Jerusalem among the old and the young about a coming war that has another meaning. These people believe that the Bible says to them today that Israel must suffer three major wars: the first was the '56 war; the second was the '67 war; and the third is yet to come. Now, it is not a fear of the third war that they talk about. Can you understand that they dream about a third war with expectations? They feel that Israel must suffer once more and that the conscience of the world must be burned once more in order to remind us all of the promise of God. And do you know what they say this promise is? They say that the Messiah will appear here in Israel. These people believe these things. And I must say, I do, too." .

As a young sabra she breathed all the hopes and ideals of her people. As she talked on, in spite of her talk of war, I somehow felt strengthened in my prayers for peace. But the irony of our situation was not lost on me. Here I was, praying for a war not to occur, because of a potential worldwide spread of a new Middle-eastern war. And this sweet young woman was praying for a Messiah to deliver her people, and mankind, and willing to pay the price of war.

I met Uri at the Sharon Hotel at midnight. I told him that my watch had been stopped for over twenty-four hours now and that I was getting tired. This time, he was unable to start the watch again. We both felt that this was an ominous sign. More effort was needed. Perhaps the prayers were not working. Perhaps Sadat was not being reached. Or maybe others in power had a more decisive role than Sadat.

In any case, it was not a good omen. Uri and I parted at 1 A.M. It was now December 25, 1971. I went to my old station at the balcony over the sea facing Egypt. Pray for peace.

As dawn came, I had some food. At 11 A.M. my watch was still stopped. I went to the bathroom to take a shower. I reached up with my hands to take from around my neck a Star of David on a gold chain given to me by Uri five days earlier. I was amazed to find that the star was missing! I searched the room and finally found the Star of David under my pillow. I had not been to bed that night. I also saw that the connecting gold link between the chain and the star was intact. There was no way that the Star of David could have come off the chain—except by the now familiar vanishing process. I felt that it was a good omen, but I wished that the language were clearer.

Uri and Iris visited me at my hotel in the afternoon. I had placed the Geneve and the Certina watches on the table side by side. Uri looked at my Geneve and said, "It is still stopped." Rather wearily, I said, "Yes, for well over thirty-six hours now." He placed his left hand, fist clenched, over it and said, "I am going to try it once more." As he said this, the Geneve started immediately. The local time by the Certina was 2:34 P.M. My watch had been stopped for a total of forty hours and four minutes. Uri and Iris left shortly thereafter. I went to bed and fell into a very deep sleep.

I woke up and looked at the clock. It was 1 A.M., the fateful day of December 26. I turned on the radio, listened to the BBC, the Voice of America, etc. There was no news of any significance. I stepped out on my balcony to get a breath of fresh air. The sky was leaden with low clouds. It had rained while I was asleep. Suddenly, at 1:45 A.M., I saw just one flash of the same blue light that Uri, Iris, and I had seen. It was right in front of me, beneath the clouds to the south. I thought that it could not have been more than a few hundred meters away. As I watched, there was a second blue flash. Then a third blue flash—and that was all. It seemed to say to me, "Good show, old chum. Go back to sleep. All is well."

I did go to sleep, and awoke at 8:55 A.M. I saw that the Geneve watch had changed to 1:45:45, but I did not know when this had happened. In any case it was stopped. So I went back to my prayer for peace on the balcony. All the rest of this December 26, I continued to pray. Uri called me once at 6:30 P.M. to report that he had lost a gold medallion from his neck chain. He said he would come to see me about 8 P.M.

Uri came in at 7:45 P.M. and sat down on the sofa. We both happened to look at the desk at the same time, and there was his gold medallion—it had just appeared on the carpet beneath the desk.

We decided to go down to the first-floor dining room to have dinner. The maître d'hôtel chose a table for us. As we sat down, Uri picked up his napkin. There under the napkin was a Mexican five-peso piece—which I often carried around with me—that had been left in the desk in my eleventh-floor room.

The fact that we had witnessed the vanishing and the appearance of gold and silver that day made a deep impression on me. Then another "first" occurred. While we were staring at the five-peso piece, the silver fork in front of Uri bent up ninety degrees. He had not touched it. When Uri tried to put food in his mouth (at 8:35 P.M.), it vanished from inside his mouth. After several unsuccessful tries, we finally gave up trying to have dinner and went upstairs to my room.

At 9:03 P.M. (Certina time) my Geneve watch again stopped at 2:45:45. At 9:34 P.M. (Certina time) my Geneve watch did a strange thing. It jumped from 2:45:45 to 3:35 instantly, and then it started to tick normally and kept running. This was the last time in 1971 that my Geneve watch was to stop in this extraordinarily precise way.

As Uri was leaving that night, he was like a man who has just realized that he is suddenly no longer a boy. One of his comments was "Now I really know that it is not me. They are doing all the work. Imagine, they come to all of my crummy shows to do the work. I wonder why they bother with all these little people?"

As midnight approached, I anxiously listened to all the news. The Arab threats continued that "Sadat has promised to liquidate the State of Israel before the week is up." There was no sign in all of Israel that an attack on Egypt was at hand. It was a strange night for me. Outside, there was the giant roar of the surf as a Mediterranean storm battered the coast. There was all the drama of thunder, lightning, wind, and rain dashing against the senses. But it was the roar of nature, not the roar of man at war.

Sitting in the dark, I was listening to the Voice of America and watching the lightning flashes over the sea. Just as the announcer said it was 2215 hours Greenwich mean time (12:15 A.M. local), I saw a bright "star" due south. I jumped up and saw that it was under the clouds; it was not a plane. Twinkling brightly with an array of colors, it hovered over Tel Aviv. The "star" shone for a minute—then went off.

I got my NIZO Super 8 camera out and ready should it reappear. Suddenly, there it was again! Then I had an astounding experience. When I pointed the camera with a 56-millimeter lens toward the light, the camera trigger locked. To test this locking effect, I turned the camera away from the light, and the trigger switch worked normally. I pointed the camera again at the twinkling colored light, and again the camera froze. I did this repeatedly and concluded that my camera was being controlled from that light—which did not want its picture taken! The light repeated this cycle, staying on for a minute and off for a minute, seven times. I noted in my diary at the time: "I strongly feel that this light appeared (seven times) to assure me that all is well. Now I feel assured that peace will begin. 12:45 A.M. December 27, 1971. Sharon, Herzliyyah-by-the-Sea."

On December 29, 1971, I read in the Jerusalem *Post,* "The public announcement of the results of President Sadat's conference this past week: *There will be no war."* To this day I do not know why President Anwar Sadat reversed his publicly avowed policy. I do not know what restrained the Israeli Government from a pre-emptive attack in the face of Arab war threats. Someday, I am sure, each side will release its own secret documents with respect to what actually happened in December 1971. As for me, the relief was enormous. As for Uri, it was his second great battle test, much more severe than in the battle for Jerusalem. I was sure that a possible world war threat was over on December 27, 1971, and subsequent history will have to confirm this judgment.[2] Without waiting to hear the words of Sadat, I now set about to find out all I could about the intelligence in the sky about whom we still knew so little.

Since I have no other name for the intelligence in the sky, I decided at this time to call it IS for short.

In the chapter that follows I will relate some of the lessons that come from IS, most of which came through or around Uri. But to avoid repetition and an unmanageable amount of material, I shall cite only those instances where a new lesson was to be learned.

[2] I was reviewing the final manuscript on October 18, 1973, and as the reader is surely aware, a war broke out between Israel and Egypt and Syria, October 6, 1973, Yom Kippur. Uri Geller and I were preparing to leave the United States for Frankfort, Germany, when the war broke out. We went ahead to Frankfort, in order to be closer to Israel should we be needed there. Naturally, Uri and I contacted the extraterrestrial intelligence to find out at the source how this new war was viewed. The judgment was succinct: "Concerning Israel: The fight and the war will be fought just like an ordinary war. This war had to come, and they shall fight it out alone. You are not needed this time. This war will be marked in earth as an important war for the human race."

I queried the intelligence as to whether this was the war that was being whispered about in the old streets of Jerusalem. The answer was in the affirmative.

CHAPTER SIX

Eye of the Hawk

On December 28, 1971, at 9:07 P.M. Uri called me while I was in the Sharon Hotel dining room having dinner with Ila Ziebell, who had just come to Israel. He seemed in such a state of alarm on the phone that I became deeply worried. He would not say what was wrong but begged me to come to his apartment immediately. I asked him if I could bring Ila along, and he said that would actually be helpful. We stopped dinner mid-course and took a cab to Uri's apartment.

When we walked in, he was alone, dressed in a bathrobe. He looked at us with red eyes. "I can't tell you what happened, but I cried. Do grown men ever cry?" he pleaded.

"Yes, Uri, I have cried when someone I loved died," I said.

He asked us to sit down. He fiddled with his hands aimlessly, wanting to talk, yet somehow constrained. Finally, it came out in bits. He had been secretly in love with a woman for the past five years. Her situation was such that they could only meet secretly at rare intervals. An hour and a half earlier she had told Uri that she could never see him again. It was torture for Uri to unburden himself of this secret. He said that he had actually placed a revolver to his head to end his life, but something made him put down the weapon and call me instead.

I was profoundly shocked at his deep depression and at the though that he might die violently, as had Arigó.

"Uri, please show me the gun!" I demanded. Uri walked into his bedroom and handed me a revolver in a brown leather case. I looked at the revolver; it was a .38-caliber Rossi loaded with six bullets.

"Uri, this gun in your hands really disturbs me. Please, may I take it?" I asked.

Uri insisted he was all right now. I offered to spend the night at his place; he refused. I invited him to spend the night at my hotel; he refused. But through all this discussion, he refused to part with the gun, insisting that he was all right. Finally, he agreed to go to the house of a friend he trusted, Sarah Bursak. At midnight we walked with Uri some four blocks to Sarah's house and left him in her charge.

I called Uri the next morning and casually inquired how he was. He said, "Fine. Why do you ask in such a serious way?"

"Well, I was concerned about what you said last night," I replied.

"What do you mean? What did I say?" he asked.

"Don't you remember?" I asked in disbelief.

"No, only that you and Ila were here and we walked over to Sarah's house," he said.

I realized that Uri was not depressed and that I could talk very frankly to him. I then repeated very briefly what he had said about his secret love and the gun. He was stunned by my words.

"Do you mean I said all that? Well, I don't remember saying any of it. It is true about the girl, but it couldn't be true about the gun. I haven't had that gun for two months; it is at Shipi's house. Please go over and ask him."

Now it was my turn to be stunned. "Okay, Uri, let's drop it," I said. "I'll come over to see you tonight after dinner."

"Good, I'll be waiting for you," he said.

I then talked to Ila about what Uri had said the previous night and what he had said this morning. We both agreed on every detail of what had occurred the night before. We were both especially sure that Uri had handed me a gun. I then drove over to Shipi's home and asked him if he had Uri's Rossi revolver. He said, "Yes, I've had it here for the past two months."

I checked to see if Uri had borrowed it recently. The answer was no. Shipi then showed me the revolver; it was the same one I had handled the previous night.

Ila and I went to see Uri at 8 P.M. He was running a fever of 38.2° C. and had the flu. In spite of the illness, he was in a good mood. None of us talked about "the night of the gun." We chatted about many things for the next two hours. Then Uri asked Ila for a coin, and she gave him a five-agaroth coin. He placed this in a wooden-match box and asked Ila to place her hands over it. Ila felt a tingle in her hands; the box was opened. The coin had vanished.

It was 10:30 P.M. The phone rang, and Uri picked it up. He said to me very excitedly, "It's her, she's calling from the Sinai!"

I said, "Who? Who is calling?"

He said, "Yaffa. Talk to her!" and thrust the phone into my hand.

Not knowing to whom I was talking, I said, "My name is Andrija; who are you?"

A woman's voice said in broken English, "Pleased to meet you. I am Yaffa. I do not speak English, only Hebrew."

Just then Sarah Bursak walked into the room, and Uri said to her, "It's Yaffa on the phone from the Sinai. Talk to her!"

So I handed Sarah the phone. She talked with great excitement and enthusiasm in Hebrew to the woman for about two minutes and then handed the phone to Uri, who talked on for several more minutes in Hebrew.

No one discussed the phone call when it ended; it all seemed so natural. Ila and I left shortly thereafter. We drove to the Sharon Hotel discussing this phone call, speculating that Yaffa must be the secret love.

The next morning Uri made a casual phone call to me to say that he was feeling better. Equally casually, I asked him about the phone call from the Sinai last night and who was Yaffa.

He stated flatly, "There was no phone call last night!"

I insisted that there was a phone call and repeated to him in detail what Ila and I had both witnessed. Uri sounded very distressed with me. "Andrija, there was no phone call. You must be getting sick! Please call Sarah; she'll tell you the same thing."

I called Sarah and repeated my story about the phone call. She, too, denied it, saying, "Dr. Puharich, I like you very much, but I think you are very strange. This is not a good joke."

I called Uri back to report on Sarah's denial and Ila's affirmation of my story. He stated flatly, "Andrija, you dreamed the whole thing, and Ila is just going along with you. Forget the whole story!"

However, Uri called me back in an hour and said, "I don't believe there was a phone call, but how did you find out that my secret love's name is Yaffa?"

These two days' events numbed me. Sarah and Uri experienced one sequence, and Ila and I experienced another, in the same time frame. I had discovered the truth about Uri's deepest secret, had had a gun in my hand that felt real, and had had a phone call experience that is real in my mind to this day. But most of all I realized that the four of us had had an experience imprinted on our minds by what could only be the agency of IS. I finally learned that, given the existence of IS, I could never again know which of my experiences were directly imposed upon me by IS and which were not.

I have never been so deeply shaken in my life as when I realized the full implication of this power of IS. I thought back to December 7 when Uri had walked toward a flashing blue light in an open field and had come back with my brass pen cartridge. All this could have been an illusion, similar to the one of the past two days. Although I still have the brass pen cartridge, I know that it could have "appeared" in Uri's hand, without lending any credence to the possible presence of a spacecraft. All I can vouch for is my experience, which I'd already come to realize could have been artificially imprinted by IS.

On New Year's Day 1972 I wanted to take a break from the heaviness of my education at the hands of IS. I invited Ila to take a ride into the countryside. We had absolutely no idea where we would go when we started. We were to decide our itinerary at any moment by the toss of a coin.

We drove north toward Haifa in the dazzling bright winter sunshine. As we reached the area of the Carmel Hills near Ma'agan Michael, an unbelievably multicolored movement of clouds came in from the sea. I stopped driving, to set up my Hasselblad camera, to take purely artistic pictures of the cloud forms and colors against this incredible sky-blue background. There were mini-tornado funnels in the clouds, patches of dark thunderous clouds; I have never before seen such a display of cloud beauty in the sky.

We drove on north past Haifa into a heavy thunderstorm. In the darkness and driving rain I got lost, but I kept on driving, since it didn't make any difference where we were going. When the air cleared somewhat, I found myself on the road to Safad, one of my favorite places in all of Israel. After Safad, we went down to the Sea of Galilee and to Tiberias. Finally at 10 P.M. we decided to return to Tel Aviv, via the town of 'Afula, in the Jezreel Valley.

As we climbed out of the basin of the Sea of Galilee over the mountains, we both saw a red disk in the sky, similar to the one I had seen in the Sinai. When we reached the top of the mountain where the sky was clear and the view unimpeded, it disappeared over Mount Tabor.

As we descended into the valley of Jezreel, we entered heavy low-lying fogbanks. Just as we left 'Afula, a white hawk cut through the fog and passed just inches in front of my windshield. This was a startling vision to both Ila and myself. As we were discussing this sighting, we encountered another heavy fogbank. The visibility could not have been more than ten meters, and I had to slow down to some thirty kilometers per hour. Then directly ahead of the car there flashed a red cometlike light. It had a trajectory like that of a baseball descending from the air toward the ground. What was even stranger was that it appeared to be one hundred meters ahead of the car, beyond the range of headlight visibility. There was something unworldly about this light as it plunged toward the ground into the road ahead, and then went out. As I approached the area of its fall, there was nothing to be seen. Suddenly I heard a cricket sound! A road intersection appeared going to the right, and without a thought I swung the car north onto this road to listen for the cricket sound. As I listened, and as Ila listened, for she had heard it, too, a white hawk suddenly flashed through the headlight glow.

I wrote later that night in my notes that "the above pattern of events—red light, hawk, red light, hawk—is highly subjective and probably has no particular significance." But I found out later that I was wrong, that very significant events were going on. In the following weeks I was approached by my friends Reuven and Jacov, who tried to hint to me very gently that there was increasing concern by the Israeli Army High Command about my presence in Israel. I was also interviewed at times by intelligence officers and knew that trouble for me was brewing. I also found out by other means that all my mail was being read, my phone was tapped, and that I was under twenty-four-hour-a-day personal surveillance. Later, I also found out that on this New Year's Day, as I was being followed, the best operatives in the country would suddenly lose me. They would radio for help, and another team in a car would locate my car and then they would lose me. The report that I had totally disappeared at 'Afula, I found out, started a major investigation about me. Of course, I was unaware of all this at the time it was happening. The Israeli intelligence people were getting the same lessons in mind control by IS that I was getting. The only difference is that I knew the lessons were from an extraterrestrial intelligence.

The major display of lights in the sky started in quite an innocuous way on January 2, 1972. I was standing on the balcony of room 1101 at the Sharon Hotel at 7:30 P.M., enjoying the view of Tel Aviv stretching away toward Jaffa. Then due south, beyond Jaffa, appeared a flashing red star, pulsing at about one pulse per second. It was stationary. The flashes continued for about thirty pulses, then it was gone. I called to Ila to witness it, and she saw the last few bursts of light. The next thing I saw I took to be some kind of meteorological experiment.

A huge orange flare burst in the air where the red light had been. As the flare plummeted toward earth, a twisted trail of smoke hung in the air. As the orange flare came to within a thousand feet or so of earth, a second flare burst a certain distance from where the first had burst—and followed the same pattern. This went on until there were seven pillars of smoke in the sky. I assumed that these flares had been released to measure wind patterns. Ila and I discussed this phenomenon as such.

Later that day we went to see Uri perform at a show at the Tzavda in Tel Aviv. I told him about the seven pillars of smoke generated by orange flares. He looked at me as though I were crazy and said, "They don't send up smoke patterns in Israel to study the wind! But let's check it out." He phoned the weather service, the Army, and the Air Force. No one had sent up any flares south of Tel Aviv at 7:30 P.M. So Uri convinced me that it was not a meteorological effect. But what was it? It did not occur to either of us that it could be connected to IS, because of the smoke. But this phenomenon was clarified the next day on a night drive. (See Appendix Four.)

On January 3, while sitting on the balcony of my room at the Sharon, Ila, Iris, and I saw in the clear daylight the same kind of hawks that we had seen two days ago to the west of 'Afula. I studied the birds carefully as two of them floated past my balcony at eye level. They were definitely of the hawk family, with a two-foot wingspread in soaring flight. The entire underside of the bird was white with darker stippling. The top side of the bird was a uniform dark dove-gray. At times one of the birds would glide in from the sea right up to within a few meters of the balcony; it would flutter there in one spot and stare at me directly in the eyes. It was a unique experience to look into the piercing, "intelligent" eyes of a hawk. It was then that I knew I was not looking into the eyes of an earthly hawk. This was confirmed about 2 P.M. when Uri's eyes followed a feather, loosened from the hawk, that floated on an updraft toward the top of the Sharon Tower. As his eye followed the feather to the sky, he was startled to see a dark spacecraft parked directly over the hotel.

We all looked where he pointed, but we did not see what he saw. But I believed that he saw what he said he saw.

I was of the opinion that the birds were peregrine falcons. But I knew that this species was probably recently extinct in the United States. I did not know if this species were known in Israel. Uri stoutly upheld the view that there were no hawks at all in Israel, only kites. He told us that the hawks were sent by IS to guard and protect me. He felt that this was simply a form taken by IS, just as they took the form of a spacecraft, because it suited their purposes. I dubbed this hawk "Horus" and still use this name each time he appears to me.

Uri was scheduled to go to the Sinai to entertain the troops on January 9 and wanted both Ila and me to go along (since there were female entertainers as part of the troupe, he felt he could get permission for Ila to go). This time he got written clearance for us beforehand. We met at Lod Airport at 6:30 A.M. and arrived at an air base in the Sinai by 9:20 A.M. Upon landing, there was a big scene with a security officer about allowing Ila and me to go to the Suez Canal with Uri and the troupe. However, Uri in his inimitable way shouted down the objections of the security officer, and we were allowed to go to the Canal Zone.

Between 10 A.M. and 1 P.M., we rode in the back of a truck with a group of entertainers. For me it was a profound experience to go through the long canyons of the Mitla Pass littered with the wreckage of the Six Day War. When we reached the Suez Canal at 1 P.M., the entertainers split into groups, each going his way. Uri, Ila, and I were escorted by an officer to the top of an observation tower where soldiers peered across the canal by day and by night. There was a dreamlike quality to this scene. The sun shone brightly and sparkled off the blue waters of the canal. The sea gulls swooped and foraged for their food. On this side of the canal the Israeli soldiers walked on top of their fortifications. As we stood on the tower in full view, one of the Egyptian soldiers shouted obscenities at us in Arabic; an Israeli soldier shouted back a choice obscenity in Hebrew. Then the quiet, the sound of gulls, and the warmth of the sun. Was this the

Eye of the Hawk

boundary across which, a few weeks ago, steel and fire were to hurtle the world into a global holocaust?

We were served a hot lunch by a proud and sweating sergeant major. At 2 P.M. a group of three dozen soldiers came from the depths of the bunkers of the Bar Lev Line to see Uri do a show in a sandbagged open area, safe from line-of-sight fire. Another entertainer, Avi, sang a lusty song with his guitar. The soldiers, with Uzzi machine guns on their backs, cheered wildly. Then Uri came on, calling upon a soldier and asking him to concentrate on his sweetheart's name. Uri thought for ten seconds and gave the name correctly as Bruriah. More cheers. Uri then had each soldier step up and think of a color, number, letter, name of a car, a capital city, etc. For every one of the soldiers Uri gave the correct telepathic answer. By now the wild cheering had subsided—there was instead a hushed awe. Uri then "repaired" a broken watch by passing his hand over it. Then he asked a soldier to hold a key in his hand. Uri placed his hand over the soldier's for ten seconds. When the soldier opened his hand, the key was bent at a ninety-degree angle. At the end of the performance, the soldiers followed Uri silently to the truck as we boarded to leave.

We went on to the next bunker, and Uri repeated the same kind of show. At 4 P.M. we headed back into the heart of the Sinai via the Mitla Pass. As the sun went down, the wind, the cold, and the jolting of the truck lowered our spirits to a state of numbed withdrawal. It was dark by 7 P.M. as we rolled into some unknown army base. We were fed dinner by torchlight. The word was whispered around that there was an air alert on; some intelligence reports said that Arab planes would enter the area. There was to have been a show that night, but since no lights were allowed on the base, it was dubious that it would be presented.

We were huddled into a small office until 9 P.M., surrounded by soldiers who mobbed and pressed upon Uri. Ila and I were practically crushed by this herd activity. I was prepared to see them start tearing at Uri's clothes in sheer admiration.

A young girl soldier offered a gold chain to Uri. He held his hand over it, and it broke in two. Uri was then pressed into doing a telepathy test over the telephone with a general from another base. The test was so successful that the general told Uri that he was going to drive over to see him personally.

It was then that I discovered the function of the base we were on. It was an elaborate decoy base designed to draw enemy bombers toward it, and away from more vital targets—a discovery that did not make me any too happy. At 10 P.M. the general and his staff entered the packed office. He made an offer to Uri to do a show at his base at midnight. Uri inquired if that meant a warm bed for the night, and the general replied that it did, for all of us.

So we roared off in two command cars into the night. I was surprised to find that we were on a tortuous winding road going up to a mountain aerie. At the top there was a forest of radar towers and antennae. It was obvious to me that we were in a most unusual electronic-warfare center. There was another hassle about the security status of Ila and me, but we were finally allowed on the base. Uri did a very impressive show. What interested me was that this was the first time I had ever seen him perform for a purely scientific and intellectual group. Everyone that I could see in the audience appeared to be of Ph.D. caliber. Yet they were just as enthusiastic and excited as the nineteen-year-old soldiers on the canal.

The commanding general was obviously very impressed with Uri and held a secret conference with him. Uri did not tell me what advice he gave to the general. We did get quarters that night with electric heaters and plenty of blankets. My bones really ached from all the jolting truck rides of the long day.

At 5:30 A.M. we were aroused and piled into a command car. Now I could see that we were in a high mountain aerie that had a clear view of the Sinai in all directions. As the sun arose, the desert became a pastel wonderland, a sight of immense beauty. I also found that we were traveling east. As we neared the region where Uri and I had seen the red eye of IS in the sky a month ago, there appeared to our left at low altitude a giant spaceship! Now Uri, Ila, and I clearly saw it. It appeared to be not more than two miles away, but desert air is deceptive when it comes to judging distances. The spaceship hugged the top of a ridge to our left and floated with the stability of a dirigible. I noticed that it did not cast a shadow on the hill.

I judged it to be double the length of a Boeing 747. In fact, it had a shape as though two B-747s, without wings, were stuck together tail to tail but with one of the planes upside down. The ship did not glint in the sun; there was no reflective surface on it; there were no windows or portholes. It had a very smooth, dull, metallic gray surface.

Uri, Ila, and I were in the back seat of the command car. The driver and two other military personnel sat in the front. Without giving these three a clue as to what they might see, Uri pointed directly to the ridge of the hill below the spaceship and asked them in Hebrew, "What is that?"

All three stared directly at the spaceship and said in substance, "There is only the hill and the blue sky. What do you see?" Uri would not reveal what he saw, but prodded them to concentrate on the spot in the sky where the spaceship floated. Not one of the three saw the ship. Finally, they asked Uri, "What's so important about that spot?"

Uri said in a joking way, "I thought maybe there was a UFO there." They accepted his words as a joke and stopped looking. Uri, Ila, and I just watched in total fascination. We soon realized that the spaceship was moving with us at the same speed as our car. This went on for a half hour, and then as we reached a turn where the road went north, the spaceship continued east, dropping out of sight behind a hill.

I recognize the possibility that there may not have been a spaceship there at all. I am aware that the three men in the command car saw nothing because there was nothing to see; I recognize that the three of us certainly had the image of a spaceship in our minds. But I believe that that image was placed there by some superior intelligence which may or may not have required the prop of an actual spaceship. The picture of that spaceship floating in its metallic splendor over the Sinai Desert is still firmly imprinted in my mind.

We arrived at the air base at which we had landed the day before at 7:30 A.M., January 10. I must confess that each of us felt frozen, dirty, tired, and aching. I was back at the Sharon Hotel by 10 A.M. I immediately took a hot bath, shaved, and made extensive notes on what had happened in the desert.

I spent the day on my balcony in the sun going over data of mutual interest with Ila before she left on the morrow. There was no question in my mind as I observed her that the experiences of the past week had destroyed all of her previous conceptions of parapsychology. She was also personally shaken up; what she had witnessed was more than she could bear. She frankly admitted that she could not keep up this kind of pace in acquiring new, unmanageable information.

I drove Ila to Lod Airport the next morning. When I returned to the hotel, there was a phone message from Uri. I called him up, and he began to thank me profusely for the most wonderful present he had ever received—the belt massager.

Now, there is a background to this story that I must tell first. About a week earlier Uri began to complain to Ila and me about his figure—that he was getting fat. We just laughed at him and his vanity. He is six feet two inches tall and weighed 172 pounds; he was not at all overweight. He exercised at least two hours every day. But he persisted in his belief that he had fat bumps on him that should be melted down. He had the idea that a belt massager would do it. Ila was very good with Uri. She explained to me that her husband had the same narcissism as did Uri and she knew how to handle the problem. She asked Uri to assemble all the specifications for the kind of massager he wanted and then to report to us. This kept him busy for a day. When he found out the kind of massager he wanted and got the price, he came to me crestfallen, saying that the cost was prohibitive. Could I find out what the price would be in the United States? I knew he had outwitted me, but I went along with the game. I called up my friend Solveig Clark in New York and asked her to send me catalogs on these machines and the prices, including air freight and duty. In three days I had this information in hand. I went over the catalogs with Uri. He picked a certain machine manufactured by Metz in the United States of a blue color. When I told what it would cost him, he was staggered by the price. Finally he said, "Forget the whole business. I don't really need the machine."

Now he was telling me on the phone, "I just walked into my apartment with Sarah Bursak. There, plugged into the wall, was a blue Metz belt massager, the same model I had picked out of the catalog. Since you were the only one who knew what I wanted, I knew that it came from you. Nobody has ever done anything for me like this in my life."

"Uri," I said, "I didn't give you that present. It must be someone else!"

"I can't believe it, Andrija. Then maybe your friend in New York didn't understand you—maybe she ordered it."

"Is there a crate there? Is there an invoice or a packing slip? How did it get in the apartment anyway? You know that it takes days to get things through customs."

"My God, you're right. My mother is away; nobody was in the apartment. How did they get in to deliver it?" he said.

"Why don't you check it out on your end, and I'll call New York and see what was done there," I suggested.

Uri came to see me at 4 P.M. just as I was getting a call through to New York to Solveig. Solveig stated that she had not ordered or shipped a Metz belt massager. She also said that she would like to come soon to visit me in Israel, which I thought was a splendid idea.

Uri and I looked at each other—we finally knew who had "delivered" the belt massager. I said to Uri, "They must really love you to humor you on this level of personal vanity. Besides, someone up there is a real joker—this is cosmic humor! A belt massager for the man who is in perfect physical shape! What will they do next?"

The massager was real, had a serial number, was made in Brooklyn, and worked with bone-jolting efficiency. The carton in which it had come had no markings on it, and there was no invoice. It looked as if it had come from a warehouse.

I returned to my hotel, had an early dinner, and prepared to go to bed early. I recalled with sweeping sadness that one year ago that day I had received the news of Arigó's death. And on that day I had resolved to change my way of life by seeking the good, the true, the beautiful: I gauged the progression I had made in the year's interim. It was more transformation than progression, and I felt that it was just beginning.

When I awoke on the morning of January 12, I glanced at the Geneve watch on my wrist. It had stopped at, or been moved to, 9:45:45 (21:45:45) while I was asleep. The electric clock showed that it was 8:56 A.M. The last time this had happened was on December 26, 1971. For a moment I had the panicky thought that something had gone wrong, that the war threat was on again. I walked into the bathroom, turned on the radio, and got ready to bathe. Right after the 9 A.M. station break the regular Voice of America program was blanked out. A husky voice came out of the radio saying, *Andrija, be prepared—in a few days* . . . It faded off in a garbled way. I knew that it was an overlay voice by IS. But what bothered me was the imperfect quality of the voice transmission. I had become used to perfection in the execution of IS phenomena. I telephoned Uri and recited what had happened, but he had no idea as to what it all meant.

The next day, January 13, seemed ominously quiet. I was driving from Tel Aviv to the Sharon along the Coast Road that goes by Dov Airport when Horus appeared opposite my car, standing still in the air heading into the wind. It was 2:30 P.M. I stopped the car to watch this magnificent hawk. Then, literally from nowhere appeared another hawk, which flew alongside of Horus. They wheeled off slowly to the right, landing about thirty feet from my car, and mated there in the field. I went on to the hotel and spent a very quiet evening there, watching and waiting.

The next day was Friday, January 14. My watch ran normally; there was no hawk to be seen. The skies darkened and the wind whipped up to gale force from the sea. The rain came down in sheets before the wind. Alone in his apartment in Tel Aviv, Uri saw a huge silent spacecraft glide over northern Tel Aviv. Then he saw the lights of the city flicker and go out. All of Israel was plunged into wet darkness. At this moment, 7:30 P.M., I was sitting in my hotel room at Herzliyyah, looking toward Tel Aviv. Suddenly I saw only blackness where there had been myriads of city lights. Now I knew the meaning of all the warning signs of the past three days.

On February 1 Uri and I were standing at 12 noon on the seaward side of the swimming pool of the Hilton Hotel. The pool was crowded with swimmers. As we looked south toward Jaffa over the sea, we saw a gigantic display in the sky. First a bright flare fell from a height of about four thousand feet some ten miles away. As the flare fell, a pillar of white smoke remained in the air to mark the fall trail.

As the first flare hit the horizon, the next flare was released some five hundred meters to the right of the first. It took two minutes and twenty seconds for each flare to fire and descend to the horizon level. In this manner seven flares were released leaving seven pillars of white smoke in the sky which lasted for some thirty minutes. Uri and I looked around us. It was quite clear that nobody else saw what we were seeing. A newspaper and radio check showed that no one had released seven flares that day behind Jaffa.

That evening Uri and I were successful in getting answers to our questions from the tape recorder. On the tape we heard a voice, new to us, which sounded rather cold and authoritative:

You may ask questions now.

AP: "Is Arigó one of your subjects?"

Yes. Do you need proof?

AP: "The best proof for me is to have him tell me about my ears."

Arigó says that he tried to cure your left side. Why did you stop taking his medicines?

AP: "I became allergic to the streptomycin, and I stopped that part of the treatment." (See page 30.)

He says to start the same medicines again; it will not hurt you this time. Arigó says that he was not hurt in the car crash. There was no pain. He left his body before the crash. He will bring back something for you.

AP: "Thank you and Arigó. I do not know your name. How shall I address you? We have been calling you the intelligence from the sky, or IS."

You may use the name Spectra. But actually Spectra is the name of a spacecraft which we use as you use a planet. It has been stationed for the past eight hundred years over the earth. It is as big as one of your cities on earth. But only you can see us.

AP: "Why are you interested in the Israelis?"

The Israeli territory is where we first landed on earth. That is why we are interested in them. Be patient—for years. You will have everything in time.

AP: "Are there other people on earth with whom you work?"

There is no other on earth that we will use for the next fifty years but you and Uri.

The tape vanished after this transmission.

On February 9, 1972, Uri and I made another contact via the tape recorder. It went as follows:

What is bothering you?

AP: "We need some clarification about what our work is about."

You must be patient, very patient. You are working twenty-four hours a day for us, but you don't even realize it. You are to help Uri. It is not important where you live; you must be on earth only wherever you are.

AP: "How is my mind being used?"

Your mind is being used twenty-four hours a day in a way that we cannot yet explain to you. You feel it now by being tired and sick. But this will not last for too long.

AP: Did you cause the blackout in Israel on January 14 of this year?"

The power failure in Israel is from us.

AP: "What use do you make of the power failure?"

It is a matter you will not understand yet.

AP: "Where will Uri and I be this year?"

I can only tell you that you will be in the U.S.A. part of the time. Handle Uri gently. He has nothing to worry about.

AP: "Can we go aboard your spaceship in order to start learning more about you?"
It will be a long time before this is possible, perhaps years. We are not ready for you yet. We are learning a lot.
AP: "When will the Knowledge Book come?"[1]
In due time, it may take years. But when it comes, it will be the most historical event that man will ever receive.
AP: "I received a phone call from you on February 5, at 5 P.M. at the Hilton Hotel. You said, 'Spacemen over West Germany! Spacemen over West Germany.' That was all. What does this mean?"
We noticed them over West Germany. We wanted you to know about it. I spoke to you on the phone about it—said it two times. We need your help in Germany.
AP: "What can we do—we are quite helpless."
You will go to Germany. We will tell you when.
AP: "Are Uri and I in any danger?"
No, nobody knows about you there.
AP: "Why has my Horus hawk gone?"
The hawk was your guard. You are being guarded in an entirely different way.
AP: "Why did Ila come here?"
She was sent to you as part of a test. The test was successfully passed. Farewell.

Now, going back somewhat in time, I want to recount my relationship to the Israeli Army.

On January 24 I had a meeting in Tel Aviv with Jacov. He informed me that there was grave concern in the Army High Command about me. He did not specify the nature of the concern, except to report that as far as the intelligence people were concerned, I had vanished from view on December 7. This sur-

---

[1] The reference to the Knowledge Book is based on a previous conversation, not here recorded. The Knowledge Book is a document which contains information important to man's future. (See page 176.)

prised me so much that I had to laugh aloud: "But Jacov—I've been living in public view first at the Hotel Sharon and then the Hotel Masada. Reuven has visited me! I have talked to you! What can they mean?"

Jacov did not elaborate on this statement but suggested that I contact a certain general. I said I would think about it. It was some three months later that I found out what Jacov's enigmatic statement meant. It was on December 7 that strange things began to happen to the intelligence operatives watching me, and to their equipment and recordings. And now the problem had reached the level of a crisis in the Israeli domestic intelligence apparatus. But again I was innocent of this storm brewing around my head.

That afternoon I was to see the hawk once again while on the beach at Ashqelon. But nothing unusual happened to me. During the next two weeks the pressures from all sides built up, and I realized that I was a source of great mystery to the Israelis. I was even told that I was suspected of being one of the great master spies of history. But I did not know what the grounds were for this building suspicion.

On February 13 I left Israel, as described at the beginning of this narrative. I previously stated that I started to reconstruct my confiscated Israeli journals in Italy. However, it was not until November 1972 that I began to work seriously on this book.

On March 29, 1972, I received in Italy a phone call from Solveig Clark, who was in New York. She said that she had received a call from an anonymous female voice which said: "The Israeli Army is not interested in detaining Dr. Puharich. Dr. Puharich is deluded by thinking that the Israeli Army considers him a master spy. Please give this message to Dr. Puharich." The phone call terminated.

Now, Uri had given me no assurance in our phone conversations since I left Israel that I should or could return to Israel. But after the phone call from Solveig, I decided that this was a clear invitation for me to return to Israel.

I went to Rome and spent Easter Sunday with Melanie Toyofuku, who was living there. I set up a plan with her to secure my release, should I be arrested in Israel. The plan was simple: If she did not hear from me by telephone every forty-eight hours by a certain hour, she was to alert officials in Washington, D.C., that I was missing.

I flew into Lod Airport on April 3, 1972. I had had a pleasant trip chatting with a Roman Catholic priest from Boston who was making his first trip to the Holy Land. We got to know each other quite well. After we landed I was standing in line with this priest at Passport Control. The page system announced, "Dr. Puharich, go to the nearest phone for a message."

The priest said to me, "Why, Dr. Puharich, that call is for you." I nodded assent and thought quickly. This could be a trick of the Shin Beth to get me to leave the crowd and then arrest me inconspicuously. Or it could be a page from Uri. I said to the priest, "I'll pick up that call after I get into the terminal."

As I stood in line to have my passport examined, I felt sure that I would be detected. But I was passed without comment. I picked up my two bags and cleared customs. There were Uri, Shipi, and Hannah waiting for me. We quickly got into Uri's car and sped away from the airport.

Uri explained that I could not stay at his new apartment; it had been wired up for total surveillance by the Shin Beth. Ever since I had left Israel he had been under continuous interrogation by the intelligence people. He was so rattled that he almost came to believe I was a spy. Finally, though, the Shin Beth concluded that I was not, but was either a scientific genius or a charlatan. They had attributed to me all the effects that IS had done to them. Uri told me about the following event, which had happened while I was in Italy.

One day there came for me in the mail a package with technical data and pricing for Xerox copiers. Uri got panicky thinking that this would be interpreted as evidence that I was a spy, so he tore up the Xerox literature and flushed it down the toilet. The next day at army headquarters, he was asked about the material he destroyed and flushed down the toilet. He denied that he had done this. Then the officer reached under his desk and placed before Uri a plastic bag containing the torn papers from the toilet flush! Uri confessed to his "crime," and everyone had a good laugh about the incident. As for me, I roared with laughter, imagining the condition of the hapless soldier assigned to this new kind of latrine duty.

I asked Uri about the page call for me when I had landed; he had not paged me. We found out later that the army people had not paged me. We concluded eventually that this page was from IS. Uri's mother later told me that she had received a phone call from "me" from Rome on Saturday, April 1, at 1 P.M. I supposedly had said, "I am returning to Lod at 5:30 P.M., Saturday, April 1, on TWA Flight 840." I never made such a phone call.

As I checked into the Hilton Hotel, loud music blared out of my locked suitcase! I opened the suitcase to find the radio playing, but the power switch was turned in the off position. I knew that I was being welcomed back to Israel and to work.

On April 5 at 12:30 P.M. the telephone rang. A human-sounding voice with a bit of an accent said in English: *Andrija, listen well! Instructions will be coming on June first.* Then silence. I immediately called the hotel operator; no outside phone call had come in for me, and no insider at the hotel had called.

The next night, in front of three witnesses, my house keys from my home in New York suddenly "appeared" on a coffee table. I had last seen these keys months before on November 17, 1971, when I had put them in the custody of my house caretaker. Earlier on the same day my Minox C camera, which had been confiscated by the Shin Beth on February 13, had appeared on Uri's bed.

One of the most spectacular feats of IS occurred on April 10, 1972, at 10:10 P.M. in my room, 1434 at the Hilton Hotel. Uri was lying on one of the twin beds talking to me; I was sitting in an easy chair listening. My Universal Geneve watch with a new heavy silver chain band was lying on a dresser near Uri. Suddenly he screamed, and there was my Geneve watch firmly clamped around his left wrist. It had occurred instantly. He had felt nothing unusual on his skin except the shock of a foreign object. Twenty-five minutes later the watch vanished from his wrist and was back on the dresser again. In both translocations of the watch the time and movement remained normal.

On the night of April 11 I noticed a red light on the seashore jetty below the hotel. I grew curious and walked to the end of the jetty, but the red light was gone. Back in my hotel room, I saw it again. Uri joined me, and we watched it for two hours. It was like the light we had seen in the Sinai, but now it was on the ground.

The next morning the sea off the Hilton was patrolled by a submarine, thirteen PT boats, and five submarine chasers. Rumor had it that radar had spotted an enemy submarine off the coast near the Hilton. That night Uri was interrogated all night by the Shin Beth as to where I was hiding. His answer was "Don't you know?" Uri believes that the Shin Beth never knew I was in Israel. But I thought things were getting warm and that I had better leave the country again.

On April 14 at 2 P.M. Uri and I were successful in getting information from IS on the tape recorder:

We have a short script for you—general guidance. Go to United States. Your work will be in Europe. Work starts in Germany with a man chosen. Main base henceforth in Israel. Detailed instructions on June first. Uri will have his powers wherever he is. Do a movie on Uri. Melanie is the one to do it. Work at it; it will come out at right time. You are not to entrust anyone with the secret of our existence—no one. Do not interfere with our educational Israel army program. We will contact you once more before you leave Israel. We showed ourselves to you in the sea by the hotel on April eleventh."

On April 15 at 8:55 P.M. the tape recorder yielded answers to our questions:

AP: "Why did you allow my journals to be taken by the Shin Beth?"

Don't ask!

AP: "Where should Uri and I be on June first?"

You will get instructions.

AP: "How can Uri and I contact you if we need help when there is danger?"

There will not be danger.
AP: "But if I think there is danger—will the hawk appear?"
You are right.
AP: "Since you do not show yourselves on earth, will we be transported to your environment so that we can meet directly?"
Someday, yes.
"Of the people who have been exposed thus far to your powers, who should we continue to work with?"
Only three. Uri, Shimshon, you. We cannot use our full powers unless you and Uri and Shimshon are together. There is a dematerialized aspect to your atoms that we can use. Farewell.

When I saw Uri off to his car parked in front of the Hilton Hotel, we first looked into the car. On the seat in front of our eyes appeared Uri's rather large Sony CR 150 radio. We had last seen it in his apartment where he had left it earlier.

The day to leave Israel finally came. As Uri and I drove to the airport, it was like approaching a potential ambush. We wondered what would happen to me and what would happen to Uri. Uri told me emphatically that based on his contacts and interrogations, he felt that the Israeli intelligence people did not know I was in Israel. I was not that optimistic because I still had to run the gauntlet of the ticket counter, baggage check, passport control, body search, and hand baggage check.

On April 16, 1972, at 9:07 A.M. the wheels of TWA Flight 841 left the soil of Israel. At last I experienced a deep feeling of safety. I looked down at the green fields, the sandy shoreline, the towers of Herzliyyah Heights, the Sharon, the Hilton—where it had all happened. Now I was on my way to Italy, to Germany, to the United States, to carry the message of Uri to the world. But I also was carrying a secret out of Israel that I was not to reveal. How could I carry the message of Uri and not the message of the intelligence of IS? These thoughts were heavy on my heart as my flight landed for its first stop in Athens. I disembarked and wandered around the terminal building. A TWA female representative walked up to me and asked me for my transit card, boarding pass, ticket, and passport. My heart sank. Had they caught up with me here in Greece? How did this woman know who I was, out of the hundreds of people milling around? I was determined not to be trapped this time.

Politely I asked, "What is the problem?"

She said, "I have a Telex here from Tel Aviv, and it says that they do not have your ticket for this flight. Did you turn it in?"

I distinctly remember that my passenger ticket was detached from my ticket when my baggage was checked, so I said, "Of course, I saw it collected." She asked to examine my documents. While she did so, I stood by in the passenger terminal keeping my eye open for her colleagues. She handed me my documents and said, "It is apparent that you don't have the ticket—it was removed—and you have all the necessary boarding cards. We shall check it out and let you know. You may board the flight."

Once aboard the plane I could hardly wait for Flight 841 to get airborne for Rome. Soon we were aloft, and I figured out what had happened. IS had "vanished" my ticket after I had turned it in so that my name did not appear on the passenger manifesto at the boarding gate. The ticket must have been found eventually, because I never heard from the TWA people again.

CHAPTER SEVEN

Seven Pillars of Fire

I returned to New York to take care of my long-neglected personal and business affairs. In mid-May I went to Chicago to attend the twenty-fifth annual reunion of my medical school class at Northwestern University. While in Chicago I found that Captain Edgar Mitchell was the featured speaker for the annual meeting of the Spiritual Frontiers Fellowship. Mitchell planned to devote his time after retirement from the Navy to consciousness research. He offered to raise money and manage a United State's-based research program whose first venture was to be a study of Uri. I promised him that he would have the right to do the first United States research on Uri, provided he could raise the necessary funds, and would manage the effort.

As June 1 approached, I got more and more apprehensive about the forthcoming "instructions." What would be the next crisis that Uri and I would work on? Where would we have to move on planet earth? How could we support ourselves? The rumor mill that had been generated in the United States about Uri's "evil powers" helped me enormously in that I did not have to explain anything to anybody about my long absence from the United States.

My daughter Illyria and I were home alone in Ossining at midnight June 1; I waited for the next twenty-four hours for the "instructions." None came. I began to have doubts. Why had they not kept the promised rendezvous?

On June 2 Uri phoned me from Rome to tell me what had happened to him in Tel Aviv the day before. On the morning of June 1 at 7 A.M. he drove the two miles from his mother's apartment to his new apartment, and when he opened his door, there was a sealed letter on the floor. The letter was from me on my stationery in my handwriting, duly stamped and postmarked June 1, 1972, Ossining, New York. He thought this very strange because at that time it was not yet June 1 in New York. He read the enclosed letter from me, which said:

Dear Uri,

I must remain in the U.S. for another three months, probably September or October before I can join you in Germany. Sorry for change of plans.

Shalom,

Andrija

Now, I must emphasize the importance of the fact that *I did not write Uri such a letter*. When Uri told me its contents, I was hearing it for the first time.

But Uri, when he read the letter, really believed that I had written it. When he got on the plane on June 2 to fly to Rome, he put my letter in the breast pocket of his shirt. On the flight he suddenly noticed that the letter had vanished from his pocket. He searched the plane but could not find the letter. Then he realized that the letter had vanished and that the contents must be the promised instructions from IS.

Uri went to Munich to work with Yasha Katz whom I had selected as his manager, and was there from June 7 to 12. One series of events that happened in Munich is worth recording. Uri was introduced to a lyricist by the name of Herr Brandin, who wished to see Uri work. On Friday, June 9, 1972, Herr Brandin and ten of his guests saw Uri do the following things: a crystal ball materialized before the witnesses; a professional movie camera weighing twenty kilograms was levitated; lead wire was transmuted into gold.

Professor Friedbert Karger, of the Max Planck Institute for Plasma Physics, witnessed some of these things and telephoned me from Munich to tell me about them. He was most impressed with Uri's powers and wanted to start a research program immediately. I welcomed his support but told him of the prior commitment to Captain Mitchell; so Dr. Karger agreed to join the newly formed Theory Group.

Uri cleaned up his affairs in Israel so that he could move to Germany, where he was told to go by IS by July 1, 1972. As a result of the June 1 "letter," I settled down in the United States and assembled a staff to carry out my scientific research program. Melanie Toyofuku came from Rome to begin the research preparatory to planning for a documentary movie on Uri; Carolyn White came from Florence, Italy, to coordinate the university research efforts; Solveig Clark worked part-time with us in the publications area; Sidney Krystal assumed the legal tasks that had to be done. With this loyal group of associates I was able to initiate and carry out a program whose specific purpose was to alert the scientific world to the existence of the powers that Uri and I had witnessed. Captain Mitchell undertook the problem of raising funds to carry out the first "validation" research on Uri. Validation meant the scientific verification of the claims I made for Uri's powers in the areas of telepathy, clairvoyance, and psychokinesis. I took on the task of mobilizing and informing some of the scientists who had been a part of the Life Energies Conference of 1970. Here I ran into my first problem. One of my Israeli colleagues had already approached this same group of scientists with a tale of "evil powers." I approached some members of this group first with a written report and eventually introduced Uri to them individually, who then gave a demonstration of his powers.

What happened among this group of mature scientists was an interesting sample of human reactions to Uri and his powers. About half of the men and women we approached believed the rumors concerning Uri's "evil powers"; by this I mean that they were fearful enough of Uri by prior stories that they did not even want to meet him personally. The other half who saw Uri demonstrate his powers believed the evidence of their own senses and judgment but were completely baffled. They could find no scientific explanations and therefore had no idea how to cope with the phenomenon.

In order to deal with the problems of scientific importance, I organized a group of scientists into a Theory Group, whose goal was to find a theoretical framework that could accommodate the effects exhibited by Uri. The leadership of this group was eventually assumed by Dr. Ted Bastin, of Cambridge University, England.

In cooperation with the Theory Group a formal proposal for further research on Uri Geller was made to the (U. S.) National Science Foundation (NSF). Captain Mitchell personally carried this proposal to Dr. Guyford Stever, the director of NSF. The same proposal was personally delivered to a key member of the President's White House staff. I might state now that this attempt at open discussion of Uri's powers in the United States failed. None of the parties we reached was prepared to consider seriously the new data that Uri Geller was bringing to science.

My next concern was to make an announcement of the verifiable scientific data that I had collected on Uri in Israel in an appropriate academic meeting. I got such an opportunity through invitations to speak at two meetings, one at Stanford University and the other at University of California at Los Angeles in late September 1972. These meetings were sponsored by the Academy of Parapsychology and Medicine.

Thus the summer passed in the preparation of lectures, reports, proposals, and in many meetings and telephone conferences. My personal conviction was that Uri and his powers would never receive acceptance in a serious way until he ran the gauntlet of scientific evaluation by established scientists in a prestigious scientific institution.

Captain Mitchell had concentrated his efforts on trying to arrange for validation experiments at Kent State University, where he had the personal support of the president, Dr. Glenn

Olds, and a professor and coordinator of graduate studies in Physics, Dr. Wilbur Franklin. However, the enthusiasm and deep interest in this experiment on the part of these fine scholars could not produce the funds and the other resources required to do the experiment. So on my own initiative, and with Captain Mitchell's permission, I opened up discussions with two scientists, Dr. Harold Puthoff and Mr. Russell Targ, about doing the validation experiments. They welcomed the idea of working with Uri Geller and agreed to accept the experimental design of the Theory Group for this study and to accept Captain Mitchell as the sponsor of the project in terms of being the funding and contracting agent. Since they had been successful in getting Stanford Research Institute (SRI) to support their plans for parapsychology research, they arranged for Captain Mitchell to meet with the officials of SRI and work out all the details of the research project. We set a target date to begin the validation experiments for the first week in November 1972.

This is merely a brief summary of the planning for the scientific research with Uri, which omits all the headaches that arose in the coordination of so many people in a highly controversial subject.

Uri's work in Germany was going well. He gave many public demonstrations of his powers, which have been adequately covered by the German press and television. He and Shipi entertained themselves there in a style that Uri had never experienced, and he enjoyed every moment. It also helped to erase from his mind the heavy burden of the knowledge of his role in the affairs of humanity. But I had to shatter this temporary "oasis" of comfort by calling him to the United States in late August to meet Captain Mitchell and some of the scientists he was going to work with.

Professor Gerald Feinberg, of the Physics Department of Columbia University, was present to see what Uri could do. He had been waiting to see him in person since November 1970, when he had heard the letter report on Uri given at the International Life Energies Conference. Uri did not disappoint this distinguished physicist as he moved the hands of a watch and broke a ring and a steel sewing needle. Professor Feinberg agreed that Uri's abilities should be the subject of careful scientific study. This opinion was shared by another scientist who was present, Dr. Wilbur Franklin.

Many other people came to meet Uri during this period, and all were impressed with his honesty and with his powers. Uri on his part began to feel hemmed in and pressured by all this unusual attention from scientists. And when he begins to feel that his freedom is being eroded the least bit, Uri reacts defensively. Captain Mitchell, who was thoroughly impressed with Uri, was the first to sense this reluctance on Uri's part to be a guinea pig for science.

When the scientists had left, we had a reading of the first draft of the documentary movie script about Uri written by Melanie. Uri suddenly began to show more and more signs of irritation as the script was read; finally he stopped the reading and went into a monologue:

"Here you are, all of you. You have been working for months on this movie script. All my life I wanted and waited for a movie about me. Now it is almost here—and I don't want it. What is wrong with me? Why am I so unhappy? Look at the chance I now have to progress in my career—yet something is wrong! Why am I behaving in this way? I now feel that something big has to happen—and I don't know what. I know it is not this movie, or Mitchell, or science. Are there two powers here who are fighting over me? They disturb some other people, or they disturb us here. They are so powerful. We have no idea why they are here. Look, I have some little powers by myself, but the big powers come from above. There's something funny about them. I still find it very funny that they will transport a bottle of cologne from Andrija's room on the fourteenth floor of a hotel down to the dining room in the basement. I think somebody is playing games with us. Perhaps they are a civilization of clowns. Or maybe one of their clowns escaped and he is playing jokes with us. And now I am coming to the main point. The things that happen like a fork bending—this has no connection with anything. They don't live in time. And who knows where they came from? They appeared on earth thousands of years ago. So they are not here to take us over. They are here to teach us something in *our* stupid and idiotic way which is why they appear to be clowns and idiotic. They are performing for us at our level."

Everyone present was shocked not only at these words but at the brusqueness of Uri's attitude. All thought of a constructive discussion of the movie script was over; for Melanie this was a discouraging rebuff.

As August 26 drew to a close, all of us were thoroughly depressed by Uri's attitude, especially about not wanting to be involved in research. Nothing that had been done, or was going to be done, pleased him. He himself said, "I am sorry to be this way, but it is not *me* feeling this way." So I had to beg Uri to sit down with me by the tape recorder to see if we could find out what was going on.

We sat together for several hours calling silently into the unknown. There was no response. Why were we being deserted in this moment of personal crisis?

At 1:01 A.M. of August 27 a large conch shell on a shelf near Uri levitated and slowly fell to the floor. We waited for a voice to appear on the tape recorder monitor speaker. Finally there came the voice of IS on the tape at 1:03 A.M., as follows:

Andrija! [Pause] *The tape will disappear.* [Pause] *For five and half months we have left you alone. You did quite a nice job. But there have been some problems.* [Pause] *You have gathered many people. All your friends that have been gathered must work in harmony. Andrija, have you been scared?*

AP: "No."

Are you prepared? Do you have any fear? Are you ready for the work?

AP: "I am ready for any work."

Uri and Andrija, listen carefully! We hope to land on your planet in a few years. We are seen more and more by people. We will enter your orbital system through [word lost] *transformation and be able to enter your environment. You may not understand this.*

AP: "No, I do not."

One of our failures is that we cannot contact you directly. We can only talk to you through Uri's power on the tape recorder. It is a shame that for such a brilliant mind we cannot contact you directly. Maybe in time we shall be able to contact you directly.

AP: "In other places you used the telephone, radio, television, etcetera. Will you still use these?"

Yes, when that is needed.

AP: "Shall I go back to Germany with Uri?"

We always keep you in contact, you are always together. You must be where the people are who support and help you. [Pause] This afternoon we heard the movie script. We used Uri to speak, although neither he nor any of you was aware of this. It is a brilliant movie, but not the story we want. We want you to prepare the earth for our landing, a mass landing on earth. We landed in South America three thousand years ago, and now we must land again. We want you to tell our story—what you call the UFO experience. Use all the collected data and literature.

AP: "How do we know which is the relevant, or true, data?"

Research the data published. You will know what is correct. Write the movie script carefully, slowly, properly, and cleverly.

AP: "Are you landing on earth to help mankind?"

Yes, but also to help ourselves. Therefore, we must land and reveal ourselves. We draw our power from this solar system.

AP: "When will you land on earth in local earth time?"

We will not reveal to you our timetable in landing on earth in your local time. It may be some years, or sooner.

AP: "In 1952 I was contacted through Dr. Vinod by the Nine. Are you part of them?

Do you remember exactly what happened in 1952?

AP: "Yes, on December 31, 1952, I was contacted by the Nine through the voice of Dr. Vinod. The message started out, 'We are Nine Principles and Forces, personalities if you will.' The equation was:

$$M_i = \frac{m_o c^2}{\sqrt{1 - \frac{v^2}{c^2}}}$$

Yes, that was us, but in different units. We are under their control. You faithfully scribed his words. The real important work is to come. The Knowledge Book is the main work. Shipi will find the book, then Uri, then you. You have many years of work on it. Then it will be released. [Pause] *One of your earth scientists, Einstein, knew about us. Just before he died, he knew the secret. You will carry on the work. Then in centuries, another, and another, to keep the data rolling—until man finds infinity.*

As the voice said "infinity," the tape recorder was switched off. The room was lit by one 200-watt lamp controlled by a dimmer switch. This lamp was slowly dimmed by some invisible hand, and Uri and I sat in the darkness. Through the north window of my study a brilliant white light suddenly flooded into the room. (My house is in a forest—away from any automobile headlights.) The light was very much of the quality of moonlight—but much brighter. We rushed to the window but could not see the source of the light, which was beyond some giant Norway spruce trees. We rushed outdoors, but the light had disappeared. The full (waning) moon was to the south—a full 180° from where we had located the light source. I went back to the tape recorder; the cassette had already vanished. So I sat down to write down what had transpired. But I cannot vouch for the word-for-word accuracy of my transcript—only the sense of this remarkable message.

What I had just heard put me into the most reverential state of contemplation that one can imagine. The weight of what I now knew stretched my load-bearing capacity to the limit. I could not sleep for two days. During the next day Uri and I were driving across the Triboro Bridge into Manhattan, and I was trying to explain to him people's reactions if they really believed that an extraterrestrial civilization was going to land on earth. I said that I thought that people would stop all normal activity; that others would sell stock holdings in panic; that a financial collapse would be triggered, leading to economic paralysis; that governments would mobilize troops and weapons; that looting, riots, and panic would spread. The reason that I went into such lurid possibilities was to explain to Uri what was involved in preparing man for an earth landing. The entire conversation was very depressing to both of us, the more so since we both realized the strong possibility that no one would listen to our announcement until it was too late.

Captain Mitchell was so interested in the things Uri had demonstrated for him that he wanted one key man to see Uri. This was his old friend Dr. Wernher von Braun, rocket designer for the U.S. space program. We went to Germantown, Maryland, on August 29 to see him.

We saw Dr. von Braun in his offices where he is vice-president, Engineering and Development, of Fairchild Industries. Uri did many impressive demonstrations for Dr. von Braun, but two are noteworthy. Dr. von Braun held his gold wedding ring in his hand while Uri concentrated on it. The ring became flattened under Uri's gaze. As we were parting with Dr. von Braun, his secretary came up to him and said, "Dr. von Braun, your pocket calculator is not working!"

He said, "Well, have you checked the battery charge?"

She said, "Yes, it is properly charged."

At this point Dr. von Braun checked the electronic calculator, and he confirmed that it was inoperative. Uri asked if he could "cure" the problem, and Dr. von Braun handed him the calculator.

Uri placed it between his two hands for some thirty seconds and handed it back to Dr. von Braun. Dr. von Braun pushed the switch to "on" and tested it. The panel lights went on, but the calculator digital display flashed like a random number generator. Dr. von Braun said, "There is power now, but the circuitry is not working as a calculator."

Uri took back the calculator and held it in his hands for another thirty seconds. This time when Dr. von Braun tested the calculator it worked normally. Dr. von Braun, Captain Mitchell, and I were most impressed by this feat of psychic repairmanship.

Uri, Shipi, and I stayed in Washington, D.C., at the Hotel Washington in suite 306. That evening I was most anxious to pursue the topics that had been brought up on August 27. We were apparently readily favored because we had no sooner sat down around the tape recorder at midnight when an ashtray floated off a table to the floor. The first statement I heard on the tape monitor phone was *The tape will gradually disappear.*

AP: "Did you send the message from "M" through Dr. Laughead on August eleventh, 1956?"

Do you remember the message?

AP: "Yes."

That was us, but not my unit power.

AP: "Can we use that message?"

Yes. It may be used.

AP: "In March 1963 I saw an ovoid light over my estate in Ossining. Was it yours?"

That was us, forcing and making your powers stronger.

AP: "In May 1968 we saw many lights in the sky in Brazil near where Arigó lives. Were they yours?"

That was ours, but a different unit.

AP: "Does anyone in the United States Government know the secret of your presence on earth?"

Andrija, many people in the U. S. Government and the Russian Government know about our existence. We do not give them any breaks to know us better. They only know that UFOs are real, nothing more.

AP: "I presume that if there is anyone in government who should know, you will have us make the contact under your direction?"

We do not need that yet.

AP: "What is the purpose of your having Uri publicly demonstrate the transmutation of metals, that is, the lead into gold?"

We have tested his powers that are given by us. Uri can do greater things, but we have to pass him, and under examination he did that successfully. And the day will come and he will use that with you.

AP: "May I now take Uri to Captain Mitchell to start experiments?"

You were not given permission to do this.

AP: "Since you indicated two days ago that I may tell everything, may I reveal your presence to any outsider now?"

Not yet. You may start a motion picture and reveal everything. You may go ahead with everything, but do not reveal to anybody yet that we are truly so near to you.

AP: "How soon after your landing will people know of your presence?"

Andrija Puharich, let me describe to you what we mean by mass landing. We need that mass landing like you people on earth call refueling, and charging up, like a huge plane of yours charges up with electricity. We do that through your barometrical and cosmic layer around earth. We shall be charging up and vanishing again. This procedure will, or might, last from two to three weeks. We people have not yet planned this big mass landing. Many, many thousands of people will see us, but we shall control that. We can almost do everything that goes off in your head. We can be visible, and invisible. You have been telling Uri on the bridge to New York that people will be selling stock and so on. That is not so. We shall do it safely, and when we say safely, that is the meaning.

AP: "Ah, so you will not stay for a prolonged period on earth?"

That is not wrong. In your further questions [see N.B. below] is useless about nations, or we taking over your earth as a playground for us. Our Hoova is sixteen thousand times bigger than your planet.

[N.B.: The following two questions were to be asked next by AP:
1. Will you rule the nations and people of this earth?
2. Will you become another nation on earth?]

AP: "I would like to know some of your history so that it will help me to prepare man for your landing."

This is not the time. The time for our history will be told to you the next time Uri and you have leisure time. That might be in Germany or that might be in America. You must use your brains. You have good and clever brains—use them! Use it successfully and you shall be rewarded.

AP: "I am rewarded by your interest and presence. I am through for the moment with questions. Thank you for clarifying the enormous personal problems I had with those questions. I now listen."

Power has been given to you. Note well this tape, for it shall disappear. If we want, and we'll take and give and pass more contacts and information, we shall do that; and if not, we will go back to Germany, and you will have another period to work—free and feel safe and well. Andrija, take care of them and take care of everybody around you. Keep, keep working.

AP: "Shalom."

Then Uri, Shipi, and I sat around the tape recorder to watch for the moment when the cassette would vanish. When this occurred, we all experienced a certain relief, because this was evidence to us that we had, in fact, witnessed a reality.

Uri and Shipi returned to Germany. I went to Stanford University to give a lecture at a conference entitled "Dimensions of Healing." I presented my preliminary findings on Uri Geller covering telepathy and psychokinesis. I believe that most of the audience was frankly skeptical about my report. However, Hal Puthoff and Russell Targ were interested in my data. Captain Mitchell, Puthoff, Targ, and I made our mutual arrangements to do experiments with Uri at Stanford Research Institute.

I went on to the University of California at Los Angeles to give another lecture on healing. While there I was introduced to John Wilhelm, the *Time* reporter who had done a cover story on extraterrestrial life the year before. He was greatly interested in the work with Geller and expressed an interest in doing a story on Uri in the future. I, of course, gave him no hint at this time about what was behind Uri's powers. We agreed to keep in touch.

While in Los Angeles I got an urgent call from Uri, who was in Munich. There were problems, he said, with the contractual arrangements with Yasha Katz. He wanted me to come there to iron it out. I arrived in Munich on October 13, 1972.

In Munich I was presented with the problem of Uri's work in Europe and how to continue it. Yasha reported that in spite of Uri's success in public demonstrations of his powers (such as stopping a mountain cable car in midair, stopping a department store escalator in downtown Munich, etc.), the German public was not interested in Uri—either as a personality or for his powers. Uri had had only one booking, in Hamburg, as a last minute fill-in in a magic show. Yasha was having difficulties in financing Uri. A prominent Swiss show producer, Werner Schmid, had appeared on the scene and he was completely taken with Uri and his potential in show business, and Yasha wanted to transfer his management contract to him. Uri approved of the whole idea. Werner Schmid's main idea was to produce a musical featuring Uri and his powers. The entire idea seemed childish to me, but I felt I could not make a move until I had better knowledge of the status of Uri's mission in Germany. I must confess that even I did not know what Uri's mission was, and for that matter neither did he. We had both accepted on faith the suggestion that he should be there.

On the evening of Saturday, October 14, 1972, I had dinner with Uri and Shipi at their apartment, 226 Balanstrasse. It was a pleasant evening after the heavy business talks with Yasha all day. Uri and Shipi were so proud that they finally had their own apartment, and they made a meal for Melanie and me. It was in fact a very good meal. However, our little family *gemütlichkeit* ended suddenly.

As we sat there, the tape recorder was switched on by an invisible intelligent energy. A voice came from the speaker output of the tape recorder:

Melanie and Shipi, you are not permitted to attend. Please leave the room.

Without a word the two of them left the room. Uri and I watched the tape recorder as though it were the Ark of the Covenant. Then in the fully lighted room first the input plug, then the output plugs, were pulled out by an invisible hand. Out of curiosity I reinserted the plugs. They came out again. I inserted an earphone into the monitor plug. There was as yet no voice on the tape, and it was not running. Then the start and record buttons were "moved," and the tape recorder was in recording operation. At 12:06 A.M. October 15, 1972, a "voice" new to me said:

The tape, keep running it.

AP: "What is Uri supposed to do for you in Germany?"

Then the voice of IS:

We have used their minds all the time, and they were successful. . . . Their work has really finished in Germany. As you go ahead with all your questions, you will get all the clear answers.

AP: "Is Uri to go ahead with Werner Schmid?"

Werner Schmid is the man that we have sent over. We have done and given him many signs, and he has checked out as a positive man. This man has been a very hard-working man, and we think that he has chosen to work with you and help you.

Andrija Puharich, what we are about to say is going to be new to you, and you must listen carefully and closely. Everything that has been done and said until today has been very important for us, but many changes have been made. We have been checking out all the human race, and we came to the conclusion that only panic and disaster may appear when we will land on your earth in a few years. We wanted to give you, and test you, how deep in conscience you can go in telling the human race that we people exist—we creatures, as you call us, in science-fictioned terms—on earth. And it has been very hard on you, on Uri, on Shipi, and everybody concerned with this whole project. You have done a good work.

But many things happened in the last month that only shows the human race is an anxious and unacceptable race. Andrija Puharich, Uri Geller, and Shimshon Strang, we still need your will of mind for our purposes, and we shall keep on using you. From today, from today, from today, you will be completely independent. You shall decide for yourselves. You shall go on with work. The way you will figure out, that is the best. But you must stay in close contact with us. Go ahead with your questions.

AP: "Are you reversing the position you took on August 29,

Seven Pillars of Fire 183

1972, that the mass landing would not cause panic, would be safe?"

No reverses are taken. There shall be landings on earth. But the landings might be invisible, and only visible to you.

AP: "Will we still have to prepare man if your landing is invisible?"

No. You do not have to prepare the human race of people who cannot accept happenings. But you must go on teaching people.

AP: "With regard to the upcoming Stanford Research Institute validation tests, are there any negatives here?"

You should not put Uri into deep scientific researches and work. You can meet these people briefly, show them his abilities, but be careful.

AP: "What is the message that the motion picture is to carry?"

Whenever Uri talks about his powers, he should mention that he believes in life in outer space. He should not go down into highly procedural things, but only what he feels. This film should have a highly interesting story. Andrija Puharich, you have a head on your shoulders, and so does Melanie, and all the workers who help you. And with their help it will be tremendous. It must come out of your head. With all the material you have studied about us in the last two months, you have a clear idea and view about us. Although we are always with you people, we shall stay away from this human race for a couple of years.

AP: "This last statement makes me feel very sad. Your help is needed more than ever."

(N.B.: At this point the voice began to sound more and more "mechanical" and synthetic, and to slow down.)

You see, the energy in your mind, that is, we must admit, that is the thing—that—we—do—not—have. W-e a-r-e c-o-m-p-u-t-o-r-i-z-e-d c-o-m-p-l-e-t-e-l-y c-o-m-p-u-t-o-r-i-z-e-d b-y m-e-c-h-a-n-i-c-a-l i-n-s-t-r-u-m-e-n-t-s-. A-s y-o-u c-a-n h-e-a-r-, w-e a-r-e c-o-m-p-u-t-o-r-i-z-e-d-, c-o-m-p-u-t-o-r-i-z-e-d-.

Y-o-u-r c-o-m-p-u-t-o-r i-s w-r-i-t-i-n-g p-o-w-e-r-f-r-o-m millions—of—light-years—away. *We also need your help."*

(N.B.: Although the sound was mechanical, there was such a poignancy and plea for life from this computer that it made me cry for pity.)

Andrija Puharich, you must understand, in this state we are computors. Long time ago, we have been touched by hands of beings. Now we must know for sure from you; it is only up to you and your own choice and your own human will to work with us. Do you regret it in anyway that you are working for us?

AP: "Absolutely not."

That is fine! We already knew the answers. But for us to be sure it must come out from you. You can take out, and we shall not harm; we shall disconnect our units, and then you shall stay a human being.

AP: "Of my own free will I serve, because in this way I can best serve my fellowman."

But we knew that you are important for us—very! You must think well and healthy. As you know we are over you, and looking at everything that you are all doing. We are not interfering in any way. We are just letting things sometimes happen for Uri. Everything you must all do alone. It is important for people to see Uri, for the younger generation to feel. It is very important for you to know all this and you are very precious to us. We can come in from our dimension by and with our vehicles which you call UFOs.

AP: "The UFO is how you enter our dimensional framework?"

Exactly. We cannot enter your earth, only appear to you through computerizing your minds. For instance, Uri Geller's mind and washing back all times our visions on his eyes. We bend, move, and material and dematerial things. That power we possess, and do possess it.

AP: "Does this include the power of healing, as in Arigó's case?"

We can do anything your mind can just think of.

AP: "With respect to your computerized format, where is the real intelligence behind you?"

The real intelligence behind us are us ourselves. We have passed our souls, bodies, and minds into computors and moved several of millions of light-years backwards towards your time and dimension. In due time we shall receive all material coming back to our main center which is zoned into a different dimension than yours. This different dimension lies beyond the so-called star, and so-called god, so-called planet that you call the sun. It is millions of light-years backwards into the dieshold [unknown word] of the ages. That is where we are originally in. The voice that you hear now has been sent many, many billions of light-years ahead of time.

AP: "How does this relate to the contents of the Knowledge Book?"

This will be revealed only to you, Shipi, and Uri as scientific and experimental knowledge. You will need it to gain this trip with us to outer space.

AP: "This promise is one of the greatest moments in life. When will the book be available?"

The book is already lying waiting just to be picked by you. But the time has not come yet.

AP: "Can you give me a good reason why I should keep Uri doing public demonstrations?"

You will also learn this in the years to come. It is very important.

AP: "May I let Shipi and Melanie hear this tape before it vanishes?"

They may, but you shall stay in this room and copy the tape. Let Shipi and Melanie on [second] thought hear only the written answers.

Tomorrow you will meet Schmid. He can be useful to you in all the world. He is a very serious and dependable man.

AP: "We shall accept him into the family. Can I count on further communication with you?"

Rely on Uri.

AP: "Could Uri heal?"

Someday he will move into that automatically. Copy the tape, Andrija Puharich! Adieu!

Contrary to advice, I allowed Melanie to listen to a few minutes of the part of the tape where the computerized voice was so heavily mechanized and slowed down; she was absolutely stunned by this experience. I worked for several hours to copy the words from the tape. At 3 A.M. I took a coffee break. Uri brought out an antique Derringer pistol neatly laid out in a velvet display case. While I was looking at it, it suddenly vanished, leaving the case intact. Uri was sick about this disappearance, and said so. At 3:10 A.M. the Derringer suddenly reappeared in the case.

I finished the copying at 3:30 A.M. and left Uri's apartment. Before I got into the car, I packed the TC 120 tape recorder into a red TWA flight bag with the IS tape cassette still in the machine. I drove back to the Schloss Hotel in Grunewald where I was staying. When I took the TWA bag out of the car at 3:50 A.M., the *entire tape recorder* had disappeared.

At 1 P.M. the same day, October 15, all of us assembled at a downtown restaurant, the Moven Pick, in Munich to meet Werner Schmid. Werner proved to be an ebullient and warm gentleman; he and I liked each other instantly and have remained the best of friends and working colleagues.

We returned to Uri's apartment at 5 P.M. It was then that Melanie missed her lovely scarf. She thought she had probably lost it at the Moven Pick restaurant. Werner called the restaurant, but the scarf was not to be found. Our discussions continued about Uri's future in demonstrating publicly, contracts, the idea of a musical, etc., until 8 P.M., at which time we left Uri's apartment—Uri, Shipi, Yasha, Werner, Melanie, and myself—to go to dinner. Before we got into Yasha's locked Mercedes-Benz, I looked into the car by the light from the street lamp and called Melanie. There on the front seat, neatly folded, was her missing scarf! When Yasha opened the door, I had a second surprise: Under the scarf was my TC 120 tape recorder in its synthetic leather case. I opened it and found that the tape cassette was gone! I took another tape cassette out of my bag, placed it in the machine, and tested its operation. It worked perfectly.

During this period neither Yasha nor Werner knew anything about the source of Uri's powers, nor about the inergy of Spectra and Hoova; all of our discussions proceeded on a purely mundane level. Then Uri got into an inspired state of oratory which I tape-recorded, and it pretty well summarizes our thinking at this time.

Uri was explaining to Werner, "You see, when I demonstrate my powers, it's not me. Somebody is trying to show us something, and by this, teaching us. They want us to show them our faith. This somebody we don't know and we just call them Spectra because that has something to do with light. I think Spectra, whoever they are, want the people to know that they exist through an example, and through that example which can be evidence for the people—such as that there is a possibility of life after death; that there is a possibility to pass the speed of light; that there is a possibility to gain powers through other things, not through Spectra; that there is a possibility to renew life and health by powers; to be strong, and so on."

Melanie asked, "Do you have a feeling as to what that example might be which we could use in a musical or movie?"

Uri replied, "Let me think now. Well, it should be an example that you can touch. Something that happened twenty years ago and remained a mystery. For example, somebody is in jail, and suddenly the bars dematerialize because he is not really guilty. Now that we can prove these things are possible, somebody in the cast will shout of something like this that happened in history that is like the bars disappearing, and then the people know. They will say, well, if that happened, why shouldn't this happen?"

Melanie inquired, "Healing?"

I said, "Healing is one of the few things that are safely international."

Uri replied, "We can use examples of things that happened three thousand years ago, and through that example, tell people that the powers showed themselves. I don't know why today the powers don't show themselves . . . maybe because people are close-minded. Is there an example of how the pyramids were built? Until today, nobody knows, and all the brilliant people disagree with each other. Well, where is the answer?

"There is another thing. You see, Andrija, I know you and you know me. I know Shipi and Shipi knows me. Melanie knows me. But nobody really knows anybody. Werner doesn't know me exactly, and I really don't know him. We believe some sixty per cent that we know you, but we don't know this Spectra at all, Andrija. But look at the foolish things they are doing. Sometimes they say 'You definitely must go!' and then they change their minds! Andrija, you understand? To us it looks like they are not stable, goddammit. They are so powerful, yet they are not stable. And maybe that unstableness that we think of them . . . maybe for them it is nothing. Maybe for them it's just a breath, you know. For them it's nothing, but we feel it—like suddenly for two to four months we don't receive anything from them because we're not together. Maybe for them it was just turning around—to see something, and back at us again. Maybe for them it was just stopping a computer for a second, a split second, and for us it was a month. Now we don't know their timing, their difference from us, their character. We don't know anything about them. So we're not allowed to! You know, Andrija, Melanie told me once—sometimes I get the feeling— what if all this is a big joke? Andrija, what if they are clowns? What if this whole thing that is happening to us—it's just one little clown that has run away from the king's garden, and he's playing with us because he has those powers? What if it's that? What if it's not at all a big, huge, godlike thing; well, yes, the powers from Hoova we have. But what if Hoova is just a goddamn little clown that is playing with us? You understand? So we have to be very flexible—very rubberish."

I replied quite seriously, "We always have to rely on our brains and common sense."

Uri said, "Yes, and that is what the little clown keeps telling us: 'Listen, man, I am also that—so be careful. I don't want to ruin your life. That's why you must always use your own brain—

no matter what Spectra says. Tomorrow I might vanish. Tomorrow you won't have any powers, and we will laugh up here, but you're going to have the dregs.' But even if they disappear today, or tomorrow, Andrija, I'm never going to laugh. I'll be satisfied. Okay. So I'll go back to some menial job. I'll do whatever I have to do. I'll work. If I have no powers, I'll go back to the export factory. But I will be satisfied with the idea that I lived with them for two years, and I knew the truth! And what I know, Andrija, nothing can hurt the truth—and if somebody doesn't believe me, or he laughs, I don't care. I know the truth. I know that I was in straight contact with them. Nothing will change that, and until I die, I will be content that I had these one, two, or three or twenty-five years in which I knew that this power exists, and if it is gone now, I know in my heart that it exists, and I know it, and I know that it won't end because when I die I really won't die, I go in a different dimension. And in that dimension, I'll be even more clever than the other guys and gals around me, and maybe in that dimension I have to teach them. Listen, guys, maybe it's that, and that! You understand me, Andrija? So let's really be happy that we're in contact with them. But, but because things are so, because one and one is two, that means, 'Come on, let's have a sign!' and suddenly falls something! Let's have a sign, something disappears! That makes me think and believe that they are not so unstable as we think.

"They have their own ideas, what they want from us, what they need from us, what we need from them, so they won't let us go, like that. But for us, but for them maybe, the world is not really important. Once in a while, I told this to Melanie, that I have the feeling, Andrija, that all we are doing, we are just goddamn slaves for them. They are using us only for their own use. They don't care about the world. They do care about this little group. But to make us a little happy because they are using us, they're throwing us little, little things. Okay. Those little things are very big for us, but for them it is nothing. Maybe they only think it.

"We don't know them, Andrija, we really don't know them.

Andrija, I forget, but you know how far away they are! They are so far that no human mind, not yours, not all the scientists together put in one place, can figure out how far away they are. Different dimensions, future, that's completely way out! That's wild! That's crazy that anything could happen! If they are so far in advance, we must be happy that we are in contact with them."

I said, "But having had that knowledge, that we know that they exist, what does that mean to you?"

Uri answered, "To my sorrow and to my disappointment, I don't really know."

I persisted, "But does it not give you the security that everything is lawful, like having a good father and a good house, that everything is properly managed, that nothing is accidental?"

Uri said, "No, listen. I don't know why they chose us; that to me means an accident. Everything is happening to us. But sometimes we ask them, and they give us answers, but the answers change sometimes also. So I figure that we with our human heads, those two little brains we have in our heads—we must work them to get nearer and nearer to the point where we think what they want. It's up to us, really."

On October 21 I had an opportunity to question IS via the tape recorder. I was assured that Uri's idea that the actions of IS were like "a clown in the garden" was wrong. I was further advised that it was desirable to have Uri meet as many scientists as possible, but to avoid too deep an involvement in research. I did not understand why we could not devote full time to probing the deep mysteries of the universe through Uri's abilities, and I knew that I would have to come back to this question over and over again until I understood the reason. I had the further impression that earth scientists were not yet prepared to enter the black void of totally new knowledge.

I agreed to release Yasha from his contract with me with respect to his management of Uri. Werner decided to join our team at his own expense. We all agreed to leave Germany and to transfer all personnel and operations to the United States in the near future.

Uri, Shipi, and I went from Munich to London on October 30. In London we stayed at the Royal Garden Hotel, which was then owned by my close friend, Tony Bloomfield. As long as we were in Europe, I wanted Uri to meet some of my scientific colleagues in England. We met with some of them, and a report of this meeting appeared in the *New Scientist* of November 9, 1972.

On the night of October 31 I was sitting alone in my hotel room making notes on the day's events. Uri and Shipi were in private rooms in another part of the hotel. At midnight my phone rang.

"Hello, is this Dr. Puharich?"

"Yes," I said.

"Well, this is Mr. Wilson of Pan Am. We processed your ticket for your flight to the United States on November 1 and returned your ticket today. Do you have it?"

"Yes," I replied.

"Well, there is a discrepancy in the ticket. Did you have trouble with the fare structure in Munich?"

"Yes," I replied.

"Please give me the ticket number, and I will Telex Munich and see if I can straighten out the problem."

I gave him the ticket number and hung up. A half hour later, Mr. Wilson called back to say there was a problem with the ticket. Could he come over now to pick it up and get it rewritten by morning? I said okay.

I let Mr. Wilson in. He looked at my ticket and mumbled some technical jargon. He assured me that the problem could be ironed out by morning. He asked to take my ticket. I asked for his name and telephone number and a signed receipt. This he did, took my ticket, and parted. Shortly thereafter, I went to sleep. In the morning I called the hall porter and asked about Mr. Wilson. Uri, who was with me, asked about the call, and I described the events of the past night.

He immediately became very alarmed. "I didn't want to say anything to you yesterday, but I felt a sense of danger in this room. Was Mr. Wilson dark? Did he look like someone from the Middle East?"

"Well yes, he did look like he was from the Middle East or Pakistan."

"That's it, Andrija. Terrorists must have spotted my presence, and they sent someone up to scout the room. If I had been here, he would have tried to kill me, us. Let's go down and talk to the manager! Remember what the terrorists did to the Israelis last month at the Olympics in Munich?" he added grimly.

I readily agreed. As we stood in the lobby talking to Mr. Ottensooser, the manager, a man came up to me with a parcel and asked if I was Dr. Puharich. I said that I was. It turned out that he was delivering a movie film that I had arranged to have shipped from New York. It had been held up in customs for five days. Uri took me aside and said, "Andrija, that package could be a bomb. Don't accept it!" He called over the manager and explained his feeling to him. Mr. Ottensooser agreed there could be a hazard and called Scotland Yard. Within an hour we were embroiled with interrogation about Mr. Wilson; the bomb squad was taking the package apart in Kensington Park; and the personnel at the hotel were involved in the case. Nothing happened. The film can was just a film can; Mr. Wilson was not to be found; my ticket was lost. It was decided that since there might be a terrorist threat we should be moved, and were transferred incognito to another hotel, the White House.

One more oddity occurred. At the White House on November 2, 1972, we were quartered in a three-room suite, number 289. I picked up my Tissot watch (with a leather strap) from my night table in my bedroom to check the time. It was exactly 11 A.M. I put the watch down and turned away from it to get a shirt out of my suitcase. Uri came rushing into my room shouting, "A wristwatch just appeared on my wrist!" There on his left wrist, fully strapped, was my Tissot. The hands still read 11 A.M. while the sweep-second hand was at the twenty seconds position. My watch was gone from the night table.

There were many other phenomena that occurred in London,

but these were things Uri had done before and that I have already described elsewhere.

I returned to New York on November 2, 1972. Uri and Shipi stayed on in London and returned to Munich on November 4. As they were flying over the area of Schweinfurt in a Boeing 747, Uri saw that the Nikon F camera at his feet had levitated to his waist level. The camera had Kodacolor film in it and a 150-mm lens. Uri felt that this was a sign for him to photograph a UFO. He looked out of his window. Neither he nor Shipi saw anything. It was a clear sky with scattered clouds below the plane. Uri started to take pictures anyway, pointing the camera out the window. This film was not processed until some three weeks later. On five of the film frames there could be seen very clear dark outlines of three UFOs. But more of the details later.

On November 6, 1972, Uri, Shipi, and Melanie arrived in the United States and came to stay at my home in Ossining, New York. We were finally again assembled in one place without distractions, to begin our serious work.

On Tuesday, November 7, the four of us were having breakfast in the dining room. The dining room has a large bay window facing east looking out onto a block-long private driveway. The opposite side of the dining room faces west and has a door to the kitchen. Lying in the kitchen doorway was my black Labrador retriever, who was named Wellington because of all of his fights with my giant black cat, Napoleon.

Shipi and I had our backs to the bay window, facing Wellington and the kitchen. Uri and Melanie, with their backs to the kitchen door, faced us, the bay window, and the driveway. At 10:05 A.M. Uri turned around in his chair and looked at Wellington and said, "Why is Wellington afraid and trembling now?"

We all looked at Wellington, who looked back at us with a shy eye. I said, "There is a mystery about that dog—he appeared one day and adopted me."

Just then the telephone rang. As I rose to answer it, heading for the kitchen phone which was nearest, Wellington was suddenly gone! As I stepped through the empty doorway, which had just been occupied by Wellington, the phone rang a second time. Then Uri said, "Look, what is that dog doing down the driveway?"

I looked down the driveway, and there, about seventy yards away, was Wellington, trotting toward the house. The phone rang a third time and I picked it up. It was the Reverend Canon William Rauscher calling me. While I was on the phone talking, Uri, Shipi, and Melanie went to the front door and called to Wellington. He entered the house reluctantly. I finished the phone call in a few minutes, and then inspected Wellington carefully. He seemed to have come back in exactly the same condition as when he had left. This demonstration of the power of Hoova made a lasting impression on all of us. We now fully realized that it was possible to translocate a living thing with safety.

I now turned to a pursuit of some basic questions that were bothering me. I was concerned with the question of whether man could understand how his brain was built, and, with some structural knowledge, could the higher powers of the mind be developed and explained? I wanted to know how Uri's brain and mind were different from other people's, and if a "normal" person could ever hope to have such powers as Uri's. As the problem developed, I was told by IS:

The ultimate powers, whether on the particle level or the cosmic level, are in rotation and drawing off of the gravitation power from the center of the system. There are special rays (which you should spell "raws") where the skin of the envelope of the cosmic rays is utilized for power. The computorized beings in space vehicles draw on this energy. This rotation energy can be used from outside the galaxy. It does not exist in a usable form at the particle level. The computorized beings are under the direction of the "controller," or what earth man calls God, or gods. In the future this general idea would be formulated in rigorous mathematical language.

I was puzzled—as people have been since the beginning of time—as to the nature of the soul. I was given a new concept which was to imagine that all souls are like a vase (i.e., a physical pot). Each vase-soul exists in a rotational, gravitational

Seven Pillars of Fire

field. When one perturbs the vase-soul, wavelets go out into the universe field. It is very much like dropping a pebble in water—wavelets will radiate outward. The perturbation of the vase-soul in the rotational gravitational field is experience.

But I needed a deeper knowledge and sought to make a contact and communication via the tape recorder. On Wednesday, November 8, 1972, a strange ashtray and a brass key appeared before Uri and me at 10:31 A.M. This seemed to be a sign, so we set up the tape recorder and waited for it to be activated. When the tape mechanism was activated, there was a surprise; a new voice sounded:

This is Rhombus 4D. People! For your own sake, after writing it, destroy the tape completely because we do not want to vanish it for you.

AP: "I promise to do that. We are all very happy to be together again and in America. Uri is happy; Shipi is happy; I am happy. This is the first time we feel that our work together is about to begin. Our learning period in Israel, in Germany, it seems, is over. Uri and I are having a difference of opinion over how best to manage him as an artist, and how best to develop him in view of your plans for him as a witness. I present our problem: I feel that Uri should be accepted by mankind as a person who is honest, trustworthy, and has genuine powers. I can only do this by going to science (as one of the few objective credible groups in the world today) and have them validate him. This will avoid trouble and friction and possibly another crucifixion. How would *you* like to have me develop him with respect to his relation with science and scientists, and with man in general?"

We shall tell you exactly how. Do you know that in six thousand million years the sun is going to cool off completely? Earth man will have to leave to a different planet. Now all about Uri. We are tuned on every movement, and every thought, and we do give you signs. And you can see, hear, feel it. Uri must not go into any scientific research! Reasons will be given very soon to you why. He can meet any scientists that you wish, socially, friendly—that is all. *Although Uri himself in his body has great conflicts with this thought against us, but we have to do it this way. Yesterday at the table we have made your dog dematerialize—and you have seen it in front of you. There is a reason for that also.*

AP: "Could you please explain?"

Not now. We are talking about experiments with Uri. If that will not happen, you yourself judged and said that you will have to take the hard way. And that is the way that we order you to take for your own good sake.

And now, many a time you wonder, Andrija Puharich, if you are protected by us or are vulnerable? Did you ever recall us telling you that you were protected?

AP: "Yes."

When was that?

AP: "In Israel, I asked you about it. You said nothing could happen to me physically, only some scares."

Yes, nothing could happen to you physically during that period of time. Now, Andrija Puharich, we are using you because you also determine and possess powers that we don't. As you see, Uri is sometimes afraid of things that might happen.

AP: "Yes. That still surprises me."

And he is doing the right thing because you have to take care of your own bodies. Do not be surprised, but things can happen. You see, although our computors are caught up onto your brain every second, that is, by using direct powers, but to detail a sufficient protection on your body, that takes a several [missed a word that sounds like "reach"] *time to arrive around your bodies. Anything that can happen spontaneously can harm you. So all we can do is do these things and give you signs. We gave you signs for two different reasons lately, and we shall state them A and B.*

A. We have sent someone to steal your ticket. You see, he could have shot Uri and Shipi if they were in the room. That was a lesson!

B. The lesson that you will lose and use more was, you are,

and you might be, in a little, as you call it, jam with scientists. Do you understand?
AP: "Yes."
Anything can happen to you while our jinns are arriving. By the time you think right now that we can move anything that we want, and fly objects around and disappear things—that is not done spontaneously. Don't you realize that you live in a space of no time? All these things are planned ahead by computors, or head device. Don't you see an ashtray and a key appeared right now?
AP: "Yes, I did."
To your own timeless situation, that means to you there is time. It looks like it happened right now, spontaneously, immediately, straightforward. But that is wrong. For us, that was planned hundred, hundreds of light-years ago, Andrija. For one little ashtray, anything that can happen to you, any third body, concerning, can damage that plan that arises by data.
AP: "There is a 'time' lag between when something is happening here, and when you can respond properly?"
Exactly. But there is more to it. If you notice, Andrija, there is a different computor talking to you right now.
AP: "Yes, I was aware. It is a different, authoritative, sharper one."
We call it Rhombus 4D. Don't forget that. This computor also covers different aspects in thoughts, on different letters of tone that you consider in your dimensions. Now, Andrija, do not forget—to you it looks like we are supermen and can do anything.
AP: "Yes, from our frame of reference."
Didn't you ever stop to think that if we could do everything, we would not use your brains?
AP: "Yes, we recognize that—which is why we call ourselves donkeys."
Do not call yourselves donkeys. For all you know we are computors, and your flesh, blood, and soul that has long passed our times. We receive messages and control from the higher power above us. Go ahead with questions.

AP: "With respect to time—is there a time lag between my speaking and your response?"

Yes, Andrija Puharich. If you consider it in your time theory down on your earth, it is approximately one and a half million light-years away.

AP: "From where Rhombus 4D is?"

Exactly.

AP: "And this takes time?"

It does not take time for us, but it does for you. Don't you see that in one little point on their way, it demashallows [unknown word] *into different aspects of dimensions where you are lost completely, and we take over. That point where powers gather through—that is the main channel of tuning into your worlds which exist more.*

AP: "Time simultaneity with time difference vanishing?"

Not quite so. Time gatherance does not vanish. Don't you see that space with energy rotation around it excludes the time question? And that time or space we gather in and use also. So that word that you said, "vanish," is also being used up by our works. That will be very difficult for you to understand. But time will come, we hope, and you will come to understand outside circumstances that you need to understand, not more than you need to understand.

AP: "This is fair enough. I would like to return to the earlier stated restriction—we can meet with scientists only socially?"

Very socially. You can go ahead as planned.

AP: "Can Uri do tasks in which his work is photographed?"

No. We have always prevented him from working with scientists—Technion, Max Planck Institute, the Weizman Institute. You are the only scientist who has been allowed to do laboratory work and experiments with him—as in Sharon Heights. You are the only one who is in this cosmic triangle.

AP: "We did not discuss the other part of my problem: how to develop Uri as an artist."

Andrija Puharich, what you do with Uri, judge for yourself. Do anything that produces energy, good works.

AP: "If Uri appears at a sport event in a stadium where many thousands are gathered—does this produce energy?"

Doesn't work. Molecules in brain cells are only positively open when excitement is not strong. Normal excitement overcomes the vibration to our powers. Brain should be in a very relaxed state to receive messages from us. For example, sexual excitement is a little, not strong enough for us. We do not exactly mean relaxation. It is a very deep knowledge.

AP: "In Israel I saw Uri create entranced audiences in small groups. Is this what you mean?"

Yes, that is the idea. Even if Uri plays in a film, it will be the same effect. Wellington has to be around you for testing.

AP: "What is the status of your advice that we use Israel as a base?"

No, do not live there. Use it only for little assignments. Don't ask questions that you can solve for yourself. We shall be soon together. Destroy tape. Farewell.

AP: "Farewell."

There were too many matters discussed in this conversation for me to comment on all of them, but I wish to tell of my feelings in one area. The prohibition about scientific work for Uri troubled me deeply. I felt that if Uri was to make his way in the world by simple demonstrations he would always be treated like a juggler, a magician. Since he also had to deliver the message about the landing, how could he ever become credible? If he tried to give the message about the landing, he would fail because no one would listen, or he would fail because he would be crucified. His mission and his life were in jeopardy, in my view, if he tried to go ahead without being validated by science. I made up my mind to take the Promethean course and plead to allow Uri to do scientific work in order to be validated.

I dare not tell all of what happened on Thursday, November 9, but I will share glimpses. I argued with Uri in an effort to persuade him to try to get permission for research. He got angry and threw a sugar bowl at me. I uttered a curse against the gods. The wind came up around the house, the trees swayed, the house rocked, then a tall grandfather clock was impelled across the entrance hall and smashed into a thousand pieces. Uri, Melanie, Shipi, and I huddled together, waiting for the wrath of heaven to take us away. Uri begged me to repent and to give up the idea of scientific work. I said I would rather place myself at the mercy of the gods than live without my principles. The minutes ticked by like bombs. This is all that I care to say of these dreadful hours. After the crash of the clock, there was no sign or word from above, only an ominous silence.

Before nightfall I got Uri to agree to fly with me to San Francisco on the following day, November 11, so that we could tell the waiting scientists that the research program was off. Uri offered to assume all the responsibility for terminating the arrangements.

Uri and Shipi used a bedroom on the third floor of the house. They were awakened from sleep by the noise of two window shades suddenly being released, rolling up with a bang. This was followed by a short silence, and then they heard a powerful voice in the room:

Rhombus 4D, Andrija must write a book!

Again an eerie silence as they listened expectantly. When nothing more happened, they came downstairs to waken me. It was 2 A.M. They told me the story and hugged me: "Andrija, they want you to write a book. That means the secret of their existence is to be revealed!"

I thanked them for the great tidings and thanked God for the mercy shown to a brash fool.

In the same morning of November 11, 1972, we prepared to leave the house to be driven to the airport. Wellington, who loved to ride in cars, insisted on going with us. Uri tried gently to persuade him otherwise. Wellington bit Uri's right wrist with a mighty snap that drew blood and caused great pain. It all seemed to add to our burden in flying out to California to deliver the bad news.

CHAPTER EIGHT

The Battle for the Truth

When we arrived at the San Francisco Airport at 3 p.m., we were met by Captain Mitchell, Dr. Wilbur Franklin, Dr. Hal Puthoff, and Mr. Russell Targ. I had forewarned them by phone that Uri was not going to cooperate in the scientific work but that he wanted to explain it to them in person. As soon as we got in the car, Uri began to tell them his story. I had no idea what he was going to say. He talked for two hours while we listened without comment. I will summarize what he said.

Uri told them that it had never been his wish to give himself to science, that that was my idea. The reason was that he did not want people to know that his powers were genuine. He preferred to keep them guessing so that they would not take him seriously. He claimed that by being controversial he had remained successful in Israel. If someone got the idea that he was genuine, it would complicate his life. He told of being approached in Rome by an unsavory character, in Tel Aviv by a Russian agent, etc. He was afraid of these political things. Then he told the story of my recent experience with the "terrorist" in London. I must confess that he got overly dramatic about the potential dangers to his life if people knew his powers were genuine. I think that everyone else felt the same way, but they listened with tolerance.

Then Uri shocked me by suddenly talking about IS and about

extraterrestrial intelligences as being the source of his powers. He turned to me for confirmation, but since I had not been released from my pledge of secrecy, I could only say, "No comment."

Uri said, "So you see, I cannot give myself to science for my personal reasons and because the intelligence that directs me does not want me to do it. I have no choice because they direct me. I can't go against that advice. Bad things happen if I go against that advice."

The talk of extraterrestrials did not appear to shock Mitchell, Franklin, Targ, or Puthoff. But they were clinically curious as to Uri's experiences and asked him questions as follows:

Dr. Franklin queried, "Are you saying that your life is not your own? That you cannot go where you want to go?"

Dr. Puthoff asked, "Have you agreed to work with this power?"

Uri replied, "I have worked with these beings for over a year now. I have very little choice—they direct me."

"He can go where he wants to go," interjected Captain Mitchell.

"I can go where I want to go. I am leading my life," replied Uri.

"Then I don't know what you are saying," persisted Dr. Franklin.

"What do you mean?" said Uri.

Everyone pitched in to clarify the issue. Was it a governing director? Was it a psychic force? Was it merely a pressure to go in a certain direction, rather than a command? Did it only veto certain things?

Uri replied, "Well, it doesn't tell me to go to the kitchen now —to eat an apple or not to eat an apple. But if I do go to the kitchen, I really can't explain whether it's me or not me who wants to get the apple. I assume that it's me, unless there's a very heavy pressure not to do it. Listen, I am in the situation that if I really were to ask that being, I could right now be in a different place—I could right now be in London, but my body would be here; I could read a letter in somebody's house in London, if I really ask the being. I just have to wish for something. But I can't bring here a million dollars, you understand. I did that—I asked that being to make me money! But then I get hit from something else! I'm not allowed to wish for things like that."

"I'm not sure I can understand that. But can you govern your own future?" asked Dr. Franklin.

"I don't know what's going to happen with me," Uri replied very soberly.

"Do you know what criteria they use if you should or shouldn't do some particular thing?" Dr. Puthoff asked. "Do you know ahead of time what their goals are?" he added.

"No," replied Uri. "You see, they are computers, which were fed millions of light-years in the future. Do you understand? They are computers, and their data are arriving at me in what I call my time, but they are in a different time zone completely. That means if I decide to do something, they decide it for me in the future. That means that if Andrija's car key appears now inside of a plastic carrot bag, it actually was planned hundreds, thousands of years in the future. It had to happen! And it happened! But if an accident happens—that I can't understand. Because they also tell me that I must take care of myself. For a while, I was living as if nothing could happen to me. Now I know I'm vulnerable. I really thought I was guarded against all possible danger! But lately I see that bad things can happen to me. That means that somehow the computers *are* on my body, but if something on the side happens that is not on their "time," they cannot control it. Let me show you something! You see, now I don't know if I am showing it, or they are showing it."

Captain Mitchell interjected, "It doesn't really matter!"

"I want to show you for twenty minutes the little things I do. Then I will go up to the bigger things."

Captain Mitchell said, "Uri, you're not saying anything to us we don't in some way already sense or understand."

"All right, that's very good. That's a good step," replied Uri. "I must warn you now. The things I know—that's reality!"

With these few words I knew that a bond of understanding had been forged between Uri and the scientists. Uri was now in the mood to show his powers to them in this informal social setting in this apartment at 9303 Middlefield Road, Palo Alto. I awaited a sign to see if IS would enter into or stay away from Uri's demonstration.

Uri then did five tests of telepathy using either numbers or drawings. He was correct in four out of five tries. He then asked for some metal objects. Dr. Puthoff took out a machined copper ring, a fork, and his silver chain bracelet, which Uri briefly touched. Dr. Puthoff put his hand over these three objects. Uri placed his hand over Dr. Puthoff's hand. Dr. Puthoff removed his hand after Uri had concentrated on the objects for some thirty seconds. The copper ring had gone from a circle to an egg shape. Every scientist present said the same thing: "Incredible!"

Uri simply stated, "It was not my body that did it. It was a power above me!"

Russ Targ asked, "Is the power happy about having this happen?"

Uri replied, "This power can't be happy—it doesn't have feelings. It is a computer. It knows if it was good or bad, I believe."

Uri then asked for Russ Targ's watch. He set the hands to twelve o'clock, and he asked Russ to hold his hand over the watch. He then asked someone to pick a number from 1 to 12. Uri was trying to have the watch hands move to the hour requested. He failed twice in a row to do this. This made him unhappy: "I'm angry it didn't go. But I hope that in the two or three days we spend together socially you may see some big things, if they allow it. But I won't work in the laboratory. What they really want, we don't know."

Dr. Puthoff asked me in an aside, "Does he have to cooperate with UFOs—is that what he is saying?"

My reply: "I can't talk. My lips are sealed."

Hearing this, Uri said, "They gain their force from the rotation of our galaxy. Isn't that right, Andrija?"

"I don't know anything. *You* are talking, not me," I replied.

Uri was both annoyed and amused at me as he said, "You see, you think that I am not allowed to say this, huh?"

"I am not saying anything," I said a bit grimly.

The Battle for the Truth

Uri looked around and said to all, "Look how he is against it!"

Captain Mitchell spoke for the group when he replied, "No, he's just being a proper skeptical scientist."

I simply did not understand how Uri could feel so free in revealing secrets that we had agreed to keep. To my knowledge, there had been no release from this pledge, in spite of what had been allowed in the writing of a book or a movie script. His attitude was all the more curious, since he was generally so conscious of security and secrecy. Was this Uri, or was it IS at work now? There had still been no clear sign.

Dr. Franklin broke the silence: "But how do you know these things? Do you hear it, see it, or just know it?"

Uri said, "I think I hear it. But I don't believe it. So I ask for a proof, a sign. Sometimes I see it on my mind's screen. There are some other ways, too. I don't know why I am telling you all these things."

Dr. Puthoff asked, "Are those forces associated with beings—live beings—or are they all programmed into a computer?"

"All in a computer, but I suspect that a being did it somewhere, sometime. The beings are not there. Because I only get what is planned; I can't ask for new things. Also, there are different units out there."

Russell asked, "Do you feel you are more in control as time goes on?"

"Yes," said Uri. "Please put some glasses of water on the table." These were brought and put on the table.

"Please everyone, be quiet now," Uri asked. "I am asking for a sign now." Everyone was quiet. The tape recorder was running, and alert to anything that might happen. We waited.

At 8:01 P.M. a bell rang! The automatic ESP test machine bell had rung, registering a hit. Russell Targ, who had designed this instrument, said, "It's never done that before."

Shortly thereafter, we examined the copper ring on the table. It had become even more flattened, going from the egg shape to a dumbbell shape. I had the feeling that this was a sign, but I needed more evidence before I could be sure.

Russ Targ asked Uri, "Do you feel that the bell and the ring are signs that they are favorably inclined toward what we are doing?"

"First of all, let me tell you. They are tuned toward us—me, Shipi, and Andrija—every second of our lives. They're tuned . . . every second. We can't escape from that. Whatever we think, they answer to that. Whatever we ask, talk, they interrupt if necessary. So I don't know for sure now whether that was the sign.

"I'm going to tell you the craziest thing. Listen to me. We were flying from New York to Munich on September 1 this year. The plane was about fifteen minutes out of New York. There were clear blue skies, about 4:30 P.M. I looked out of the window and I said to them, 'Please, just for once, give me a sign—not little things—please appear before me now.'

"And I swear to you on my mother—and Shipi would swear on his mother—they came from the right side of the jumbo jet. I'm not going to tell you a flying saucer came—but a black object came flying, zooming, no smoke came out! I said, 'Shipi, look!' It was round. He saw it; I saw it. Then it passed—it disappeared.

"Now we landed in Amsterdam. I went to the captain and asked him if there was any object flying to the right of the plane fifteen minutes out of New York. He said, 'No.' I said, 'Please listen to me,' and asked him again, just to be sure. This was a proof to me that they cling to every thought of mine! I tell everyone I was born with these powers, but I wasn't born with them. No. What happened to me was when I was three years old. Andrija, I am doing the right thing, okay? Then I realized I had these powers. They were given to me then."

Puthoff asked, "A very specific event?"

"Yes," said Uri. "I won't talk about it. I'll never forget it. But I didn't really know it until I met Andrija. Before that I was always trying to prove it and to figure it out. There were times when I thought I was going mad with my powers. Sometimes I revolted against myself. Are you with me?"

Everyone nodded assent.

Uri went on, "Why? For what? Things—one thing is going to happen for sure. Then people will know we are not mad."

"Do you know when the event will happen?" Dr. Puthoff asked.

"In a few years," Uri replied. "It will happen. Things are going badly."

Suddenly a copper ring fell to the floor, under the table around which we were sitting.

"Where did that ring come flying from?" asked Targ.

"I thought it was underneath the table," said Dr. Franklin.

Uri said, "No, it was right there by Hal Puthoff."

"It was, a little while ago," said Captain Mitchell. "It fell right by my toe, underneath the table—I felt the impact!"

Uri took me aside and said, "Am I blabbering off my mouth? Am I saying the right things?"

"Uri, I feel that you are saying exactly what you are permitted to say. The bell going off and the ring going through the table convinced me. I'll give you more support from now on."

We returned to the table around which we had been sitting. Uri said he wanted one more sign. He asked if he could hold Hal Puthoff's silver chain bracelet in his hand. Then he requested Hal to hold the bracelet in his own hand. Uri concentrated for a few seconds. The chain broke in two. Inspection proved that one of the heavy links had vanished. Dr. Puthoff was the first to observe that the copper ring had now assumed the shape of the mathematical symbol for infinity.

By 9 P.M. we had been together for six intense hours. We had met with the purpose of bringing about an amicable divorce, and now we were reaching a point where a scientific enterprise seemed about to be born. There was a relaxed, expectant atmosphere in the room.

Russell Targ reiterated what Captain Mitchell had said before our meeting began. "What we are doing here could be as important as *Sputnik*."

Captain Mitchell said, "Uri, however much you may feel you have been directed, I feel we have all been directed. We have all converged."

"Let's go higher," said Uri. "Andrija, Shipi, and I know. I am at the head, a generator—they are batteries. All that is happening has one reason: education—they are preparing us for something. Everything they do is an education for us. Flowers bloom from a bud in a second in my hand. Things disappear. This is the difficult part. But we do not talk about these things. People get fearful."

Uri paused for a long time before continuing. "First of all, when I got here today, I thought I couldn't tell you anything. Now I feel everything is open and possible. Then the forces we deal with seem funny at times; they joke and I think they are not serious. This is hard for me to understand. Then they are not consistent; they seem to change their minds. Sometimes Andrija and I think that they are playing jokes with us.

"Now, how did I get out of Israel? I was about twenty miles out of Tel Aviv. There was Shipi, me, Andrija, and two girls. We were trying out a new walkie-talkie. It was February 11 of this year. They said, 'We're over West Germany now—things don't look so good down there!' That was all. That afternoon Andrija received a phone call in which a voice said, 'Spacemen over West Germany.' The next day I ran into a singer friend who said her manager in Germany would like to have me work in Germany. Then we got orders from these beings to go to Germany when an airline ticket materialized for me. Andrija found the man in Germany to manage me. I was there for five months, and nothing really happened there. I felt I was being used there all the time by them, but I never knew the reason. They are somehow using our energy for their use. We are being used somehow. Sometimes I have the worst headaches—and I am not doing anything, just resting. But that's not it. Then the work was finished, and I had to go to America. That's why I think they are changing their minds."

"Did you ever think that it may have been just to get you out of Israel?" asked Captain Mitchell.

"Well, they tell us; don't ask us how they tell us. Andrija knows that my powers had to be validated. He had an idea it should be done through science. Then there was a movie to be done on me. And boy, I like the idea of doing a movie about me. That's great. Melanie worked for three months on a movie script. It was a beautiful script. Then cut—they suddenly said, 'No movie.' I was crushed. Andrija and Melanie were disappointed.

"They don't have feelings, but they control my feelings. They put us through heavy tests all the time. I suppose you are all being tested. I guess we must be purified. Sometimes these tests have to do with women—you go way down in your feelings. Then you pass and you go high. Once we were in debt and we asked for money—all we got were things falling from the roof on our heads. I hope you all remember what we are hearing. The earth people—if they are put together in masses—are building an energy that they use. I know how it was in Israel. When I performed, you could hear a pin drop. I could feel something was happening to people, an energy was being used. I don't know what they want from me now. They are jumping from one thing to the other. I have to follow it—I can't say no. I like adventures, but sometimes this tires me."

"I could tell you a series of events that is analogous to what you are talking about," said Captain Mitchell. "The effort I have been putting together in research has had the same ups and downs as you're describing. And for absolutely no reason, about six or seven times in the last three months my efforts would go counter to any rational outcome."

Uri went on, "In the past few months, hundreds of strange things have been done by the powers. When I got to Germany, I got instructions on a tape, from a clear slow-motion voice, but it was a mechanical voice. After we heard the tape, it vanished before our eyes. They use every known communication means to reach us. I was supposed to contact a certain man by these instructions in Hamburg. The next day I got a show in Hamburg. A man came up to me and said, 'I'm Werner Schmid, you flipped me. I wrote a musical about a man just like you. I need you.' It got so serious that Andrija had to come to Germany. For Schmid, I was getting signs forty to fifty times a day, things like objects appearing, a flower bud blooming in my hand, and so on."

"How do you know that wasn't just a man, a lot of coincidences, and not those powers?" asked Mitchell. "It may not be as 'directed' as you think."

"Well, I check it. I took a spoon in my hand and asked it to bend and melt in my hand, if he is the right man. I did it and it bent. That's the only way I can be sure it's not a coincidence. I know one thing that bothers me right now. Why am I not allowed to validate myself by science?"

Of course, nobody but Uri and I fully understood what was meant by this question. As soon as Uri raised this question, my trusty TC 120 tape recorder stopped running. The cassette would not turn. A few minutes later it began to run all by itself, without my doing anything.

Russell responded to Uri's question. "I thought the signs were very positive earlier when you were asking questions."

"I think there is a difference between his showing you what he can do, and being publicly and scientifically validated," I tried to explain.

"But he did that in Germany before large crowds, did he not?" asked Dr. Franklin.

"Yes, but that's show business," I said.

"We couldn't have a better situation for experimentation than at SRI," said Dr. Puthoff.

Dr. Franklin said, "You know everybody I have met who is in charge here at SRI has Promethean views. Do you know what I mean by that?"

"No, what does Promethean mean?" asked Uri.

Dr. Franklin replied, "Prometheus brought fire from Zeus. He brought fire from the gods to man."

"Uri, let me explain," I interjected. "The gods had fire, and this fellow Prometheus said, 'Look, man is cold. He could use fire. How come you don't give it to him?' They said no. He went ahead and stole the fire in order to help man. The gods got angry and punished Prometheus by hanging him on the side of a mountain in the Caucasus. And every day a big vulture would come and eat out a piece of his liver. He would recover, the vulture then would eat more. They would not let him die, and they would not let him live. This means that a man who sticks up for his ideas, in spite of what the gods say, takes a beating."

Russell said, "Well, Gary Feinberg wrote a book called *The Prometheus Project* in which he says that psychical effects may be pivotal in our understanding of man."

Uri went on. "You see, those computers form a network that monitors the universe. These collect into centers which control those below. Then those are under the control of still higher powers."

Hal Puthoff said, "I've heard Andrija describe your powers of making things disappear. Suppose only half an object disappears. Can you use that as a tracer into another dimension?"

Uri replied, "I never tried that. Things have never happened halfway like that; it's all or nothing. But I know one thing—there is one place where there is a hole, and I must find the place. And if I find that place, then I am in a different world. There is someplace a leak, a hole I can slip through. But they have not showed it to me yet. I don't have to walk to it; I can bring it to me and go through it. Even if my body remains here. But my body might also disappear. I am afraid of that; I could disappear from here."

Captain Mitchell said amusedly, "We were going to ask you to do it to one of us."

Uri hastened to reply, "I am not allowed to do this to anyone else! I wouldn't do it to you. For us it would be a loss; for them it wouldn't. Listen, when I went, and it happened to me only twice in my life. Listen to what happened. The first time, we were in Israel. I was driving the car, and Andrija was giving the instructions where to go. And my girl friend was with me. Andrija doesn't know Tel Aviv, and he was telling me to go out of Tel Aviv. 'Where?' I said. 'Drive,' he said. We were going out to the suburbs about fifteen kilometers. He said, 'Stop!' I stopped near a field. We went in; some force was pulling us to the center of the field. I think there was a moon, because it seemed so bright."

Uri's voice dropped to a hushed whisper, as we hung on his words: "First we followed a sound, like the sound of crickets.

There at the end of the field we saw a light shining, bluish, like a strobe light, about forty-five meters away. Andrija had his camera and he started shooting. So I went ahead. I was drawn to the thing. I remember everything until I got near it. I don't remember the shape, believe me. All I remember was that something was handed to me. Then I went back. I was completely in a trance. I handed something to Andrija; it was a ball-point pen that had disappeared a few days earlier under controlled conditions. That's the first time I ever lost time—from my earth time. Andrija, what happened to the camera—would you finish that?"

"I shot the roll of film," I said. "It vanished out of the camera."

"The biggest experience of my life, though, was the day before yesterday—was it? It was at the top of Andrija's depression about the research. It was something terrible! It was something awful! Andrija, Shipi, Melanie, and I were all in the kitchen. You've got to bring them to the point where it happened to me, Andrija!"

I said, "Well, I had a dispute with the friends he's talking about. I was challenging them, I suppose."

"Was that your idea—or did somebody else say that?" asked Russell.

"I was shocked how Andrija was talking to them," said Uri.

"It was my idea," I said. "Uri was afraid I'd vanish any instant. Then Uri jumped up, saying, 'You're wrong!' and hurled a sugar bowl at me which missed. In two seconds he sat down."

"In two seconds—three seconds— I was gone, an hour to me!" said Uri. "I know what's time. But I vanished from there. Of course, they saw my body. It was the first time that Andrija shouted at these beings. I'm still shook up from what happened. In those two seconds I was gone for one hour. Shipi was on my left side; Andrija was on my right. We were walking in a long corridor for half an hour. Nobody can wipe that out from my mind. There were yellow lights all around. It was so real—in these shoes. It was so real, I haven't been able to sleep since then. I entered a round room, through a door, like a light going up. The three of us were there. There was a purple light going

The Battle for the Truth

around the room from a slit. We went downstairs, and there were three couches there. We sat down, and the couch thing went back. I have marks on my hands from the two knobs. My head went back, then a thing came down before us like a screen with some orange lights. Then a voice came, a mechanical voice, and it said, 'It's only the beginning. It's only the beginning.' It went on and on."

"In English?" asked Russell.

"Yes, in English. When I came to, my hand was still in the air from throwing the sugar bowl. For me, it was an hour. They said it was two or three seconds."

"What did you say was on your hands?" asked Russ.

"I touched two balls—which were on the arm rests of the couch. I told this to Andrija. There were two round patches on my palms, with three notches on each round patch."

"When you were walking with Andrija and Shipi, did you talk?" asked Dr. Franklin.

"No," replied Uri. "But everything that happened is as clear as I am in this room with you."

"Did it seem like a strange or dangerous place to you?" asked Russell.

"No," replied Uri. "It seemed like a peculiar place. What bothered me was the walk—the long, long walk. I hate walking. This was not a dream. This was real."

"Uri, what do you make of all this?" asked Russell.

"When I came back? It feels like I came back from another dimension."

"It sounds to me like you had an out-of-the-body experience," said Russell. "Some of what you experience depends on what you expect."

"Listen, there's one thing here that divides us. Someone made me do this!" said Uri.

"Uri, something you haven't told us—when we have signs tonight, what makes you think you should not undertake a validation?" asked Russell.

"Because I still know it. I'm not fighting them. They still tell me no," replied Uri. "Here is why I think this is going on. It happened to me in Israel. They don't want me in a laboratory. I don't know why."

"Well, we're not going to ask Uri to do anything in the lab that he has not done here tonight," commented Dr. Puthoff.

I stated quietly, "I think other places and other people who could have validated Uri were 'edited' out. They were not the right people. What is important here is to build up a community of fellowship and interest first. Then the validation will follow naturally. Maybe the major event that is coming has something to do with it."

Uri asked the scientists, "What is validation for you?"

"For us, it is having a clear Plexiglas table on which you do your things. The camera shoots what you do. That's validation," replied Dr. Puthoff.

"Let's say I do it—tomorrow," said Uri. "And the camera shoots. And all of you saw it, one, two, three, four, five people. You are sure you saw a ring bend. Then nothing comes on the film. You have a fact. Then what would you do? You have a broken ring."

Russell replied, "I don't believe that would happen."

"I would consider that a significant experiment," said Dr. Puthoff.

Russell pursued the question; "I cannot imagine the camera wouldn't run."

"The camera may run, but it will pick nothing up," said Uri.

"Then I think you're right," said Russell firmly. "We're not ready to validate it if that should happen."

"But there are other things we could do. We can set up a laser beam, shine it on the wall," said Dr. Puthoff. "You could try to bend the light."

"That's easy to describe," said Russell gravely. "But that would be an earthshaking event. I don't know whether you realize that."

"Everything Uri does is an earthshaking event," added Captain Mitchell.

"You have seen about five such events here tonight," I said. "What we must try to do is to understand Uri and accept what he says as true until proven otherwise. We should work, but be sensitive to timing in the world at large. Then we may make it."

Everyone chimed in, "Oh, we'll make it."

Russell added, "We'll encounter obstacles beyond belief—but we'll do it."

Captain Mitchell added, "We'll be successful."

Uri added, "If I do it, I'll only do it one time. But maybe they'll change and let me do it."

"Could you remember any former lifetimes?" asked Dr. Puthoff.

"No," replied Uri.

"How about in-between lifetime periods?" he persisted.

"No," replied Uri.

"Are you a religious person?" asked Russell.

"Well, I believe in God," said Uri. Then, as an afterthought, he said, "What happens if nothing shows on the film?"

"We have a world-famous cameraman, so that's not likely to be the case," said Russell. "His name is Zev Pressman."

"Let's try to figure out what to do tomorrow," requested Dr. Puthoff.

Russell said, "Why don't we look at the lab briefly in the morning. Since it is Sunday, why don't we go to Santa Cruz—the beach, horses, the amusement park?"

Uri suddenly shouted, "Look, I picked up this spoon, and it snapped off." Everyone inspected the new specimen. Then all discussion stopped while a log was made of these and other unusual events of the evening.

By midnight an unusual rapport and camaraderie had been firmly implanted in this group. But in spite of the many signs that had occurred, Uri still felt he would not be permitted to work in the laboratory at Stanford Research Institute. In spite of his feeling, everyone else was optimistic not only that this was the right group of scientists but that Uri was right for them.

I went to bed that night with the prayer on my lips and in my heart that wisdom would prevail.

Sunday, November 12, was a day of relaxation. We drove toward the Santa Cruz beach on Highway 17. Hal Puthoff was driving; next to him was Adrian Kennedy, his girl friend. Uri, Shipi, and I were in the back seat. Uri asked Hal if he had one of those machined laboratory rings with him. Hal said, "I'm always ready for research. I just happen to have a few in my pocket."

Uri said to him, "Take one out. Look at its number and place it in my hand. Now put your hand over my clenched fist." Uri then said, "I have an empty feeling in my hand!" Uri slowly opened his fist, palm up. As he did so it was evident that his hand was empty. The ring had vanished! For some time we drove along in silence.

After an afternoon at the beach, we returned to Hal Puthoff's apartment. The car was parked at a lower level of the apartment complex in Mountain View, California. Hal led the way up the stairs, which were surrounded by trees and shrubbery. At 6:36 P.M. the brass ring that had vanished some hours earlier fell out of the air in front of him, on the stone steps. Dr. Puthoff was profoundly moved as he grasped what this small event meant for the picture that scientists had developed of physical reality—it would, quite simply, have to be revised. When the scientific crew assembled that evening for dinner, we had an exciting hour-long discussion about this remarkable event. No one questioned its genuineness, but everyone knew that this event could not be used for scientific proof. The event would have to be repeated under the controlled conditions of the laboratory—and replicated many times.

The next day was Monday, November 13. Uri cautiously began to feel his way into laboratory work, knowing full well that he had received no mandate to go ahead. His first test was on a laboratory instrument called a magnetometer, which measures the strength of magnetic fields. As he concentrated on this instrument, he was the most surprised person in the laboratory when the needle deflected, indicating that his mind had simulated the same effect that a magnetic field would produce. The test was repeated many times. There was no question in anybody's mind: Uri could create effects on the magnetometer that were impossible, according to science. However, we observed

The Battle for the Truth 217

that Uri had to make an excruciating effort to simulate this "mental magnetic field."

On the next day, Tuesday, November 14, an effort was made at SRI to see if the deformation—or vanishing—of a metal ring could be documented. To do this, an elaborate recording apparatus was used, called acoustic holography. This means that one of the scientists held a bonded metal ring underwater. Uri touched this ring with one finger. The entire procedure was scanned by sound waves which made a picture similar to an X-ray picture showing the bones of the hands and the metal ring. The test was such that this "acoustic X-ray" picture was monitored on a television screen and videotaped. This was considered a "cheat-proof" method of validating whatever effects Uri produced on the ring. As Uri concentrated on this test, he exerted great effort, as he had with the magnetometer. As he did so, it was observed that Uri also affected the video tape recording and the image on the television screen. These two records showed a distortion of the TV screen image related to Uri's exertions. In addition it was seen that the brass ring was being flattened by Uri's "mind power."

As this experiment was being run for several hours, the scientists on the floor below Uri were having great problems. On this floor was located a bank of computers that belonged to the Advanced Research Projects Agency (ARPA) of the United States Department of Defense. One of these computers began to perform so badly on Monday, November 13, and Tuesday, November 14, at those hours during which Uri was working, that it began to be useless. As the word spread through SRI about Uri's mental power over the magnetometer, the metal rings, and video recording systems, somebody got the idea that the computer malfunction might be caused by Uri. However, there was no proof that this was the case.

My chief concern at this time was whether or not Uri would continue to work at the laboratory. All the signs seemed to indicate that he was being given all power and support. But my tape recorder did not give me any clear text assurance that there had been any change in policy.

Finally on November 15, as Uri and I were resting from the day's work at our apartment, my tape recorder started to run, and the following brief message was recorded:

One more test to do tomorrow, then it is finished in the laboratory. Start writing a book on Uri immediately. The rotational energy that we use is on a galactic scale and we use it from outside the galaxy. It does not exist on the particle level. Farewell.

I discussed this instruction with Uri. He felt that since things were going so well in the laboratory he would go on working until no more effects occurred. I agreed to this idea of gradual disengagement. However, I had pressing business back East, and I left Uri and Shipi at SRI and returned home on November 16.

I would hear from Uri each day from California, and each day he continued the laboratory testing successfully. He was still amazed that he had been allowed to continue to work in this scientific laboratory.

On November 18 Uri remembered that he still had the film in the Nikon F camera, which he had shot over Germany on November 4. He got special processing of the film just in case there was a UFO picture. When the film was returned, the Kodacolor prints—five of them—showed UFOs on them.

Uri called me up in great excitement about these photos, which he said, Hal Puthoff was then examining. I begged him to get the negatives and the prints from Hal as soon as possible. He said he would do this immediately. Hal told Uri that he had the negatives and the prints at home. When Hal looked for them, they were all gone except one print showing three UFOs, which I still have in my possession. How the negatives and prints disappeared, no one knows. It was a great loss of data.

Uri went on working, saying each day that this was his last day of laboratory research.

This day-to-day procedure was also hard on the SRI researchers, who found it difficult to make plans for extended studies with Uri.

On December 1, I received disturbing news from Uri by

The Battle for the Truth

phone. It seemed that the computer bank of ARPA was giving more and more problems when Uri was working in the laboratory.

Certain investigators from Washington, led by George Lawrence, of ARPA, deliberately started the rumor that Uri was a charlatan who had deceived the SRI research staff into believing he had genuine powers. This rumor came to John Wilhelm, of *Time* magazine, in Los Angeles, and he initiated a reportorial investigation.

I heard from two sources in San Francisco that laboratory reports of the Geller experiments had been stolen from SRI and offered for sale to Charles Peets, of the San Francisco *Chronicle*, and to James Bolen, of *Psychic* magazine.[1] Some idea of the rumors circulating at this time is given in a quote from a letter report written by one of the ARPA investigators, Dr. Ray Hyman, professor of psychology, University of Oregon, dated December 28, 1972. Hyman said that the story of Geller was not yet over, and that since he had come back from SRI, he had talked with a high official on the phone to give his report. The official told him that new information had come in about Geller, but that he could not tell him about it because it was "too complex." Hyman thought he meant it was too complicated to talk about on the phone. No, he meant it was complex in the sense that it was highly sensitive and must be kept secret. Hyman got the impression that the new information was embarrassing to certain important individuals and had to be kept confidential.

The true fact is that the new information which "must be kept secret" is that the researchers proved that Uri could concentrate on a video tape record and wipe it out or distort it.

Uri completed his work at SRI in the middle of December 1972 and returned to Ossining. We compared notes as to his experiences at SRI and the rumors that had come to me. There was no question in our minds that we were caught in a national

---

[1] James Bolen, as publisher and editor of *Psychic* magazine, refused to buy these purloined documents. Bolen was also the first person to capture on motion-picture film Uri's bending and breaking of a fork. See *Psychic*, June 1973 cover story.

security issue in the United States, as we had been in Israel a year before. We had no idea why IS had created this situation. Uri told me that he had had no intention, consciously or unconsciously, of affecting any instruments other than those he was concentrating on in an experiment. Now there were two governments in the world who had become alerted to Uri's powers—why? Both Uri and I were as much in the dark about the purpose of IS as were the officials in the U. S. Defense Department. There was nothing we could do but sit and wait for further developments.

On December 18 Uri, Shipi, and I were sitting around the dining room table after dinner. I was telling a story about the solar system and some of its movements. Uri was deeply interested in what I told him, especially when I dramatized the vast distances that exist in our galaxy, and between it and other galaxies.

We retired to the living room to watch an 8 P.M. television show. I walked up to the TV set to turn it on. As I backed away from the screen, my heel hit something on the floor which had not been there a moment before. I looked down, and there was a drinking glass made from a 7Up bottle. My daughter Illyria had made it for me. I knew that this glass had been in the kitchen after dinner, and now it had been transported here. This was a sign to get the tape recorder, which I did, and I placed it on a table near me; it was in the off condition. I knew that if there was a message, the recorder would be turned on by the power of IS. Then I sat down by the fireplace some ten feet from the TV set to watch the show.

In a few minutes I had to get up from my chair to adjust the color on the screen. I walked across the empty carpet to the set, tuned it, and backed away, checking the image on the screen. My foot bumped into an object. I looked down. It was a twelve-inch globe of the earth, which moments earlier had been in my study upstairs on the second floor. Uri and Shipi had not seen the globe appear—it was suddenly there! Uri began to feel uneasy and said he felt that a UFO was near. We went to a large bay window looking west into a clear sky. We saw a single red light in the sky but could not be sure that it was a spacecraft. Then we heard the tape recorder being switched on behind us. This is what appeared on the tape, in a mechanical computer voice:

Andrija Puharich, we heard your talk at the dinner table. You are right. The human mind is too small to grasp the immensity of the cosmos. You cannot know its secret. Andrija Puharich, at your insistence we completed the experiments. You were under test for your loyalty then, and you passed. Now you are under test again. You are on the right track with your ideas about how to present Uri. But our computors will always be with you. Uri will always be prepared to answer your questions with our advice. We leave you now. Farewell."

Uri, Shipi, and I discussed the meaning of those words. This was the first comment we had received on the scientific experiments since November 15, and it was gratifying. I personally felt the weight of this new test mentioned by IS, especially since, as always, I did not know what the test was and had to rely purely on my inner sense of the truth. The loyalty referred to above was, I think, my loyalty to Uri and to the welfare of man.

The globe was still on the floor where it had appeared. At 9:25 P.M. we were talking about it, trying to figure out its symbolic meaning, when it suddenly vanished. We started a search of the house to find out where it had gone. We found it on the dining room table, placed exactly in the center as measured with a ruler. Alongside it had appeared a German five-pfenning coin.

That evening I began to suffer a headache and extreme fatigue. I did not know whether I was getting a case of the flu or whether this had something to do with the test. This became a kind of nameless agony without content for me. It hung on to me by day and by night for three days. I must confess that all I could do was to pray for help through this crisis of the soul.

Finally, on December 21 relief came. Uri and I were sitting in the kitchen having a cup of coffee and comparing notes on the aches and pains we had both been experiencing since the evening of December 18. At 2:57 P.M. Uri got up without saying a word. He looked strange to me. I asked him if he felt all right. He said not a word but marched off to the sitting room. I hastily got my tape recorder and followed him. He sat quietly facing north. I placed the tape recorder on the coffee table and waited. At 3 P.M. it switched on, and I placed the monitor earphone in my ear. This is what I heard:

Andrija Puharich, in the past twenty-four hours you have passed the test successfully. This is the last time ever in your life that you will have to be tested.

AP: "Please, tell me what the test was."

The test had to do with the control of your mind—and it was successful.

AP: "Is that why I have felt so exhausted not only during the past twenty-four hours but for the past two weeks?"

Yes, that is the reason. You are on your own now. Use your brain. Use your ideas. Be clever. We will be in touch with you more readily now. Farewell.

I looked at Uri. He was still sitting in deep meditation. He did not seem to be aware of me. I transcribed this short segment of tape. I could scarcely bear to wipe out the message on the tape, but I had no other choice. What can a man say after he has heard such words? I observed that this taping was not preceded before or after by a physical sign, as in the past. Uri's behavior was like that of a Praetorian guard; this time it was not as if his actions were meant to be a sign. I entered into Uri's silence by bowing my head and my will before the Ruler of the Cosmos. Not only had my transgression been forgiven, but I had been blessed.

A new phase of communication seemed to open up on the next day because I was allowed to ask questions, and got answers, however cryptic:

AP: "I need information about what you did at Stanford Research Institute and its purpose."

After you insisted that Uri be validated, counsel was taken higher and higher, and it was decided that Uri could be validated

The Battle for the Truth

just this once. And he may never be allowed to do such work again under laboratory control.

AP: "I need advice as to how much I am allowed to tell people about Uri's work on earth."

You must tell the world everything about us. Tell how the information comes through all sources—tape is a good example.

AP: "I need to know more about the history of your role in earth life if I am to be effective."

You are close to the answer in all that you are thinking. You must tell the world what you deduce to be right. But we cannot tell you all of our secret history.

More fragments of information appeared on January 12 while Uri and I were driving in my car south on Lexington Avenue in New York City. The time was about 11:30 P.M. when the tape recorder was actuated invisibly:

Andrija Puharich, you are free for two years to make all moves and decisions on earth. You are no longer under test. But we also need the brain of Uri, Shipi, and you to help us with many other civilizations in space.

AP: "Can you tell me roughly what the goals are for the year 1973?"

We cannot forecast for you.

AP: "I do need more help about your history."

We cannot reveal our history yet to you.

AP: "Are there other civilizations in our galaxy?"

Yes, within this car there could be twenty hundred thousand civilizations in an inner space. There are untold millions of civilizations in the galaxy. You cannot possibly understand all this.

AP: "But do any of them interact? Or are they sealed each in his own compartment?"

A few do interact. Write the book. The Knowledge Book will not be given in the next two years unless our computors change. Farewell.

While these bits of instruction were coming in, there was a great deal of trouble brewing around us. The tapping of our telephone in Ossining was extended, it was reported, to our friends and colleagues in New York City. We were being followed everywhere. *Time* magazine was increasing its interest in the SRI work with Uri. John Wilhelm, of *Time*, called from Los Angeles to tell me that he had obtained a copy of a report by George Lawrence, of ARPA, in which Lawrence was trying to discredit both SRI and Uri. Wilhelm was unable to get information from SRI—they had refused to talk to him, so he asked to come East to see me and Uri in New York. I told him that I had given my word to SRI not to talk about the research but that Uri and I would be prepared to talk to him on a personal level.

John Wilhelm arrived at my home in Ossining on the morning of January 18, 1973. We learned from him for the first time of the vicious nature of the accusations being circulated against Uri and SRI. It appeared that ARPA personnel were making every effort to discredit the scientists—Mitchell, Targ, and Puthoff personally—in order to discredit Uri. Wilhelm said he was trying to get at the facts but SRI would not reveal any. He found that his people at *Time* had already concluded that Uri was a fraud. In fact, he said, Senior Editor Leon Jaroff had already bet him a blue German folding bicycle that Uri Geller was a charlatan and a fraud.

John Wilhelm spent twelve hours talking to Uri and witnessing a few small demonstrations of his powers. He was perspicacious, fair, open-minded, and persevering in his interview. When he finished his interview, he told us that he accepted what he had seen, and was willing to continue to examine Uri's work objectively. But he commented that no one would accept his findings at the headquarters of *Time* magazine. Since John was so open to Uri, Uri opened up to him and revealed that his powers were due to the presence of an extraterrestrial civilization. John reminded us of the cover story he had done a year before for *Time* on extraterrestrial life and of his deep interest. He said that if we ever had proof for this claim, he would like to be the one to report it to the world, but he would need overwhelming proof for such a historical event. We told him that we had no way of knowing if proof would be allowed. We did not explain

The Battle for the Truth

that there was still a contingency as to whether man would be allowed to know of, and view the landings. I believe that we honestly revealed to this good man all that we were permitted to say and that he was free to report whatever he felt able to tell his people. He was quite frank in telling us that he would not yet dare to report to his editors about the powers behind Uri. He left us that evening and caught an 11:36 P.M. train back to New York City. I drove him to the station in Ossining, and when I returned home, I found a most unusual thing at the foot of the outside stairs to my house. It was my large Farquhar clear plastic astronomical globe. It had been last seen in my upstairs study. I took the globe indoors to inspect it. Now, I must explain the construction of this globe. There was a large clear plastic outer globe with the stars on it. Inside was a smaller one of the earth, also of clear plastic. Inside of this sealed earth globe was a foreign object, which had never been there before. It was a piece of my own printed medical stationery. On it was typed a message—and the type was the same as that of my Selectric IBM typewriter. I could read the message through the two plastic globes. It said:

    YOU ARE ALL ALONE NOW
    ALL OF YOU FOR A LONG TIME
                S

I called Uri and Shipi. We read this letter sealed inside of the globe. There was no way to get it out. The message depressed us. What did it mean? It was true that I had been told that I was to make all judgments and decisions on my own for two years. But that had already been said. Why was a new message being sent? It even occurred to us that Uri's major powers might be withdrawn. This discussion went on and on, and we became more and more depressed.

On January 21 Solveig Clark and I were taking a walk along the nearby Highway 9A with Wellington. Wellington suddenly stepped in front of a car and was mortally wounded. I held him in my arms, and he looked at me with astonishment, as he died.

I had lost my friend; but somehow I knew this was meant to be. However, it was not a good omen, with all the storm that was brewing around us.

Hal Puthoff and Russ Targ arrived in Ossining on January 27 to show us the movie film they had made of the experiments with Uri. They told us that the management of SRI had decided to stand firm, to back Hal and Russ, and to make a public announcement backing their findings with Uri. This was heartwarming news for us.

On February 2 we were driving from New York City toward Ossining at noon on the New York State Thruway in a driving rainstorm; as we were turning into Exit 7A at Elmsford, New York, we both saw a welcome sight. There, some thirty feet in front of and above our car, was Horus. He was fluttering in the rain and air, hovering over us so that we could see him. I slammed the car to a skidding halt. Horus glided to a nearby dead tree, landed, and looked down upon us from his imperial height. How happy Uri and I were to see him, after a whole year! We looked at Horus for some ten minutes, then he glided silently down into the woods and vanished. Uri and I looked at each other; we both knew the meaning of Horus's appearance. We were in danger again! But we were also protected.

When we got to the house, Uri and I sat in my study to discuss our situation. The tape recorder started to run. But this time there was no message. The tape recorder ran on and on, blank. Then a letter appeared on top of the tape recorder. I picked up the letter. It was dated 1949, with no month or day. It was from my departed friend, Dr. Eugene Milne Cosgrove. The letter was still in its original envelope addressed to me in Camden, Maine, with the stamp of that vintage on it. I read the letter; it was most poignant. Dr. Cosgrove was describing to me the nameless terror that struck him when he realized he had just suffered a heart attack while alone in Flat Head, Montana. I remembered having recieved this letter some twenty-four years before, but I had not seen it since. Where had it come from? With Horus on the scene, and this acute reminder of the nameless terror of impending death, what was in store for us?

The next day I received a phone call from Charles Reynolds, who represented himself as a photographer for *Time* magazine. He said he wanted to meet with Uri. I put him off until I could check his credentials. I found out that he was a magician and a free-lance photographer. He was part of a *Time* cabal to lure Uri into a confrontation with magicians in an attempt to discredit him. I talked the problem over with Uri. I advised him that every indication I had showed me that a lynch was in the offing. I even suspected that someone at *Time* was being pressured to do a hatchet job on Uri and myself. Uri decided to go ahead and demonstrate for *Time*, and that no matter what happened, it had to be for the best. I called Charles Reynolds back and made a date to have the *Time* staff meet Uri on Tuesday, February 6, 1973.

We met in the offices of John Derniak. Present on behalf of *Time* were editors Fred Golden and Leon Jaroff, magicians Charles Reynolds and James Randi, photographer Peter Basch, some secretaries, and Uri and I. I opened the meeting by stating emphatically that Uri was not a magician and had submitted his claims to science for judgment. One of the magicians immediately made the statement that Uri was known to be a magician, based on material in "our Geller File." Uri explained that he was not a magician; that he had appeared in Israel and Germany in stage shows where magicians had performed; and that his powers of telepathy and psychokinesis were real. One of the *Time* editors informed us that everything was being taped; we consented.

The atmosphere was that of a kangaroo court. Uri was damned if he refused to demonstrate and damned if he did demonstrate; he chose to run the gauntlet and demonstrate. He asked me to leave the room so that the charge of collusion would be eliminated. I did not observe what Uri did for these people, so my report is secondhand. Uri was annoyed by the hostile atmosphere and made a slow start with a telepathy demonstration, but he did eventually succeed. The magicians said they could *duplicate* this "trick." Then Uri bent a fork by lightly stroking it. The magicians said they could duplicate this "trick" by using sleight of hand and misdirection. Then Charles Reynolds offered his own apartment key to be bent. Uri bent it by concentration, and it continued to bend after it left his hands. No one said a word about this "trick," and it has never been mentioned to this day by the editors of *Time* or by the magicians. A secretary from *Time* called us later that day to tell us that the key had gone on bending by itself after we left.

Uri was in deep gloom as we left the offices of *Time*. Now he felt the full weight of the lynch that was being organized against him in the United States. We also found out that the *Time* correspondent in Jerusalem had filed a report on Uri which said that scientists from Hebrew University claimed they had caught him cheating. This, too, proved to be a lie, but it suited the policy of the editors of *Time*.

Since the war was clearly on, I had to mobilize my forces. My goal was simple—to keep the human race from talking itself into a "crucifixion" state of mind. I officially informed the editors of *Time* that Uri's powers were real and that science would affirm this in due time. I organized a group of prominent citizens who believed in Uri's powers to act as an Operations Group. The Operations Group was to raise funds for research, keep in touch with media executives at newspapers, magazines, television, etc., and spread the word among leaders in American society that a major issue was in the making. The Operations Group consisted of Judy Skutch, John Tishman, John Douglas, Stewart Mott, Maria Janis, Byron Janis, Ruth Hagy Brod, and others. One of the first tasks of this group was to counter whatever *Time* did. The editors of *Newsweek* were approached, and they assigned Charles Panatti to do a Geller story. After several weeks of work Panatti turned in to the editors of *Newsweek* a favorable story about Uri. [This story has still not been published at the time of this writing.]

I activated the Scientific Theory Group that had been in existence since the Life Energies Conference of 1970. They were apprised of the pressure being built up by the editors of *Time*. They knew that the scientific stakes were high—just as high as they were when Copernicus startled the medieval Church of

Europe with his findings about the earth and the sun. The influence of this group was enormous in the councils of state; they gave authoritative assurance to the National Science Foundation that Uri's powers were real and that scientists had best keep open minds. Another member, Dr. Gerald Feinberg, invited Targ and Puthoff to dispassionately present their findings on Geller at a Physics Department Colloquium at Columbia University on March 9, 1973.

In the meantime *Time* magazine had requested the results of the SRI research. Leon Jaroff of *Time* told the president of SRI that if SRI did not give them a report on their findings with Geller, *Time* would go ahead with an unfavorable story about both SRI and Geller. The president of SRI said that *Time* would have to wait, like everyone else, for the report on their findings, to be given on March 9, 1973, at Columbia University. Neither man would budge from his position. For me the last few days before the final showdown were packed with action.

On Sunday, February 25, at 7 P.M., I handed Uri a Mexican five-peso silver coin that weighed thirty grams. This was the same one reported on in Israel. I asked him to bend it in his left hand. As he clenched it in his fist, it vanished. We talked about what IS might do with the coin, and I suggested that it be made into a "thought transmitter" and returned to us. At 8:30 P.M. a 1925 silver dollar fell by my right foot. I examined this coin and it turned out to be a silver dollar given to me by Henry Jackson in 1948 as a token with which to start the Round Table Foundation. It had been in storage in a jewelry case in my bedroom on the second floor. However, the silver dollar had been bent by means unknown since I had last seen it.

At 9 P.M. the phone rang and Uri got up to answer it, crossing in front of me. As he went past me, a coin fell from the direction of the ceiling, hit his shoulder, and fell at my feet. It was the Mexican five-peso silver coin—but now it too was bent.

On Tuesday, February 27, Uri and I went to Philadelphia for a meeting at the home of Arthur Young with the chairman of the Scientific Theory Group, Dr. Ted Bastin, of Cambridge University. Dr. Bastin was most impressed with the genuineness of Uri's powers; the Scientific Theory Group was now fully prepared to back Uri.

We returned to New York on February 28 when we received the latest "news" from our friend Judy Skutch. She had found out that *Time* had decided openly to attack SRI and Uri, based on reports they had received from George Lawrence, of ARPA; Ray Hyman, of the University of Oregon; Martin Gardner, of *Scientific American*; the magicians; and others. Leon Jaroff was to write the *Time* story. John Wilhelm called me up to say that he disagreed with the policy of the *Time* editors and he was publicly dissociating himself from it. *Newsweek* had said it would eventually run a story defending Uri. SRI had made a decision to make a press release for Saturday, March 10, 1973. Reports from Israel told us that Leon Jaroff was relying on reports he had from Jerusalem for the main thrust of his attack. We now had to consider the possibility that the Israelis were involved in all this plotting; but for this suspicion we had no evidence.

I had been scheduled for many months to give a speech at the University of California at Berkeley. I was to speak before some fifteen hundred students about recent advances in parapsychological research. I was thinking seriously about using this as a platform for a public rebuttal to the charges of *Time*. On Friday, March 2, I got a reliable report informing me that *Time* was going to press that day with an all-out attack on Uri. I made up my mind, then and there, to fire the first salvo publicly in defense of Uri in my speech at Berkeley.

CHAPTER NINE

Why

On Sunday, March 4, 1973, I appeared on the stage of Zellerbach Auditorium on the Berkeley campus before some fifteen hundred students. The Bay area was abuzz with rumors about the heavy pressures on SRI because of their support of research into the psychic. The student rumor was that the government was trying to suppress the psychic research at SRI. This, of course, was not true, but the temper of the students was angry and I thought I detected the faint smell of riot in the auditorium.

After giving them the basic information about Uri's powers, as witnessed by me (no mention of IS, of course), I said the following: "Let us accept this story at its face value without trying to breach the credibility gap, which is enormous. What does it mean for a piece of metal which has a definite mass, a definite atomic structure, a definite macroscopic form, to disappear in a human being's hand? We can write several equations, very elementary, of what kind of energy it would take to make that coin vanish. We can think of infinite compression and reduce it to the size of a neutrino; a kind of neutron gravitational collapse situation. We can think of infinite expansion where all atomic forces are released, and the parts fly off into space. One can think of all kinds of possibilities, but they all require enormous amounts of energy, and the human hand could be badly damaged in the process. There is no question in my mind or in that of my scientific colleagues that we are dealing with a genuine phenomenon. We absolutely believe in the validity of what we observe. Not only do our eyes tell us that the event occurred, but recording instruments tell us as well.

"The committee that has been formed to study Geller and to design future experiments is made up of quite well known and distinguished physicists, both theoretical and experimental. We have had a number of conferences during this past year about how to handle this kind of data. We have reached a consensus that there is no possible physical explanation of what is going on.

"I want to give a label to this phenomenon—the intelligent control of energy, or inergy: something related to the inner workings of the human mind. The next event that I want to go over with you is about the object that has disappeared—parked in a space that we cannot begin to define—and the return of that object. To the best of my knowledge, when that object returns, there has never been any difference in the temperature of the object compared to the local ambient temperature. So far all studies have been done at room temperature. This is of great interest. One realizes that we are dealing with one of the most extraordinary phenomenon that man has been exposed to in recent times. One physicist has said that the Geller effect, inergy, pulls out the material platform on which science rests, and also challenges every fundamental principle of science. I know that this is an enormously powerful statement to make.

"But in order to face this problem we have had to consider this awful thought. Normally we go into hysteria when there is even a weak violation of a principle of nature, and here I am talking about all of them as being suspect. So we have planned a series of studies which test Geller's inergy against known experiments which were once used to establish the laws of physics. These will come out over the years to come, I hope.

"The experiments done on Geller to date were carried out within a well-established research institute, but the results have not yet been published. I have seen the data, the movies, and I am convinced that the proof for the reality of what I am telling you is sound. This work was done initially in August 1972, and then resumed in November and December 1972. You will see the results eventually in published form. I don't want to name the institute because a controversy has developed with respect to this work with Geller and the claims. This is the reason I have dropped my prepared talk for this occasion. Since I run the risk of saying something libelous, I will refrain from using names. But the social situation that has developed based on the Geller phenomenon, that is, inergy, is quite extraordinary, in my opinion. . . .

"Now, what does this mean for all of you who are hearing my particular position? You have to appreciate that this is my position; it does not represent the full story, it does not represent the truth—it is only what I see. I think that as a trained observer my observations have some merit. I did not trust my observations in such an important matter. I'll backtrack a bit in order to tell you of some of the things I did to insure to myself and to my peers that we are dealing with a valid phenomenon. I had Geller checked in Israel by others, and by some authorities from the government as well. I then took Geller to Germany and had scientists check him, one of them being Dr. Friedbert Karger, of the Max Planck Institute for Plasma Physics, who has already put his favorable opinion in print. I also let Geller publicly work before journalists in Germany, and a series of articles were published. I took Geller to England where scientists of great repute examined him and reported favorably on his work in the *New Scientist* of November 9, 1972. I brought Geller to this country and introduced him to many individual scientists, and to my knowledge to date, there is not one of these scientists who will not vouch for the reality of Geller's effects.

"Geller is willing to submit to all the conditions of science and prove his case. I am personally responsible for Geller's welfare while he is in the United States. I am certainly in favor of making any arrangements with any responsible group of scientists to continue this study until all the facts are in. If Geller is a fraud, as has been alleged, I will be the first to admit it, because I am only interested in one thing and that is, the truth. I also want to bring that truth out in the open for the advancement of knowledge, and hopefully and ultimately, for the benefit of mankind.

"There are other implications of these effects which should not be ignored. If one can do these things, others will surely come along who can do the same thing. If we can study this long enough, and it really is a formidable problem, we may open up the fifth force in nature, we may open up new ideas of dimensionality, of space. We may have completely new notions of how this human transducer can tap into regions of nature that our instruments at the moment cannot reach. This gives mankind an enormous, incredible potential that even the gods of old did not have. In this scheme of nature, which I foresee as true, we should really be humble. We should look at what nature has allowed us to see and not become fearful, not to avoid the facts, not try to get rid of the implications before the solution is found."

The students cheered wildly in behalf of Geller's cause. The next day I got a telephone call from New York and was read an advance text of the *Time* story. My worst fears were realized; it was a scathingly critical article. Very little comment is needed. *Time* states that Hyman "also caught Geller in some outright deceptions that Targ and Puthoff apparently did not discern." Hyman was so observant that he wrote in his report from which *Time* quotes about Uri: "His swarthy complexion sets off his blue eyes." Any casual observer could tell you that Uri has brown eyes. In addition to Hyman's incredible sloppiness in observation, there was the unsubstantiated, wholly untrue statement that "Geller left the country in disgrace."

However, all this nonsense was laid to rest when the SRI researchers made their report to the scientific world on March 9 at the Physics Department Colloquium in Columbia University. The tone of the meeting is reported by Peter Gwynne, science editor of *Newsweek*, in the *New Scientist* of March 22, 1973.

> The colloquium had all the trappings of a grand scientific occasion. The hall was crowded with physics professors, the parapsychology establishment of New York, journalists, and gradu-

ates and undergraduates attracted either by genuine interest or cultish curiosity. Murmurings of excitement greeted the appearance of the SRI physicists—Russell Targ and Harold Puthoff. Their presentation was certainly spectacular in a scientific sense . . . According to Targ, he and his colleague took just about every precaution imaginable—including consulting with a professional magician—to make the experiments cheatproof.

The audience was generally friendly, and questions were concerned more with improving the experimental procedures than with attacking the concept of studying psychics in the laboratory.

In his opening remarks, Dr. Targ said, "The work we've been doing is in the field of so-called psychical, psychoenergetic phenomena. It is our understanding that these phenomena were not invented in the laboratory, but are found occurring spontaneously in the field. They are found in the state of nature. And the purpose of our research is twofold: First of all, we set out to find if these phenomena do in fact exist. And if they do exist, we want to find out whether they can be investigated in the laboratory under well-controlled conditions. The work that we are reporting on today was carried out with two individuals in particular. The two people who acted as subjects for our work were brought to our attention as a result of experiments in which they had participated in the New York area with other researchers.

"The two subjects with whom we worked are Ingo Swann and Uri Geller. The work that had been done with them was done at other universities and research organizations. . . .

"Now, Dr. Puthoff and I entered this research area half a year ago and we entered it as physicists. Both of us have been doing active research in physics for about fifteen years. For a good part of that time we have had an avocational interest in psychic phenomena. And it is this avocational interest that, I think, qualifies us more than disqualifies us to do this research. There are two things that are evident when you try to do psychical research and interact with subjects. The first thing you discover is that any person with whom you work who claims to psychic powers is highly motivated to *cheat* [*laughter*]—because the thing they are trying to do is at best making use of those perceptual abilities over which they have the most marginal control. And it is the universal experience of people trying to do research in this area that the subject will try to supplement whatever ability he might have, if any, with whatever he can get away with.

"The two criteria we had in designing experiments were as follows: First of all, the experiment should be as cheat-proof as possible. That is, we designed our experiment in such a way that it was not possible to cheat. And as we went along, and we analyzed our experiments and looked at our film and video tape records, and if we decided that if a subject could, in principle, *could* have cheated—even if there was no evidence for cheating —we threw that experiment out as void. And we did not criticize the subject, but considered that our own experiment was inadequate, because it didn't have sufficient safeguards against cheating.

"The second point that was a criterion for experimental design was that the experimental output of any work we did should contain objectively analyzable data. The ideal kind of output from an experiment from a physicist's point of view is graphical output obtained with a chart recorder. And this was our favorite kind of data. . . ."

After some further remarks about Uri, Mr. Targ prepared to show the SRI film: "Dr. Puthoff and I were not alone in the experiments with Mr. Geller. In addition to the scientists listed on the film, we had the services of a magician which is a valuable part of any research activity [*loud laughter*]. All the data that you will see was observed by the cinematographer who recorded it on film, and by an assistant in a separate room who observed and recorded everything with a video tape recorder. This latter was very valuable in that it allowed us to immediately replay that particular experimental protocol. We will now let the film record speak for itself." [The complete text of the film appears in Appendix Two.]

Dr. Targ was, in the words of the *New Scientist* article, "subdued in his conclusion." "We do not claim that either man has psychic powers," he said. "We draw no sweeping conclusions as to the nature of these phenomena or the need to call them psychical. We have observed certain phenomena with the subjects for which we have no scientific explanation. All we can say at this point is that further investigation is clearly warranted."

I left the crowded and cheering festival atmosphere of the Colloquium at Columbia early so that I could report the outcome to Uri. He had been advised by myself and many others that he should not be present in the physics building, Pupin Hall; there were too many press, radio, and television reporters present, and there was a possibility that one of them might trigger Uri into some immoderate statement.

Uri was still smarting from the false allegation by *Time* that he had left Israel in disgrace. However, none of us realized how hurt he felt by being excluded from the Colloquium.

When I reported to him that the SRI scientists had given him solid endorsement for his work, he did not seem pleased. When I told him that the work with Ingo Swann had been reported, and favorably received, he pouted. When I reported in detail which of his experiments had been reported and which had been excluded, he began to argue with me. He said, "Why didn't they report on the experiments when I broke the piece of crystal without disturbing its electronics? Why didn't they report the experiment when I dematerialized the stop watch from a doubly locked case and made it reappear on the test platform, all of which they captured on video tape? Why don't they have the courage to report all the things I did for each of them personally? And the most important thing they are afraid to tell—that I proved over and over again that I can do things to magnetic tape. Are they afraid that the world will panic if they know what could happen to all man-made computers that are strangling the life out of humanity? I'm really sick and tired of the inefficiency and weakness of scientists. I'm not going to give myself to research anymore!"

Uri's frustration was beginning to boil over. He secretly knew that a small group of scientists believed that his powers were genuine, but these men and SRI walked cautiously in telling the world. On the other hand, *Time* reached millions of people all over earth, and those who would read the story could only conclude that Uri was a clever magician at best and a fraud at worst.

When his good friends and supporters came from the Colloquium a little while later, Uri greeted them with stony disdain. As they sat around discussing their individual feelings and opinions about the Colloquium, Uri would break in with unpleasant comments, implying somehow that everyone present had been responsible for getting him into this terrible position before the world.

Now, everyone present knew how hard Uri had worked to produce his effects under controlled conditions. Everyone also knew that Uri was not responsible for what had happened with *Time*. We all felt that IS had somehow contrived to bring about a controversy and that Uri would be receiving more attention in this way than if he were accepted as being genuine. But Uri had none of this detached perspective. He was personally hurt, and this, too, we all had to try to understand.

But Uri's anger mounted as he listened to the trivia of our conversation. At one point he chose Werner to be the scapegoat for all his pent-up frustration. He went into a shouting, towering, abusive rage. Although Uri is very volatile and mercurial in his moods, none of us had ever seen him truly angry. And since we all knew of his great powers to bend, break, and dematerialize things, it became a fearful scene. We all took the abuse in silence, knowing that Uri had to blow off all the pressure of his emotions. We parted from our friends around midnight in New York, and Uri and I drove home to Ossining. I was deeply shocked at Uri's behavior, and for the first time in our relationship began to ask the question "What hath God wrought?" As we drove homeward in the wintry night, Uri's gloom became heavier and heavier in its silence.

Why

I went to sleep with a heavy heart, and did not sleep well at all. Since IS had not produced any signs throughout all of Uri's rage and gloom, I felt that they, too, were ashamed of his breakdown. During the restless night the conviction slowly built inside me that Uri's querulousness, negativity, anger, and frustration would sooner or later defeat our work. The events of this night were to me a foretaste of failure, that we would not be able to intervene successfully on behalf of mankind with our superior beings out there. Somehow I had always felt that Uri, Shipi, and I were test subjects for the rest of man; that is, if we who *knew* could not make it, then how could anyone else make it? And here we were failing because of simple combat fatigue. In my subconscious I realized that if I did not at once bring our human relationship to a fruitful crisis, with a positive outcome, failure was inevitable.

In the morning my daughter Illyria, Uri, and I were having breakfast in the kitchen. No one was saying much of anything. The gloom of the previous day had not yet worn off. Suddenly words came out of my mouth for which I did not feel responsible. They came out with a vehemence that no one had ever heard from me: "Uri, I can't go on with all this emotionality and negativity. You better go back to Israel! Let's forget the mission!" I was shocked by my words but made no effort to retract them. My daughter was petrified by the power of my feelings. Shocked, Uri stared at me, then left the room. We did not speak again until the next day.

I isolated myself in my study. Everyone stayed away from me. Now it was I who had become the tyrant. I tried to understand what I had done. I must have screamed out from my deepest subconscious. I knew that I should not try to carry on the commission unless I had complete control over myself. And here, in a short time, Uri and I had both broken down before our mentors. I really knew now what it meant to be a zero, a nothing.

Uri on his part was more depressed than he had been the previous night. Not only the world but his best friend had let him down. Through Solveig, who was a house guest, he sent me peace offers. But I sent back word that I could not talk until I had re-examined and weighed the entire personal situation and the value of our work for mankind. In effect, I went over everything that is in this book, and more volumes of experience that will never get into books. On Sunday, March 11, at about two in the afternoon, I was still in my study placing myself on the scale of judgment. Was I capable of carrying this message to my fellowmen? Should I step aside now, before it was too late, in favor of someone stronger, wiser, and more pure than I?

As I thought these thoughts, the answer arrived on my desk top in front of me, where there suddenly appeared the Farquhar astronomical globe. It had been in a room across the hall, and it had somehow entered my locked study. On my desk blotter pad nine pens appeared and formed into this pattern:

$$WHY$$

The nine pens all belonged to me and had been on my desk in a stone jar that contained some fifteen pens and pencils.

The globe was the same one in which had appeared some months earlier the typed message "You are all alone now, all of you for a long time." As I have said, the Farquhar globe is made up of two nested globes. The small inner globe is of the earth and is about nine inches in diameter; the outer globe is a star map of the sky and is about twenty-four inches in diameter. One uses this globe to identify any star or constellation. A complex mechanism is used to align the two globes for a given day and hour of sighting of the sky. Then, with the use of a compass to fix direction and a goniometer to measure the angle that the star makes with the plane of the earth, one can locate the star in question on this outer globe. The effect of doing this is like standing on the rotating earth and looking out into our galaxy with a map.

To me the symbolism of this globe was clear: "Please look out into the heavens for your answer; your earth-bias, earth-based reasoning is too limiting." The use of "why" was, of course, a very personal reproach, but the use of nine pens sharply reminded me who was asking me this question.

I felt ashamed of myself for being so frail, so petty, so weak, so childish. I called Uri into the privacy of my study and showed him what had happened. We both looked at each other with brotherly love and understanding, and we wept. We were thoroughly ashamed of our emotionality and weakness. We promised not to indulge ourselves again in such childish breakdowns. Then my ever-present tape recorder was switched on by an invisible hand. The voice said:

What has happened? Why? We will enter Uri's brain and examine it. [Long pause] *We find everything in order and pure. There is absolutely no negativity or evil in you, Shipi, or Uri.*

AP: "Thank you. Is it possible that an outside force entered one of us?"

It is not possible for any other power to enter the body, mind, soul, or work of you, Uri, or Shipi. We guarantee that. It must be due to your human weakness. Both you and Uri must be stronger, and in better control. The one who speaks to you now has come from the farthest reaches ever, because of the seriousness of this situation. Farewell.

As the voice ended, the tape cassette vanished immediately from inside the tape recorder. I sat down to write the above words from memory, and I believe that every word is accurate. As I finished these notes, a large metal cabinet three feet high with nine file drawers vanished from alongside of my desk. I called this cabinet my bric-a-brac drawers, because it contained hundreds of little objects that I treasure: jewelry, coins, stamps, special documents, awards, mementos, and leather goods such as billfolds. Everything that was personal or precious was there. So its disappearance was a loss, but I was pleased at this countersignature of intelligence and power. We searched the house to see if it was on the premises. The last place I looked was in my second-floor bedroom, and there it was, neatly placed alongside my bedside bookshelves. I searched it. Everything had survived the transformation without obvious change. There was only one thing missing—a gold Parker pen that had great sentimental value to me.

At 3:45 P.M. I returned to my study, where I found Uri doodling at my desk. I looked at what he had just doodled. It was a set of very advanced tensor equations describing the nature of the gravitational field. Uri did not know what he had just doodled, and he asked me where this came from. Since I recognized the equations as being of the form written by Albert Einstein, I replied, almost facetiously, "Einstein." As I said this, there appeared a piece of paper on the floor some ten feet away from me. I walked over to pick it up. It was a newspaper photo of Albert Einstein! I remembered seeing such a photo in the *New York Times Magazine* some ten years earlier. I had clipped it out but had not seen it for several years. At this vantage point I was looking at my bed across the hall from where I was standing. In front of my eyes there had appeared a book on the white bedspread. I walked over to examine it. It was a book I had last seen in the basement; it was by Edwin F. Taylor and John Archibald Wheeler, entitled *Spacetime Physics*, published by W. H. Freeman and Company in 1963. I looked through it carefully, but the equations that Uri had doodled were not in this book, although the general subject matter was there.

Throughout all this activity I had left the nine pens on my blotter pad intact spelling out the word "why." I returned to my study with Uri—holding the book. As we approached the desk, right in front of our eyes the nine pens flipped simultaneously in the air and settled down into a new pattern as follows (though I did not understand the symbolism or meaning of the configuration):

Why

Peace reigned over our household and descended into our souls. Having walked through the seven pillars of fire, were we at last prepared to mediate between heaven and earth?

> Thy will is done, O God!
>   The star hath ridden high
> Thro' many a tempest, but she rode
>   Beneath thy burning eye;
> And here, in thought, to Thee—
>   In thought that can alone
> Ascend thy empire and so be
>   A partner of Thy throne—
> By winged fantasy,
>   My embassy is given,
> Till secrecy shall knowledge be
>   In the environs of Heaven.*

* Edgar Allan Poe, *Al Aaraaf* (lines 106–17), 1829.

EPILOGUE

"It Is Only the Beginning"

As I sat down in the springtime of 1973 to write a book for publication, I found myself haunted at every turn by a thousand questions. How could I expect people to believe my story, when every bit of supporting evidence had vanished? I hoped that if I could approach truth closely enough, she would sing her song directly into the heart of man. The reader must be the judge of whether or not I have succeeded.

Then I was faced with the problem of finding a publisher. I had good contacts not only with my publisher but with key people in other firms. When they read my five-page outline of this book, they all gently backed away as though they had just been confronted with the work of a deranged mind. Some asked me to water down the story to the simple facts that could be substantiated scientifically. I would have done this as a first step, except for the time pressure of only a few years before the mass landing. For this reason I could not water down the truth. I decided not to try to sell the book until after it was written. Then a publisher would know exactly what he was getting into.

My other problem had to do not with what I was going to say, but with those basic questions that had not been answered in the narrative and that people would want to know if this work was to be credible. So I made up a list of such basic questions, hoping that my mind would be scanned by the computers, and thereby convey to my mentors the importance that I attached to these questions.

The issue was now firmly joined. The genuineness of some of the Uri Geller effects was upheld by one of the world's greatest research institutes; yet he had been labeled a fraud by one of the most powerful journalistic voices in the world. Magicians began to appear on all the prominent television talk shows, denouncing Uri as a fraud; one magician went so far as publicly to accuse Stanford Research Institute of "criminal negligence" for supporting Uri.

To counter this negativity, Uri and I leaped into battle. Uri appeared in leading universities and colleges from coast to coast in the United States. Here he was immediately popular and a kind of folk hero with the students for standing up to the Establishment. He appeared on national television and for the first time in his career was able to produce his major effects for millions of people at the same time.

Within two months after the *Time* attack was published, the magicians began to fade away. We had won our first major battle and were now in a position to begin a more constructive and educational phase of our work. That work continues to this day.

One day Uri was watching me work at the above-mentioned list of questions, which were on a clipboard, and he asked me what they meant. In reply, I simply read to him from the list. When I had finished reading the list, Uri and I, at his request, went from the first floor to the third floor of the house. I left the clipboard on the first floor.

As we examined a bowling ball (which Uri wanted to use to go bowling), my clipboard with the questions suddenly appeared on a cot behind us. Uri and I immediately went downstairs to get my tape recorder. We had no sooner set it up when it went into operation by itself:

AP: "May I have permission to ask my list of questions?"

This is Hoova. Yes, we heard, and will answer what we can.

AP: "What is the history of Hoova in the evolution of the human race on this earth?"

We first interfered with the human race twenty thousand years ago. We came on a planned mission from our own solar galaxy, and our first landing place on earth was at the place you were at in Israel, at the Oak of Mamre in Hebron where Abraham met us. That is the origin of the legend of the ladder to the gods, because they saw us come out of our craft on a ladder device. However, we found traces of the presence of other visitors from other spaces who had been on earth millions of years earlier. But we found man in much the same animal condition that you see him in today.

AP: "When was the last time that you actively tried to upgrade the quality of man's self and of his civilization?"

We give advice actually about once every six thousand years. The last time that we did this was six thousand years ago to the Egyptians. Our advice is usually given gently and is not too strong, and we do it more for our own purposes than for man's benefit.

AP: "Was this in the period of Imhotep?"

Yes. He was a man very much like Uri, and he brought to the Egyptians all of their civilization.

AP: "Was this the period of Tehouti also?"

Yes. He was better known for his powers of healing.

AP: "Were there others?"

Yes.

AP: "Were there other places where you tried to help man by stimulating the process of civilization?"

Yes. Six thousand years ago we tried to help in other places. The area that you now call Alaska—this culture passed on to what you call China. We also did this in India.

AP: "Now that I understand the pattern, I can fill in the details from archaeology, mythology, and history."

This is the time in which humans were allowed to see us physically. They abjectly worshiped us, which we could not tolerate.

AP: "I am deeply concerned about a problem that lies heavily on the mind of every man: Is there a soul?"

Yes. Did you ever really doubt it?

AP: "No. But I need your view in order to illuminate my opinion. What is the nature of the soul?"

It inhabits different worlds at different times in its existence. When the physical body dies, it goes with all of its being to its own world. There it carries on with the next phase of its existence. It may go on to other spaces, or it may even return to an earth physical body for another round of existence—what humans call reincarnation may occur. There are higher powers that divide these people (souls), and that decide where they shall go. The purpose of all existence is to move toward God. However, no one can know God. We ourselves can only know God by reaching him as an idea—not physically.

AP: "How does the soul relate to you?"

We occupy our physical bodies for about a million years at a time. However, our computers do not have souls and they do not die. We, too, as souls, move on toward God; everything that exists moves.

AP: "What is the life track of a human soul like?"

The soul goes through at least one hundred thousand life tracks as it climbs up toward God. There is no way to tell you about time. You see, you can never understand the vastness of time, and there is no end to time.

AP: "May I repeat? Can you reach God?"

Yes, with ideas, but not physically. We die, for we last in our physical bodies about a million years of your time.

AP: "Well—speaking relatively—is our human life short or long?"

Only powers higher than us can answer all these questions of mortality. Some questions, for humans, and even us, are totally unexplainable. There is a vastness to the universe that never ends.

AP: "Once I asked you in Israel for the definition of a light age. You didn't answer. Can you answer now?"

Yes. It is one hundred thousand million earth years.

AP: "You do mean earth years—not light-years?"

Yes—earth years.

AP: "In the total time track of the human race—all past,

present, and all of its future yet to come—where are we now? Are we along it ten per cent, fifty per cent, ninety per cent? Where?"

Ah, we know the past of the human race. But this is one of the secrets—we cannot tell it to you. As to the future we are not permitted either. But remember all that people need to do—God has written on stone, the Ten Commandments. Thus shall it be done. Remember you are working for us in ways that are important to us, and which we have not yet explained. Actually, there is no special message for you to pass to the human race. It is possible that should there be a war impending, as between Russia and China, there may be a message to prevent it. But you may try to open their minds with things like telepathy and psychokinesis—things which we have almost forgotten. Yes, they are to be helped.

AP: "If your secrecy is related to your principle of nonviolation of free will in humans, why is there to be some revelation now?"

Our secrecy has only to do in very small part with the free will of humans. Mostly it is because we don't want to reveal our intentions. In the past we have even landed before masses of people. But we cannot afford anymore to land visibly on your planet. It is because of your tendency to panic, to worship, to react abnormally to us.

AP: "During the past quarter of a century there have been many space visitations reported. Are these yours?"

Most of these reports by humans are due to hallucinations and aberrations. But some of our units have landed. But most of the reported landings have been from other visitors from space—some of whom we do not see, but which you can see. They are of different vibrations, different spaces, different velocities. We are the only ones who are mostly here. The other visitors come and go. We stay. This tape will vanish when you hear it. Farewell.

My prime concern in writing this book has been to alert the world to this historic series of events, and not so much to describe their minutiae. These details can be filled in later if the reception of this work warrants it.

It is obvious that I am personally convinced that superior beings from other spaces and other times have initiated a renewed dialogue with humanity. But it is equally obvious that my case for this conviction can be carried into the heart of every person largely by the sense of truth my words carry, and not on the basis of objective proof. It is my hope that as Uri continues his research efforts at the hands of science, and as he carries personal testimony to people, the truth of what he and I say will take hold. And of course, it is up to the Nine and their various controllers and messengers to decide who shall be witness to their presence.

Much of this kind of revelation in the future will undoubtedly appear from day to day in news reports, television reports, and other media. This will consist largely about other peoples' experience with the kind of things herein reported, as more and more sightings occur in the coming years. It is only when a large number of other people experience to some degree what Uri and I experienced that our credibility will be enhanced.

I want to make it clear that I have as of this writing never met a being from the Nine, Spectra, Hoova, Rhombus 4D, or others of this genre, in a face-to-face sense. My meetings have been only through the message systems I have described. Furthermore, I have not been inside one of their craft. While I do not doubt that superior beings exist out there, I do not know what they look like, how they live, or even what their goals are with respect to humankind. Considering that I have had two years of intermittent experience, I am remarkably ignorant about these beings. On the other hand I have complete faith in their wisdom and benevolent intentions toward man and living things on earth. My lack of hard knowledge about them is the kind of deficiency that does not erode my faith in their essential pursuit of the good, the true, the beautiful, and the just.

The relationship described in this book between these superior beings and Uri and me continues to grow deeper and mutually more meaningful. Yet I can honestly say that there is no conflict between my loyalty to them and my loyalty to my own kind on earth. Many people have felt that in serving the interests of these beings who are trying to reach mankind, I have somehow sold my soul in the process. Nothing could be farther from the truth.

In the last analysis, how much more we discover about these beings from space is dependent on how coolly and openly each human being receives them. If there is fear, panic, or hysteria, we will not find out much more. If we interpret the presence of these beings in terms of our pet theories, religions, tribal and racial beliefs, or other preconceptions about life out there, we shall surely distort the truth. If we regress toward cultish practices, or abject worship of these beings or anything connected with them, we shall cut ourselves off from further knowledge. The healthiest attitude that we can take is to go on tending our gardens, shops, and other affairs while being sensitive to the idea not only that we are not alone in space but that benevolence and guidance may come to humanity from beyond our planet.

Uri and I will continue to bear witness to this new presence in men's affairs, and if people so wish, we will share our small knowledge with everyone for the benefit of all mankind.

APPENDIX ONE

The Nine

This is a continuation of the philosophy of the Nine, introduced on page 15.

CH *is a principle which is the revealing principle of knowledge and law. CH is the principle of timeless knowledge as revealed through the time process.*

R *is the principle of art and rhythm.*

M *is the principle of the human and intimate.*

The language, the method, and the logic—that belongs to this body or brain [Vinod] that we use. CH presses the buttons and releases the forces. We strive to bring about the required correlation, which is to say, it is in explicit fulfillment of our purpose that we are meeting here tonight. This is a planned performance. Planned to the minutest moment.

If the velocity of light is approached to ninety-nine per cent, the increase in the mass is in the range of seven. This is one of the physical proofs of why we want sevens. Perhaps you have not noticed this before."

AP: "No, I haven't."

That is partly an inference from Einsteinian analysis light velocity. Even there this seven range—it is not exactly seven, but it is the range of seven; it does not go beyond eight. It doesn't go beyond six, but it hits around seven and such microscopic aspects of velocity. If seven can be so perfectly deter-

mined, you will notice why the seven has been detected even in the physical as well as psychospiritual dimensions. The acceptance of the Law of Seven. Now, that's a clue which will keep you absolutely convinced and you will not ask me again what is the rationale of seven. If we tell you that it is the occult number and the seven chords of being as known in ancient occult literature, you will continue to have a veil of suspicion. But now that the increment in the mass is exactly to the range of seven by an approximation of ninety-nine per cent to the velocity of light, that is a kind of indicator how mass is related to high velocity. Related in this way, that it achieves an increment of seven—achieves an increment to seven, not of seven. Beyond ninety-nine per cent we cannot go because it becomes infinitization, as you know.

AP: "Yes, that's what I was going to ask you, whether the change in increment beyond ninety-nine per cent becomes enormous rather rapidly?"

Yes.

AP: "It approaches infinity between ninety-nine and one hundred per cent?"

Yes. Now these are only theoretical indications. We cannot really go on with experimentation in this direction, but if we get seven times the electrical equivalent of the human body—if we get it seven times—do you know what would result? It would result in sevenon of the mass of electricity. That's a very strange term, but it's true. If it gains sevenfold, corresponding approximation to light velocity will be ninety-nine per cent. That is the point where human personality has to be stretched in order to achieve infinitization. This is one of the most secret insights. Our problem now boils down to this, how to get the human body seven times what it is in electrical terms. One more tremendous secret. Copper is a phenomenon which succeeds in giving half of seven resultant to human body particular. That is why your copper cage succeeds. Tremendous secret. That is why the idea of a copper cage is so revolutionary, so enormous in its possible effects on parapsychological effort.

Somewhere, somehow, we have to now work out the cosmic

ray properties. We don't know where it can be done, but it has to be done very urgently because that will determine the next phase of actual human life, consciousness, unfoldment, and evolutional process. The atomic fission or fusion is expected to facilitate human comfort, if it does not just result in the elimination of all life on earth. But a more important source of facilitating human comfort is the exploitation of the cosmic ray.

AP: "Will you define what you mean by cosmic ray?"

That is what we are worrying about.

AP: "I mean define it simply."

I will say that cosmic ray is the channelized direction, rather than directed channelization of the basic energy that constitutes the essence of cosmos. That is the definition of it.

AP: "I don't believe that that is what is meant by cosmic rays in a physics book."

Yes, it is in a slightly different way. To our view, the cosmic ray energy is more fundamental than the solar systems themselves.

AP: "May I ask if the formula and its undetected implications implies the discovery of as yet undiscovered energies?"

No, I must admit one hint. Just as there is a time dimension, there is a timeless dimension toward which Einstein is groping. A hint as to the method:

The leap is not in the dark, but in the light, which could be taken. Take what I say only as a proposition or axiom. The fact of every knowledge experience is timeless, although the act of knowing is in time. To experience knowledge is a timeless experience. We have to discover a formula which will illustrate the correlation between the act of knowing and knowledge. The spotlight of consciousness is something so tremendously powerful. This spotlight of consciousness is a sunlight by itself.

AP: "Do you mean it has the growth power of sunlight?"

Yes. We make it grow, we make it live, we illuminate it.

AP: "You started to elucidate 'the leap in the dark.'"

Yes, we use the phrase "leap in the dark," which is common, but here the leap is in the light because it is expected to take us to an understanding of the supersense. It is light because it is the consciousness problem, not just subconscious or normal conscious inclusive of the superconscious which is the light per se. Perhaps you can understand the beautiful phrase.

Then the following poem was given by M.

> Shadows are receding in a slower rhythm.
> The song is bursting out of every atom.
> In the rainbow hues the multiple one is dissolving itself.
> The thrill of surprised happiness is coursing
>   through the veins of the earth.
> The trans-lunar dream is incarnating itself through
>   the bones of the body.
> A teardrop from the human eye becomes starlight
>   in the darkness of the night
> And the silver dew on the cheek of the new morning,
> And itself again reappears on the horizon of the human
>   creativeness
> As an immortal moment of discovery.
> Through a series of labor pains in time God is the
>   timeless birth and mart of human aspiration.

Remember, all this is a real guidance from God. God is nobody else than we together, the Nine Principles of God. There is no God other than what we are together. And just for once in your lifetime believe this to be the truth. If God ever spoke, if God ever made an instrument of a human being—it is now that he has made it; and look upon this as the most precious moment in your lives. These are God's words.

You see, the procedure is this. We accept the thesis that we are here and that we want these things done, we can do them through you. You have also to struggle—we have also to struggle. Supposing all healthy biologic events surround the birth of a child; it will take nine months and it will take mating. The greatest of men were not born in an instant. All the birth pangs that any other mother would undergo, their mother had to undergo, too. But the point is this: Supposing tonight I sit down here—which is perfectly possible—I can sit here for one hour and tell you what is going to happen to the minutest detail—how often you are going to sneeze, how often you will sit—that can be done; but it is not the way to do it. What you are doing is just the right thing. Struggling a little, getting creative imagination into exertion, awaiting a certain little point for guidance. We are satisfied that every step is being taken in intense sincerity. Failure and success is in your hands. But we also have to do these things. You have to do them, we have to do them—putting up the very best effort in intense sincerity. It's so pleasant to be deluded and to be surprised and to be flabbergasted. All these things are very pleasant and necessary. But if we were not pleased, if we had detected that you are making enormous mistakes or failures, I would have told you before.

We have to look upon this as a long-term contract between you and us. Your cooperation is so very urgently needed. If we develop these techniques, we shall have taken long strides, because what we can do is just this much: indicate the formula and the method—but we understand how much labor, application, patience, it involves to get into operative focus. We have full realization of how much you have to work. So our plans are definite. We feel that you must put in some real effort. We shall cooperate, but your will has to exert itself. On a long-term basis, together we shall achieve some wonders, capital W.

"So, go in full trust and in full hope towards us and more towards yourself that these things definitely come out, and no matter what other things happen, they will only help the cause.

The major aspect of this type of work which you have felt already for several years and you have a ripe view of it although you may not perhaps feel so. But if you will begin to think, idea it, and put it down, you will produce something remarkably valuable. So go ahead and do that as quickly as possible.

What you have been groping toward with some real certainty was that there must be a parapsychological dimension that can throw definite floodlights on the new horizons of science.

AP: "Yes, that is the idea I started out with some time ago."

We know. That is what we have proved to you, perhaps for the first time, in a manifold, simple, lucid, and condensing manner. In case you have questions in reference to this mantric method the certainty of the presence of which you had already known—you had known that there must be a way, a parapsychological way, which can lead us to wider horizons of science. And if parapsychological knowledge will not help that way, what good on earth is it?

Parapsychology, if you want to accept it as a science, has to be impersonal, it has to be methodological, it has to achieve an increment in human knowledge, it has to give really the right lead to the present human mind.

AP: "By the 'lead' you mean the direction man has to take in his evolutionary course at this particular stage in his development?"

Yes. You see, as we will progress, we shall tell you why war-mindedness is generated, why it is fostered. Obviously, how war-mindedness could be counteracted without propaganda and the threat method and mutual competitive method. For instance, we might tell you how atomic explosions, even when they are produced, can be silenced. We don't have a counter-atomic weapon to fight with, but no atomic weapon will ever have any effect.

We'll silence the atomic weapons of the world. Whoever produces them, they will have no effect. Let them go on producing. You see, just as sound could be produced, it could also be silenced; just as light could be burned, it could be extinguished. The method of production is the method of destruction obversely applied. There is a kind of immunity, physical immunity—just as there is an immunity from diseases. Matter has potential for counteracting almost anything that has taken shape. So, supposing we manufacture a silencer of atom bombs —and one silencer would be enough—let Russia go ahead producing atom bombs in endless quantity. The silencer won't permit it to have any action within say—what is the world's diameter?

AP: "The circumference of the world is about twenty-five thousand miles at the equator."

Circumference is better. Oh dear, twenty-five thousand miles

is nothing. We can protect twenty-five thousand miles like we can protect a fly. If one million atom bombs exploded, they can't touch twenty-five thousand miles.
AP: "That is a staggering concept to our limited imagination."
Yes, it certainly is.
AP: "Is the atom bomb a real threat to the world peace? In the sense in which you have just described it, it doesn't seem to be any threat at all should you so choose to deflect its energies, or silence its energies."

I think I must tell you this, that it's not going to happen. The world is not going to be allowed to be atomized. The fear is there, the threat is there. Human nature is so wretched today. But on the other hand, human nature is so beautiful also, so sacrificing, so understanding. What we have really to fear is not only the fear itself but the tendency to regiment. That's why the Russian approach to world problems is not acceptable to the scheme of things, to ourselves, for instance, because it regiments. There is an element of regimentation in all evolutionary processes, but it is the degree that is unfortunate over there in Russia. Regimentation that insults human will, that we cannot ever associate ourselves with. But everything else, we don't mind. So precisely our plan is set.

In our scheme, we also go on experimenting. We have to experiment in a sense that we never force any will that we get. The wills of humans have to lend themselves; in that lies their growth and maturation. We go to the limit of persuasion but there we have to stop. Our persuasion is quite often very effective, but we must notice the limit; if it is resistive, we just leave it alone.

We don't force in our scheme of things. These forces—principles and personalities—we have to get them into direct service to mankind. We appreciate the desire in you to catalyze this power for serving the man.

We have no access to the human world. We have manufactured this body [Vinod] for our work, atom by atom. We have got it to travel across fantastic spaces, but lest we get confused there is one thing which we slightly hinted at yesterday, which is this. The sort of teleology which is active in this work is not exactly the human purpose way. It is like the implications of laws; it is teleology in a very mysterious sense. Though M and CH are responsible for the idea that you got, it is not to say that you had nothing to do with it. We are terribly happy to note your attitude; we also are very discriminate. We are not putting an idea on barren rock.

Our side of the problem is very pathetic, if you will permit me that word. We don't come across wills, points, foci, where without offending their freedom we could do our work. It is not easy. As we reported to you, we can achieve an extraordinary amount of conditioning, but we cannot plant a foreign urge to anyone. That is the way evolution works in regarding the wills of individuals. Unless that is done there is no growth. If I act for you, if I sort of give you dates, or give you money by precipitation (that can be done), you don't do anything—it is we who do it. We don't want to do that thing—all that has to be done is really by you. Although very strange occasions arise when you rightly feel that there is not the guidance in this crucial anxiety or blank wall against, or impasse, or financial stress, absence of human cooperation—if the help didn't come from us in these hours, what good is it? Sometimes it is very clearly felt, and we don't blame, but the tragedy is shared by us. Around the eleventh or twelfth hour of the night, if the richest person around us wanted instantaneously five dollars—he can't get it from the bank; all that could be done is to wait until nine o'clock in the morning. That is what happens with us with far more precision, because he or she can go to the phone and borrow money. We can't borrow human wills, we can't borrow evolutionary processes, impulsions, and we accept these limitations for the fulfillment of the law. It's not that we can't overcome them. What is the sense of the law, the sense of gravitation; if now the table has this times the weight, and five minutes later twenty times over? The gravitation law itself gets frustrated. So the laws which we have set in operation which we illustrate throughout, they might not be offended but you might. If you care for a little phrase from us—Delays are not denials. Patience—that's all.

In all great adventures of ideas the only prayer which we can address to God is "Grant me patience." Because God will work, to give you the fruits, for that you need not ask.

What is the meaning of sense? Unless we understand the import of sense itself, the supersense will not be intelligible to us, and since we have to formulate a basic ideology for our work over here, it is important for us to get a glimpse into the real meaning of sense itself. Related words are "absence" and "nonsense." Nonsense really means sense out of reference. Absence, or the out-of-sense, away-sense, has a reality, but there, too, the emphasis is on normal elements. Supersense is the discovery of the fullness of sense, of the full stature of sense. The important point is this—that the two words of sense and supersense are in no way divided. There is a continuous spectrum. If sense and supersense were two different worlds, there would not be that real flow between the two. It's not crossing the border because the borders do not exist. It is just a rising on the scale. The capacity to react, that is the feature or characteristic mark of sense. If this were absent, the supersense or the infinite itself will never be realized by sense. That is the purpose of evolution. Now, coming to understand the exact meaning of sense itself. It is really the capacity to react, even physical objects have that capacity of reacting, but the apparent distinction that could be made is that when sense reacts it has the feeling and experience and knowledge of having the reaction. The whole growth of our nature lies in this—to know how to react and to be wakeful at the moment of performance.

AP: "Does this imply conscious awareness of knowing?"

Self-knowledge, if you like. This piece of knowledge is described as reflective knowledge, that is, to know that we know. Knowledge is sense; it is never a handmaid. If this is grasped, it should be clear why supersense, which is the supreme knowing, is itself present in all acts and facts.

I have manufactured a word; I will call it subsistentiality: Subsistence—the physics of supersense. Just as there are laws for sense, there are also laws for the supersense.

"An aspect of human consciousness is to produce the pair of

the sense and the supersense. It must evidently approach something like the nucleus of the atom, the matrix of high velocities —the equation for that is.

$$Z = X \cdot o$$
Where Z is the superconscious, X is the sense.

The sense life of a master symbolizes the unity of integer, and by analogy in pair production the electron and positron as resultants of the annihilated individuation.

AP: "Is the gamma ray to be thought of in analogy to individuation before it has differentiation into the spectrum of supersense?"

Right.

AP: "Would that be preconscious individuation, or highly conscious individuation?"

The whole gamut of individuations—pre-, all the way to the highly intellectualized level where it is annihilated. In masters' lives we have every sense—alert, responsive, even enjoying—but it functions from a different plexus and the peculiar result being this: that it leaves no trace of sanskar or karmic latency. It creates no seeds for further repetition of the will act. That is the secret of released action. All of us have to learn that. To some extent we have known it. You have known it. Quite a few of us have known it. Peaceful action—action without passion—this is not self-expression as some of your modern educationists have thought it to be, because the so called self-expression is a process of manifesting the dormant needs or instinct. In a masterly conduct, there is no self-expression, unless you capitalize the S and make self into infinite itself. But there is no point in calling it self-expression, because there is only one way to do it, and all masters will do it the same way. So one masters self-expression. For practical purposes, what is the use of this particular principle? When we act, let us act in terms of not our self-expressing urges, not even in terms of our so-called ideals, but in terms of infinite peace. Infinite—which is the same as peace. But how to do that? Is it just words? No. When we are inspired by Peace, our actions are not limited to our own personal aspirations or fulfillments. They are as the terms in a process which lifts us into action. For instance, when we let the law find itself through our thoughts, words, and actions, we act in terms of peace and as inspired by the Infinite. How to discover the Law? Do we get to it by an analysis of situations? By an understanding of the causes and reason? No. Emphatic no! Though, by all means, these do supply a guiding light on lesser levels of action. We can know the Law if an inner tranquillity is presented towards its reception. So the process is one of silencing yourself—the exact opposite of endless thirst for articulation to which we are so vulgarly bound. It is not, therefore, the education, but tranquilization, that we should keep in view. A withdrawal, a sanctifying silence, an exposure rather than an education. That is the secret. We, who are dedicated to such—I mean you and we who are dedicated to the Law—we must practice this masterly way of life."

AP: "Does that mean that if we find tranquillity we automatically open the way to the Law? That is the first step? To move through every situation in life with equanimity and tranquillity?"

Right. Achievement of exposure. You see, we attribute motives to others in terms of our own personal lives. Most often this is ludicrously unjust, and the one who suffers is just ourselves. Because if I slap the ground suspecting a scorpion, which is not there, it's my hand that is going to hurt itself. Most philosophy is like that. Famously it is the search for the black cat in a dark room which is not there. We do need symbols of Law, but let them be symbols and not concepts. For instance, in a tranquilizing attempt let us use symbols like the "Nines" or the liberated consciousness of mankind. That's all that matters with us—nothing else does. Then we will tranquilize. But if you put more successes in doing this or that—one thing—they never come about; second, even if they come, they are concealed failures; thirdly, they lead us into new shapes of successes, an eternal maze, an ever-receding horizon. How to clean a muddy pool of water? A challengeful problem! You can throw in some other chemical; you can wash the water with waters; you can strain it. But you know the simplest and most scientific way? Leave it alone, and the dirt will sink down to the bottom. Don't fight with your mind. Leave it alone. Then it will reflect Law; the full-orbed light of Law. This is not difficult. These are not just words. All of you have known this as a matter of fact, but we have to make it the One Law of our life. The sense world is a great distraction. Simplifying our ways, eliminating the non-essentials, is so very urgently necessary for those who are sold on big ideas. Asceticism is really a wonderful trait—only this is that it has to be natural. It should not be the result of a fight. That's why I do not insist on your leaving alone smoking or drinking once in a while. It should be left alone by itself. We shouldn't make it into an end, because that involves too much fight, and a useless fight at that. Success means nothing if it is come by that amount of fighting, because the attention itself which we give during the fight builds up a vast attachment to the things we seem to have conquered. They live deep down inside you. So let us expose ourselves to asceticism, renunciation, simplification, withdrawal, tranquilization. But let us expose ourselves—let us not fight into it. It has to come through. It must come. When the dried leaf on the tree just drops down, it doesn't need to be torn away like the green one has to be. Let us do these things under social, official, or external compulsions if they are necessary; but let our hearts not be enthralled by them.

AP: "Yes, I think in that sense all of us have a far greater challenge than the man who lives simplicity; that is, if we can achieve some degree of tranquillity amongst complexity, it is a far greater test and challenge for us, is it not?"

It certainly is. So in reference to our program everything is settled almost. What we have to do is to fight peacefully. To fight peacefully means to strain and struggle in a mood of tranquillity. So that's our message to you. Fight peacefully.

APPENDIX TWO

Text of Stanford Research Institute Film*

Throughout mankind's history there has existed a folklore that certain gifted individuals have been capable of producing physical effects by means of some agency generally referred to as psychic or psychoenergetic. Substantiation of such claims by accepted scientific methodology has been slow in coming, but recent laboratory experiments, especially in the Soviet Union and Czechoslovakia, and more recently in our own laboratory, have indicated that sufficient evidence does exist to warrant serious scientific investigation. It would appear that experiments could be conducted with scientific rigor to uncover not just a catalog of interesting events, but rather a pattern of cause-effect relationships of the type that lend themselves to analysis and hypothesis in the forms with which we are familiar in the physical sciences. SRI considers this to be a valid area for scientific inquiry.

As scientists we consider it important to examine various models describing the operation of these effects so that we can determine the relationship between extraordinary human functioning and the physical and psychological laws we presently understand. It is not the purpose of our work at SRI to add to the literature another demonstration of the statistical appearance

* Used with the permission of the Stanford Research Institute.

of these phenomena in the laboratory, but rather we seek to achieve an understanding more compatible with contemporary science and more useful to mankind.

This film describes a five-week investigation conducted at Stanford Research Institute with Uri Geller, a young Israeli. The film portrays experiments that we performed with him just as they were carried out. Each scene has been taken from film footage made during actual experiments; nothing has been restaged or specially created. It is not the purpose of the film to demonstrate any purported psychic abilities of Mr. Geller but rather to demonstrate the experiments done with him and his response to the experimental situation.

Meet Uri Geller. One of the types of demonstration that Geller likes to do is to sit with a group of people and attempt to send a number to various people in the room. With Uri Geller, this is Edgar Mitchell, who with his eyes covered is trying to pick up the number that Geller is sending. Also, we see Wilbur Franklin, of Kent State, Harold Puthoff and Russell Targ, of SRI, along with Don Scheuch, vice-president for research at SRI. Dr. Scheuch is trying to receive and then write down the number that Geller is sending. In this case, Scheuch is successful in picking up the number.

Of course, this is not a laboratory experiment, since the activity is totally under Geller's control. It was set as an absolute that experiments, to be worthy, had to be under institute control. Here we show a series of experiments where, previously, fifteen drawings were placed in double-sealed envelopes in a safe for which none of the experimenters had the combination. It took signatures of both the key researchers to remove a drawing at random from the collection in the safe. One of the researchers would then, in this case Targ, look at the drawing outside the experimental room, reseal the envelope, enter the experimental room, whence Geller's task was to draw what he perceived in the envelope.

This is Geller's representation of what he believed was sealed in the envelope. At no time during these experiments did he have any advance knowledge of the target material. As far as he is concerned, these could be drawings of any kind, whether a design or a representational picture. In fact, this is the most off-target of the drawings that he did.

Here—the experiment is repeated, this time with Puthoff as a sender, just to check that the identity of the sender is of no significance in the experiment. Additionally, all experiments are tape-recorded to guard against any verbal cuing on the part of the experimenters.

This the drawing that Geller has made to correspond to the target object. The rectangle on the clipboard represents the TV screen in Geller's mind on which he claims to project the image he is trying to draw. As you can see, he is quite elated about getting the right answer. Before he does this, it is usually preceded by several minutes of "I can't do this—it's impossible. I want to stop. Let's wait."

Here in the laboratory notebook on the left side of the page you see the original targets, and on the right, Geller's responses. This is not a collection of correct answers out of a long series of correct and incorrect responses. This is actually the total run of pictures in the series. It is interesting that there is often a mirror symmetry.

In this particular case, neither Geller nor the experimenter had knowledge of what the target was. This is a double blind experiment. Here, on the upper left of the page, is a picture that was brought to SRI by an outside consultant and sealed in his own envelope; Geller's representation is at the lower right. This was by far the most complicated target picture encountered during these experiments.

This is a typical target carrier used in the experiments. The inner envelope is opaque in its own right; the outer one is a heavy manila envelope. A floodlight behind these envelopes would not permit the interior to be seen. This type of communication experiment was repeated many other times during the five weeks, with Geller choosing to pass about 20 percent of the time.

It is interesting that when he drew his response in this case he didn't recognize the object as eyeglasses—it seemed to him to be an abstract drawing. In general, these drawing experiments were not double blind as one of the experimenters knew what was in the picture in the envelope.

Here, however, we present a case of a double blind experiment, in which someone not associated with the project comes into the experimental room, places an object into a can chosen at random from ten aluminum cans. Numbered tops are also put on at random. The randomizer then leaves the area, and the experimenters enter the experimental area with Geller, with neither the experimenters nor Geller knowing which can contains the object. In this particular case, the target is a three-quarter-inch steel ball which now resides in one of the ten cans in the box.

The ten cans having been arranged neatly, Geller's task now is to determine which of these ten cans holds the steel ball bearing. He is not permitted to touch the cans or the table. The experimental protocol is for experimenter to remove the cans one at a time in response to Geller's instructions as he points or calls out a can-top number. Eventually there will be just two or three cans left, and Geller will then indicate both by gesture and in writing which one of the remaining cans contains the target. It is only at the end of the experiment that Geller touches the can that he believes contains the object. The protocol included the possibility that he might touch a can accidentally. In such case, that would have counted as a miss. Here he writes the selected number.

This, you might say, is a kind of ten-can Russian roulette. He has made his choice. The steel ball is found.

In later repetitions of this same experiment, he was finally weaned away from the dowsing technique where he runs his hands over the cans. He got to the point where he could walk into a room, see the cans lined up on a blackboard sill, and just pick up the one that contained the target. We have no hypothesis at this point as to whether this is a heightened sensitivity of some normal sense, or whether it is some paranormal sense.

Now we are repeating the experiment with a different target object. One of these cans is filled with room-temperature water.

Again, the can was filled by an outside person who randomized the position of the cans. Then the box that contained the cans was rotated by a second person so that there is no one person in the room who knows the location of the target can. As you can see here, there is less hand motion by Geller over the can. The protocol as before involves his calling out the number or pointing and one of the experimenters removing the can at Geller's call. At this point in time he is asked to make his choice both by writing the number down as well as making a selection by hand. You will note that he is making a final test to be sure of his selection. Tentatively, he reaches and having made the selection now looks to see whether water is inside the can. He now waters the plant with the contents of the can. You will note he is very pleased with finding this target because he had doubts at the outset whether he would be able to locate a can filled with water.

We repeated this type of experiment fourteen times; five times involved a target being a small permanent magnet, five times also involved a steel ball bearing as the target. Twice the target was water. Two additional trials were made—one with a paper-wrapped ball bearing and one with a sugar cube. The latter two targets were not located. Geller felt that he didn't have adequate confidence as to where they were, and he declined to guess, and passed. On the other twelve targets—the ball bearing, the magnet, and the water—he did make a guess as to the target location and was correct in every instance. In subsequent work with another subject, we found the subject experiencing a highly significant difference in his ability to find the steel ball bearing as compared with finding other targets.

The whole array of this run had an *a priori* probability of 1 part in 10^{12}, or statistics of a trillion to one. Here is another double blind experiment in which a die is placed in a metal file box (both box and die being provided by SRI). The box is shaken up with neither the experimenter nor Geller knowing where the die is or which face is up. This is a live experiment that you see—in this case, Geller guessed that a four was showing but first he passed because he was not confident. You will note he was correct and he was quite pleased to have guessed correctly, but this particular test does not enter into our statistics.

The previous runs of ten-can roulette gave a result whose probability due to chance alone is one part in 10^{12}. We decided at the outset to carry out the die-in-box experiment until we got to a million to one odds, at which time the experiment was terminated. Out of ten tries in which he passed twice and guessed eight times, the eight guesses were correct, and that gave us a probability of about one in a million.

We would point out again, there were no errors in the times he made a guess.

This is the first of two experiments in psychokinesis. Here a one-gram weight is being placed on an electrical scale. It is then covered by an aluminum can and by a glass cylinder to eliminate deflection due to air currents. The first part of our protocol involves tapping the bell jar; next tapping the table; then kicking the table; and finally jumping on the floor, with a record made of what these artifacts looked like so that they could be distinguished from signals. In tests following this experimental run, a magnet was brought near the apparatus, static electricity was discharged against parts of the apparatus, and controlled runs of day-long operation were obtained. In no case were artifacts obtained which in any way resembled the signals produced by Geller, nor could anyone else duplicate the effects.

The bottom four signals show the type of artifact that results from tapping or kicking the table. They are small AC signals with a time constant characteristic of the apparatus. The upper two traces, on the other hand, are apparently due to Geller's efforts. They are single-sided signals, one corresponding to a 1,500-mg weight decrease, the other corresponding to an 800-mg weight increase. Those types of single-sided signals were never observed as artifacts with any other stimuli.

We have no ready hypothesis on how these signals might have been produced. The width of the signals produced by Geller was about two hundred milliseconds. The chart ran at one millimeter per second. It was of interest to note that Geller's performance improved over the period of experimentation, starting with 50-mg deflections and arriving at 1,500 mg.

In this experiment Geller is attempting to influence the magnetometer either directly or by generating a magnetic field. The full-scale sensitivity of the instrument is .3 of a gauss, and, as is clear in this instance, his hands are open. Throughout the experiment, his hands do not come into contact with the instrument. The magnetometer itself was used as a probe to go over his hands and person to make sure that there were no magnetic objects in his hands or on him. Here you see substantial fluctuations both to the left and to the right—almost full-scale in certain cases—on the magnetometer meter. These fluctuations are sometimes uncorrelated with the motions of his hands.

This is the chart recording of the magnetometer fluctuations produced by Geller. We see here full-scale fluctuations of .3 of a gauss, which is a significant magnetic field, comparable to the earth's field. After each of these experiments we would in general discuss the results with Geller, show him the strip chart recording, and talk about the significance of his experiments. He was very interested in the experiments we were doing because he had never taken part in laboratory experiments of this kind before.

The following is an experiment which in retrospect we consider unsatisfactory, as it didn't meet our protocol standards. Here the task is to deflect the compass needle which, indeed, Geller does. Before and after the experiment, he was gone over with a magnetometer probe and his hands were photographed from above and below during and following the experiment so that we are sure there were no obvious pieces of metal or magnets in his possession. However, according to our protocol, if we could in any way debunk the experiment and produce the effects by any other means, then that experiment was considered null and void even if there were no indications that anything untoward happened. In this case, we found later that these types of deflections could be produced by a small piece of metal, so small in fact that they could not be detected by the magnetometer. Therefore, even though we had no evidence of this, we still considered the experiment inconclusive and an unsatisfactory type of experiment altogether.

A look at the lower mirror affords one the best view. It can be seen that his hands are completely exposed to photography from above and below with different cameras.

These are a series of unconfirmed physical effects that need further investigation. One of Geller's main attributes that had been reported to us was that he was able to bend metal from a distance without touching it. In the laboratory we did not find him able to do so. In a more relaxed protocol, he was permitted to touch the metal, in which case, as you will see in the film, the metal is indeed bent. However, it becomes clear in watching this demonstration on film that simple photo interpretation is insufficient to determine whether the metal is bent by normal or paranormal means.

In the laboratory, these spoon-bending experiments were continuously filmed and video-taped. It is evident that some time during the photographic period this stainless steel spoon became bent. However, unlike the things we have heard about Geller, it was always necessary for him in the experimental situation to have physical contact with the spoon or for that matter any other object that he bends. It is not clear whether the spoon is being bent because he has extraordinarily strong fingers and good control of micro-manipulatory movements or whether, in fact, the spoon "turns to plastic" in his hands, as he claims.

Here are a number of the spoons that were bent by one means or another during the course of our experiments. There is no doubt that the spoons were bent. The only doubt remains as to the manner of their bending. Similarly, we have rings that were bent by Mr. Geller. The rings that were bent are shown here. The copper ring at the left and the brass ring at the right were manufactured at SRI and measured to require 150 pounds force to bend them. These rings were in Geller's hand at the time they were bent.

This brief recap is to remind you of those experiments we feel were best controlled. They are the three perception experiments, including the hidden drawings in envelopes, the double blind hidden object experiments, and the double blind die-in-the-box experiment. The two psychokinetic experiments—the depression or raising of a weight on an electrical scale and the deflection of the magnetometer—also do not seem to admit of any ready counter-hypothesis. What we've demonstrated here are the experiments that we performed in the laboratory and should not be interpreted as proof of psychic functioning. Indeed, a film never proves anything. Rather, this film gives us the opportunity to share with the viewer observations of phenomena that in our estimation clearly deserve further study.

APPENDIX THREE

Clock, Time, and Prayer

On the Instructions of Spectra to Pray for Peace Whenever My Watch Stopped (See page 136.)
Tel Aviv, Israel; December 21–24, 1971

On December 21, 1971, as I drove to Uri's apartment in Tel Aviv, I started my prayer. I had got into the habit now of going into prayer consciousness as soon as the watch stopped. When I arrived, Uri looked at the stopped watch, put his hand over it, and it started to run, at 1:21 P.M., local time.

We discussed the experience he had had with the brown suitcase. There was no question that it was my suitcase which was stored at the Sharon Hotel. Later on when I checked the storage closet, I found my Taperlite suitcase in place, and not in any way changed. We could not come to any conclusion as to the meaning of this event. I felt that it was only an assurance of continuing presence to help allay our recurring doubts. Feeling very tired from my all-night vigil, I left shortly to return to my hotel.

I lay down on the sofa in my room, and I remember looking at the watch as I was dozing off to sleep. I remember seeing it come to a halt at 2:45:45 P.M., just before sleep overtook me. I awoke at 4:39 P.M. (electric clock time) and saw that my watch was indeed standing still, at 2:45:45. Fortunately I was alone,

Clock, Time, and Prayer

with no one to disturb me, and was able seriously to apply myself to peace prayers. The watch remained stopped for twenty-one hours and twenty-seven minutes. I did the best I could to stay awake and keep the prayer for peace and love for Mr. Sadat going. However, there were distractions. At 10:15 A.M. on December 22 I turned on the RCA radio in the room. There was only one station on the air, at 760 kc, very loud and clear, and all in Hebrew. All other stations were absent on this radio. When I checked the other stations with my Sony battery radio, they were all on the air normally. I found at 10:49 A.M. that all other stations suddenly came through normally on the hotel radio. I reasoned that I was being shown yet another aspect of the intelligent control over electronic communications systems.

Reuven came to see me at noon. At 12:12 P.M. (electric clock time) my watch began to run normally while he and I were looking at it. I left the hotel at about 1 P.M. to go into Tel Aviv to attend to some business at the American embassy. While I was at the embassy, my watch stopped, at 3:45:45. But I had no local time clock to check against when this occurred. After sitting by the seashore for some three hours in quiet prayer, I went to see Uri. While with him, at 6:06 P.M., local time, my watch started to run again by itself. We left his apartment at 6:50 P.M. to drive to a place near Rehovot where he had a show in a theater.

As we drove in the darkness, a cold, driving rain beat against the car. We were discussing our deep concern for the danger of a war. I was in the middle of the following sentence, "I believe that Mr. Sadat will make a decision tomorrow about going to war," when the car horn gave one short blast of sound, all by itself! Uri and I looked at each other, realizing that every word of ours was somehow being overheard. A few minutes later the headlights switched off by themselves, forcing us to stop. A few minutes later the lights switched on by themselves.

The show was in a large theater with no heat, and the feeling of cold had a bone-chilling effect. The crowd was young, rather wild, and very noisy. At 8:30 P.M. the show started; my watch stopped at 5:45:45. While the variety show went on, I pretended to be asleep, but was in fact engaged in my peace prayer. Uri's part of the show was on from 11 to 11:30. During this period I had the feeling that the power of my prayer was being amplified. We left the theater at 11:30, and when Uri and I met, my watch began to run again.

On the road back to Tel Aviv, the car lights suddenly went off, and the engine went off suddenly. We parked at the edge of the road and waited. In two minutes an invisible hand turned the lights on again. It was then that we discovered that the ignition key had been turned off by counterclockwise rotation. This was how the engine had been turned off by our invisible friends. We drove back to Tel Aviv without any further occurrences, except that at some point during the drive—I do not know when—my watch had been stopped at 7:45:45.

Because of this incident and earlier such incidents, I borrowed Uri's very fine Certina watch, just to have a reference clock on me.

When I returned to the Sharon Hotel at 1 A.M., December 23, 1971, I had no choice but to resume my prayers, since the watch was still stopped. The watch remained stopped until 10:04 A.M., December 23, and until that moment I remained vigilant at my prayers. I no longer suffered from exhaustion; it was as if I were drawing on some reserve of energy.

When the watch started running, there was not time to go to sleep. I had to go to Tel Aviv to have a meeting with one of the Israeli army officers. I got there early for my appointment so that I could have breakfast. As I was eating breakfast and reading the newspaper, I got an impulse at 12:03 P.M. (Certina time) to stare at my Geneve watch, which was now running normally. The minute and hour hands were almost precisely at 9:45 setting, and the small second hand was coming around clockwise from the twenty-second marker. As I watched this second hand, it moved normally until it got to the forty-five-second marker, and there it stopped instantly before my eyes. This is the first time I had ever seen the hands come to a stop instantly under direct observation. I checked the operation of Uri's Certina on my right wrist; it was operating normally. Al-

Clock, Time, and Prayer

though I should have prayed then and there, I could not, for at this moment, the army officer arrived. We met for some thirty minutes and parted. I regret that I am not able to disclose the nature of our conversation, except to say that the "coming" war was discussed.

I then went to see Uri at his apartment and talked about my all-night vigil. He was sympathetic. He wanted to do an experiment with the two watches. Both were placed face up on the table, reading:

Geneve: 9:45:45 (stopped)
Certina: 2:00:00 P.M. (normal)

Uri placed a sheet of paper over the two watches. Just then the local air-raid sirens went off with a crescendo of sound, just a practice alert. The paper was lifted off. The Geneve was running normally again.

I left shortly thereafter to take care of some business at the National Car rental office in Tel Aviv. While I was sitting there at 3:00:00 (Certina time), my Geneve watch stopped at 10:45:45. So I drove to my hotel immediately to begin my prayers. This time I sat facing Egypt and facing the sea for many hours. Uri walked into my room at 9:29 P.M., placed his hand over my Geneve watch, and it started to run immediately. Without knowing why, Uri was unconsciously being directed to come along and release me from each of my long prayer vigils.

Uri remained with me during the next hour. It was during this hour, from 9:30 to 10:30 P.M., December 23, 1971, that Uri became a Magus—a man sure of his powers from on high.

It began with Uri testing his power on the Silva compass which was lying on my study table. He had just started my watch with casual ease, as I have just described. He placed his hand over the compass, and the needle literally spinned. He took his hand away, and as we talked about the ease with which he now moved a compass compared to his efforts just one month ago, the compass vanished before our eyes. We searched the entire apartment, and I found the compass lying on the floor of the bathroom. I put it back on the desk.

As Uri and I stood at the desk, he opened the desk drawer and almost unconsciously picked up the Minox flash gun which had appeared in his hand on December 20. He took the flash out of the leather case and asked me to tell him once again the story, and I assured him that this flash gun had not belonged to me before—that it was a gift from an unknown source. I handed him the flash gun, and he put it back in its leather case and dropped it into the drawer. A few minutes later Uri was drawn back to the desk drawer and opened it while I watched him. He picked up the leather case. "My God, it's gone!" he shouted. I opened the case; the flash gun had indeed vanished.

Uri was feeling his power as a newfound gift. He said that he now consciously wanted the flash gun to reappear. He placed the empty leather case inside my heavy large steel camera case and snapped all the locks shut on it at 9:50 P.M. At 9:55 P.M. we opened the steel camera case, and there was the Minox flash gun, neatly placed inside its leather case!

Uri was having great fun with his newfound power. He was holding an unlit cigar in his left hand as he said, "I wish I could now make something disappear from my hand." As he said this, the cigar instantly vanished from his hand. We laughed uproariously at what had just happened—it was like some vaudeville act. Two minutes later the cigar reappeared on the microphone part of the Sony TC 120 tape recorder, which was on a table.

I admonished Uri about how careful he had to be from now on with respect to his thoughts. He had just expressed a simple wish—and it had been fulfilled. It was like rubbing Aladdin's lamp. But we knew that our genie was an intelligence from a superior civilization. Uri said he would be very, very careful about his thoughts from now on.

We had a serious talk about the war threat. I said, "There are only about seventy-two hours left. I wish we would be given more information now."

Uri said, "Don't worry—it will come, if it is needed. But I don't think there is going to be a war. I feel it now." As we discussed this war problem, we began to look at my Geneve watch lying on the table. The minute and hour hand had reached the

Clock, Time, and Prayer

11:45:45 position. We looked at the second hand and saw it go from 42 to 43 seconds to 45 seconds—then it stopped. The Certina clock time was 10:30 P.M. Uri left a few minutes later.

I settled down to a long prayer vigil. But I did not know how long it was going to be this time. It was to last forty hours and four minutes before my watch started to run again. As the hours wore on, and Christmas Eve approached, my thoughts turned more and more to the Prince of Peace.

APPENDIX FOUR

Spacecraft Sightings

January 3–8, 1972
(*See page 151 for context.*)

On January 3, 1972, Uri had a show at a theater in Yerucham which was southeast of Beersheba. We headed south from Tel Aviv at 6:35 P.M. on the road to Rehovot. As we passed the sign on the road that pointed to the Sorek Nuclear Research Center, we—Uri, Ila, and I—saw a huge red star to the west. Actually, if we had not known about spacecraft, it would have looked like another star.

Uri slammed the car to a sudden stop on the shoulder of the road. We scrambled out into the mud to look.

The red star was gone. About a thousand meters away at twenty degrees elevation was another long red light, about three hundred feet long. There was one red light trailing it about one hundred yards to the right. I looked at my watch; it was 7:15 P.M. Uri took one look at this long red light and said, "Let's get out of here!" and drove away furiously.

We now saw dozens of lights and craft in the sky, but Uri would not stop to observe them. He kept driving at a fast pace. I shall try to describe as best I can what we observed. At 7:23 P.M. there appeared ahead of us a bright star that was only about two hundred yards above the road, always staying about a quarter of a mile ahead of us. This star flashed color sequences, red, blue, yellow, green, etc. This "flasher" lasted until 7:26 P.M.

At 7:40 P.M. two yellow lights appeared to the west as we approached Kiriyat Gat. These blanked out, and three orange flares appeared exactly like the seven I had seen the night before. These were only a half mile away and lit up the whole countryside. Pillars of smoke rose from the orange flares which did not hit the earth but hovered in the air. I could not help but think of the Pillar of Fire that guided the Israelites in the Sinai, during the Exodus.

At 7:41 P.M. the moon, very full, rose over the hills to the east. To the south of the full moon we saw four disk-shaped red-gold lights that moved slowly to the southeast. Then one winked out, and only three remained for another minute. Then at 7:43 P.M. from the region where the last red-gold lights had disappeared came a magnificent spacecraft. It was huge, at least a thousand yards long. It was definitely circular as it tilted up slightly so that we could see its underside. The rim of the circle was a flat wall covered along its entire length with what had the appearance of portholes, but what was actually seen were flashes of light that had the appearance of a porthole. These flashes lit up the length of the craft with colors that encompassed the entire spectrum of light. The lights were so bright that the countryside below the craft was lit up as it passed about a half mile due east, moving north.

Other cars were on the highway going in the direction we were, as well as in the opposite direction. We three soon realized that no other drivers were looking at what we were looking at. I knew from previous experiences that this display was "for our eyes only." What I couldn't understand was how others could not see what we saw when the flares, or the craft, lit up the entire countryside so brightly? This at times included the road ahead of us. While the huge spacecraft silently moved north to our left, there appeared directly in front of us, about two hundred yards away, a bright burning yellow ball. It came right at us soundlessly, and then exploded laterally into a mouth shape. Just to the right of the road, two yellow flares were following our progress on the road. The also gave off smoke. Then behind these two flares, two more briefly winked at us. Then another ball flare came from the east side of the road and exploded over us. All of this was silent, and there was no smell of burning substance in the air. The display was awesome, in that each flare seemed to move with a guidance related to the movement of our car.

Then on each side of the road, yellow flares flashed for a few seconds, like giant eyes winking at us. Then for the next thirty-five minutes we were surrounded above, to the right, and to the left by these smoking flares—yellow, gold, red, and golden red. It was impossible to keep track of all these lights at once.

At 8:25 P.M. two red flares appeared to our right, to the northwest. They followed us like two red eyes at a respectful distance, always hugging the edge of the horizon. As they moved, they lit up the fields and woods below with an eerie fiery glow. Most amazing, they followed us right through the town of Beersheba, hugging the rooftops and lighting them with a red glow. This was an incredible experience, and this pair of eyes followed us all the way to Dimona.

At Dimona we picked up a hitchhiking soldier who was going to Yerucham. As soon as we picked him up, the lights winked out, to be seen no more that evening. We were so excited about what we had seen that Uri could hardly concentrate on his show. But he did his show with ease, demonstrating telepathy, repairing watches, and bending metals. We drove back to Tel Aviv from midnight until 2:30 A.M. without seeing a single light. There was no question in any of our minds that we had seen at least one giant spacecraft that night. We had seen dozens of colored smoky flares that followed us with a kind of animal faithfulness. The seven pillars of smoke that I had seen the night before were only a forerunner of what we had seen this night. There remained the mystery of why no one else was seeing what we saw so plainly. I did not even attempt to take movies, knowing full well that my camera would be jammed. We checked the newspapers the next day. There were no reports of strange lights in the sky such as we had seen. If what we saw was an hallucination, it was a beautiful spacy trip for the three of us!

The next night was January 4. Uri had another show in the direction of Beersheba in a small town, Ofakim. We went out of Tel Aviv by the same road as the previous night. In the car were Uri, Iris, Ila, and myself. As we passed the Sorek Nuclear Research Center, we saw our first red light in the sky that moved slowly to our west in a sinusoidal path. I do not want to bore the reader, but we all saw the same kind of aerial display as we had seen the night before. We saw the giant spacecraft with the multicolored flashing porthole lights, the flares, the explosions, and always being followed by these eyes in the night. Again, no one but we seemed to see this awesome display.

When we reached Ofakim, Uri was to perform in a lovely modern theater. The night was warm and balmy for a change. I decided to stay outside the theater and keep an eye on the sky for further aerial displays. By the loud booming public address system in the theater, I could tell exactly when Uri appeared on stage to start his show. As Uri began to speak, I and Ila saw a red light and a spacecraft approach Ofakim from the east, settle down over the town, and land somewhere just beyond our range of vision. It was really hidden behind some buildings about a half mile away. I watched the area where it had become invisible all the while that Uri was doing the show. As Uri ended, the red light arose from its hiding spot, and a red disk-shaped craft moved away toward the east.

On Wednesday, January 5, Ila had stepped out on the balcony of room 1101 at the Sharon Hotel just after sunset, about 5:20. She called to me in panic. I joined her. There coming from the south flying low over the Tel Aviv-Haifa Highway was a huge spacecraft. It had a steady white light at the front and at the back. Between these two lights was a dark hull, perhaps one hundred yards in length. It was about two thousand feet to our east and moving slowly at about two hundred miles per hour. It was a majestic sight as it moved unchallenged over Israel, and probably, unseen by any except us.

The same evening Uri had another show to the south at

Beersheba. As we were driving just south of Rishon Le Zion at 8:40 P.M., Uri stopped the car to point out a spacecraft to Iris, Ila, and myself. It was the most spectacular performance I had seen to date. The spacecraft was high in the sky and very far away. It was located just above the belt of the Hunter in the constellation Orion. We could not tell how far away it was because it seemed to be way out there in the star field. Whatever the distance, it was a huge rotating disk with a red light at each end. What was spectacular was that it was going through complex maneuvers. First it moved sideways in circles or loops like a coiled spring. Then it would move back in complex figures just like script writing loops and swirls. Then it would oscillate in straight line lateral movements. It seemed to be skywriting, but none of us could read it.

I wanted to try to take a movie of it, but Uri dissuaded me—this was sacred, he said. Watching this spacecraft had a strange quieting effect on all of us. Personally, it made me feel very small and alone in the universe. The display lasted four minutes by clock time, but to me it seemed like an eon.

When we were somewhere in the area of Ashqelon at 9:35 P.M. we got lost on a side road. There appeared a small spacecraft (diskoid) with a steady red and green light on it. This resolved into a single red light which took a position over and ahead of our car. We followed the light, and it led us through a maze of small roads. When we found our road again, the red light winked out.

Uri's show was a rousing success. On our way home to Tel Aviv, we saw no lights or craft in the sky.

Author's Biography

Born on February 19, 1918, in Chicago, ANDRIJA HENRY PUHARICH, M.D., has made significant contributions to medicine, neurophysiology, mind sciences, and medical electronics through his researches and inventions in these fields.

Puharich graduated from Northwestern University Medical School in 1947 and completed his residency in internal medicine at Permanente Hospital in California. His interest in psychic research developed from an academic curiosity about telepathy.

Puharich established in 1948 the Round Table Foundation in Maine. There he conceived and developed a series of experiments to enhance ESP in sensitives by means of electronic systems. Among his colleagues and research associates were author Aldous Huxley and Dr. Samuel Rosen, world-renowned ear surgeon. Puharich's first research subject was Eileen Garrett, the late medium who founded the Parapsychology Foundation, and the results of this research convinced him that telepathy existed.

Puharich brought the Dutch sensitive Peter Hurkos to America for investigation and was the first to study this gifted psychic. His experiments teaming Hurkos with another sensitive, Harry Stone, produced extraordinary results when both subjects were in an electrified Faraday cage. These experiments are now regarded as classic in the field. Puharich also studied the Indian sage and teacher Dr. D. G. Vinod, whose powers of materialization and contact with nonterrestrials opened new possibilities in preparing the way for Puharich's future work.

In 1958 Puharich moved his laboratory to Carmel, California, where he continued his researches and served as a consultant to industrial corporations, foundations, and universities.

In 1960 Puharich headed a research expedition to Oaxaca, Mexico, to study the sacred mushroom rite of the Chatino Indians. He is the first known outsider to participate in the sacred rites of the Chatinos and to document it on film. The following year he went to Hawaii at the invitation of David Bray, last of the royal line of Kahuna priests. After intense training and development, which awakened his own powers of consciousness, Puharich became the first non-Hawaiian to be initiated into the Kahuna priesthood, a tradition dating back thousands of years. While in Hawaii, Puharich discovered the first hallucinogenic mushrooms ever found in the islands.

Later that year, Puharich moved to New York and founded Intelectron Corporation (with J. L. Lawrence), to develop electronic systems for aiding hearing in nerve deafness. He served as president and director of research for ten years and holds fifty-six United States and foreign patents for his inventions. He has also applied for patents on his systems to enhance ESP, which have become the issue of a long-standing debate with the U. S. Patent Office and are assuming the stature of classic cases in the legal literature.

From 1963 to 1968 Puharich led a number of medical research expeditions to Brazil to study the healer Arigó. Arigó's totally unorthodox surgery and healing powers defied every rule of medicine. While in Brazil, Puharich first became aware of UFOs, where he saw and photographed a number of them.

In 1971 all of his previous professional training and skills, investigative researches, and field studies led him to Israel, where he became the first scientist to investigate seriously the phenomena of Uri Geller.

Puharich is listed in Who's Who in the East, American Men of Medicine, Leaders in American Science, Biographical Dictionary of Parapsychology, and many other biographical listings

for achievement and contribution. His numerous professional memberships include the New York Academy of Sciences, American Association for the Advancement of Science, Aerospace Medical Association, and the American Association for Humanistic Psychology.

Puharich has published over fifty papers and articles in scientific and professional journals and written two books, *The Sacred Mushroom*, 1959, and *Beyond Telepathy*, 1962, both published by Doubleday & Company, Inc., and both reissued by Doubleday in paperback editions (*The Sacred Mushroom*, 1974, and *Beyond Telepathy*, 1973). He has collaborated on a book by John G. Fuller, *Arigó: Surgeon of the Rusty Knife*, T. Y. Crowell & Co., New York, 1974.